The Archaeology of Change: .

History and Archaeology are both methods c   ... the
aim of discovering what happened and wh   ciosely related
disciplines and practitioners of either ignore .ock emanating from the
other at their peril. Through both, it has long been clear that human
societies have been undergoing a continuous process of change from as
early a date as it is possible to investigate. Indeed, change, be it slow or
rapid, is almost a sine qua non of man's history and development.

Only by exploiting this process has it been possible to break up the past
into 'period chunks', each distinguished from those which came before
and after by easily identified characteristics and identifiable whatersheds.
Hence 'Roman Britain' has been singled out as a discreet period of study,
separated from the 'Late Pre-Roman Iron Age' and the 'Sub-Roman
Period' or 'Dark Ages'.

In many respects this compartmentalization of the past is inevitable.
Such is the detail in which we now undertake research that no individual
can hope to master more than a relatively narrow period of history. The
break-up of the past into chronological chunks is at least a consistent
method of proceeding, and it does have the virtue of allowing specialists
the sort of oversight of a whole society, over a short space of time, which is
unavailable to the thematic historian.

As a general approach, it does, however, have its dangers. One such is
the tendency to assume that long periods of the past which lie within a
single, conventional compartment (such as the three and a half centuries
of Roman Britain) were periods which saw little change. To develop this
example, a description of British society in, say AD100, could be thought to
be only marginally less accurate when applied to the same community in
AD350. This is demonstrably untrue.

Another danger, closely allied to this is the tendency to assume that
change was concentrated at the interfaces between different periods. In a
sense there is an ambiguity in this situation in that the chopping of the
past into periods has naturally occurred precisely where such breaks seem
to occur. Since these breaks have tended to been seen as co-incidental
with either conquests or settlements (as in those of the Romans, Saxons,
Vikings and Normans), there has been a strong tendency to explain
periods of rapid change in ethnic terms – even as a consequence of the
replacement of one population by another.

This Series seek to re-examine the interfaces between the different periods into which modern scholars have divided the past. Each concentrates on a single period, or the break between two periods, and explores the processes of change therein, seeking a broad oversight set against as wide a cultural and social context as is possible. Processes such as acculturation will be discussed, and elements of change set alongside evidence for continuity which seems to bridge even the most dramatic of such period-breaks. Once consequence may be the recognition that our retrospective system of managing the past by dividing it into periods has created a false impression of discontinuity and hiatus between those periods. The choice of different criteria would allow the drawing of period boundaries almost at will, with very different results for the way we look at the past. In this respect, as in so many others, the past is shown to be a product of the present.

Each volume is written by a well-known specialist of the period under review. The results will challenge many of our more uncritical assumptions about the past, about the processes of change and about continuity from one period to another.

Further Titles in this Series

Rome, Britain and the Anglo-Saxons

Nicholas Higham

LONDON

DEDICATION

Felicitati

© Nicholas Higham 1992
First published 1992

Typeset by Setrite Typesetters, Hong Kong
Printed and bound by Biddles, Guildford, England

for the publishers
B A Seaby Ltd
7 Davies Street
London W1Y 1LL

ISBN 1 85264 022 7

A CIP catalogue record for this book
is available from the British Library

Cover illustration

*The Snape Anglo-Saxon gold ring, set with
a late Roman intaglio. Found in a boat burial
at Snape, Suffolk. British Museum.*

Photo: Peter Clayton

CONTENTS

LIST OF FIGURES

NOTE

All carbon-dates are offered in a form which has been corrected to calendar years after the tables published in *Radiocarbon* **28** 2B (1986). Dates are all AD unless stated otherwise.

ACKNOWLEDGEMENTS

This volume has grown over many years, and the views expressed within it have evolved and crystallized even during the process of writing over the last six months. During this period I have benefited enormously from the opportunity to discuss their own recent research with Paul Bennett, Glenn Foard, Peter Hill, Mike Hughes, Chris Morris, Dominic Powlesland and Tom Williamson. My colleagues David Hill, Alex Rumble and John Peter Wild have helped me in many ways and Paul Holder has, as ever, been of great assistance concerning bibliographical matters. I am grateful for the encouragement given me by Charles Thomas, Chris Taylor and Rosemary Cramp. A work of synthesis of this kind is necessarily dependent on numerous studies by a host of different scholars, and I have attempted to attribute opinions and evidence wherever appropriate within the text.

Since the completion of the text of this volume, Martin Miller has published his *The Romanization of Britain* (C.U.P. 1990) which deals with the subject matter of chapters II and III in far greater depth. Reading this stimulating volume is highly recommended. My thanks are also due to: Petra Day for her correspondence concerning her research of the site at Shotover Forest, and for her permission to mention her conclusions prior to full publication; Frank Chamtess of Keele University for permission to refer to his palynological research at Tattan prior to its publication; John Manley for providing me with interion reports of excavation of square-dithed tarrows in Chvyd; Paul Bennett and his staff at the Canterbury Archaeological Trust for discussion of sites and access to final reports prior to publication.

Notwithstanding the enormity of my debts, all opinions and suggestions herein expressed are my own, however outrageous they may appear. Likewise must I own to the errors.

I would like to thank the University of Manchester who contributed to my expenses in several research visits in England and abroad, and funded a temporary lectureship to replace me for an entire year to enable this volume to reach typescript. To a generous employer my grateful thanks.

N.J. Higham
Manchester
April 1992

CHAPTER ONE

HENGEST AND THE HISTORIANS: AN INTRODUCTION

In Colonel Archer's lands at Tanworth in Warwickshire are two entrenchments, or camps (I have not seen them) which were (it seems) the entrenchments of Vortigern and Hengest....

(John Aubrey 1665–93 (1980 ed): 302)

Bede presented his *Historia Ecclesiastica* to King Ceolwulf of Northumbria in 731 and the *Historia Brittonum* was written within the century following. One consequence was the dissemination of stories concerning Vortigern and Hengest, which rapidly assumed the status of incontrovertible fact. John Aubrey, writing almost a millennium later, could take for granted the acquaintance of his audience with such stories and record without fear of correction their responsibility for earthworks still then visible but not otherwise explained.

It has been the task of far more recent scholarship to question these stories and subject them to the more vigorous historical criticism which has exposed them as myth, the stuff of romantic literature, however venerable that literature may be. Setting them to one side, it has been possible to amass and organize a far more complex and challenging body of information concerning the 'Dark Ages'. The result is a debate concerning the origins of England which is livelier and better informed than at any time in the past, to which scholars have brought a developing range of specialist studies — textual history, place-name studies, palaeobotany and archaeology, to name but the most obvious — yet the very nature of that settlement remains at issue. Was it a mass movement of large tribes, which swept before it the disordered survivors of Roman Britain into the refuges of Wales, Cornwall and Brittany? Was it a small-scale movement of Germanic warriors who became the new estate-holders of Britain's lowland zone and imposed their religion, language and material culture on the British peasantry? Or was it something between these two extremes, with some of the characteristics of each?

The English settlement has always been an emotive topic, both within the academic world and without. The work of early medieval Welsh scholars, Geoffrey of Monmouth, Wade or Layamon, presents a literature which has been nurtured by the depth of feeling created by the interface of the Celtic and English worlds. For reasons which are far from obvious,

Arthur eventually emerged as the principal character of twilight Britain, but only after Norman interest in his exploits blossomed after the Conquest. From the *Fight at Finn's Burg* fragment in *Beowulf*, it is clear that the name Hengest was familiar to later Anglo-Saxon audiences, for whom this allusion presumably touched a rich vein of myth and legend. By the ninth century he was credited, by English and Welsh commentators alike, with the leadership of the first English settlements.

In the modern period the battle lines were drawn up at an early stage in the emergence of history as an intellectual discipline, during the second and third quarters of the nineteenth century. From the beginning the issue was divisive and attitudes tended to polarize. For those enamoured of the splendours of Rome, the newcomers heralded the decline and fall of the long and civilized peace of the Roman period. Yet for medievalists, the Anglo-Saxons rapidly came to provide the proper starting-point for English history. From their arrival dated the inception of English culture and language to the early law codes of the English, constitutional and legal historians could refer back the basics of the common law and the peculiarly English brand of mixed government, which they deemed to have evolved from a form of noble savagery in England's heroic age.

> She [Britain] was subjugated by the Roman armies; but she received only a faint tincture of Roman arts and letters...
>
> The scanty and superficial civilisation which the Britons had derived from their southern masters was effaced by the calamities of the fifth century...
>
> Rude English pilgrims... returned [from Rome] with awe deeply impressed on their half opened minds, and told the wondering inhabitants of the hovels of London and York that, near the grave of St. Peter, a mighty race, now extinct, had piled up buildings which would never be dissolved till the judgement day...
>
> (Lord Macaulay 1867, I: 2−5)

It is to J.M. Kemble that we owe the foundations of the modern study of early medieval England. In *The Saxons in England*, Kemble displayed doubts concerning the reliability of the narratives of Bede and the *Anglo-Saxon Chronicle*, and he was prepared to allow considerable ethnic continuity from the British past:

> Steadily from east to west, from south to north, the sharp axes and long swords of the Teutons hewed their way... The mass of people, accustomed to Roman rule or the oppression of native princes, probably suffered little by a change of masters, and did little to avoid it.
>
> (Kemble 1849: 20)

The axes were for the virgin forest and the swords for the British aristocracy. However, contemporaries found his views at odds with their perceptions of themselves. In the intellectual cauldron of the mid-nineteenth century, developments in biological sciences had led to a focus on the distinctiveness of animal and plant species. From Africa and the East, colonial administrators and missionaries were sending back ethnographic studies of tribal societies which reflected their cultural, linguistic and ethnic separation from the rest of mankind. In Europe, belief in the inherent superiority of the white man over all other races was finding intellectual support, particularly among Teutonic philosophers from whose ideas was eventually to emerge the belief in racial superiority which characterized German thought in the 1930s.

In such an intellectual climate it was only natural that historians should adopt a comparatively uncritical reading of the early English texts and opt for an interpretation of the English settlement which rested on the mass migration of entire German tribes. The ethnic interpretation was resurrected initially in lecture form by Edwin Guest in the mid-century and then enthusiastically wrought in prose by JR. Green in 1881. Thereafter this view was given academic credentials by William (later Bishop) Stubbs (1891). Stubbs collected together early documents for teaching purposes in a volume of *Select Charters*, which achieved rapid success in the training of both historians and lawyers, for many of whom it was the only work on the period consulted. He included a brief introduction which summarized his view of the interface between Britons and Anglo-Saxons:

> [the]... inhabitants [of Britain] were enervated and demoralized by long dependence, wasted by successive pestilences, worn out by the attacks of half-savage neighbours and by their own suicidal wars; whose vast forests and unreclaimed marsh-lands afforded to the newcomers a comparatively easy conquest, and the means of reproducing at liberty on new ground the institutions under which they had lived at home.
>
> This new race was the main stock of our forefathers: sharing the primaeval German pride of purity of extraction... and strictly careful of the distinction between themselves and the tolerated remnant of their predecessors...
>
> Our whole internal history testifies unmistakably to our inheritance of Teutonic institutions from the first immigrant.
>
> (Stubbs 1870: 1−3)

A comparatively literal reading of Tacitus, Gildas and Bede, a low enumeration of the British population and a high estimate of the area still under ancient woodland − all had become hallmarks of early English history. It was unashamedly ethnocentric at a time when ethnicity and culture were seen as indissolubly linked and ethnography and ethno-anthropology were flourishing. As an explanation it was entirely in tune with English perceptions of themselves and it attracted numerous adherents who were content to adopt an apocalyptic view of the origins of England:

Thus you see that our forefathers really became the people of the land
in all that part of Britain which they conquered. For they had killed or
driven out all the former people, save those whom they kept as mere
slaves.

(Freeman 1878: 28)

The English migration, then, was perceived as a folk-movement of
entire kinship groups and tribes, living within a comparatively egalitarian
tribal society but under the rule of kings, who spread across England
driving the Britons in front of them like land crabs before an incoming
sea-tide. Expressions of this view were to retreat from the overtly racist
language used by Stubbs and his contemporaries, as European notions of
racial superiority were savaged by the Second World War. Yet the central
explanation of the English settlement — often dubbed the 'Germanist'
view — survived, virtually unscathed.

This was not because such views were unchallenged. In the early
decades of the twentieth century, a series of articles and books by Hector
Munro Chadwick offered a rather different view of early English society
which was far more hierarchical than that envisaged by the Germanists,
and within which there was far more room for Celtic survival. Analysis of
the early legal codes revealed large numbers of Welshmen in Anglo-Saxon
society at various different levels and the handful of slaves who survived
Freeman's bloodbath were amplified into as many as half a million
(Chadwick 1905: 373). The notion of a conquest, as opposed to a settlement,
was ably supported by Lennard (1933–4). Even among non-specialists,
that successive cultures reached Britain on the backs of '"waves of population" perpetually pressing the aborigines westward' was not everywhere
given easy credence (Belloc 1904: 21).

However, the Germanist view prevailed, both among the scholarly
community and in more popular volumes. This was largely because the
general conclusions reached were compatible with contemporary political
and social attitudes, but also in part because they seemed to be supported
by the results of research coming out of new areas of study, which
gradually became better organized and more influential during the early
twentieth century.

The emerging research area which had the most immediate impact on
works of historical synthesis was the study of place-names. Place-name
studies were given a firm foundation by the work of Eilaart Ekwall and his
contemporaries, who brought to their efforts a detailed knowledge of
Anglo-Saxon and, less commonly, the ancient languages of Scandinavia.
From their studies a series of basic assumptions concerning the chronology
of English place-names passed from the status of hypothesis to that of
fact. Detailed examination confirmed that the majority of English place-
names were of English extraction; of those which were not, the vast
majority could be assigned to the Scandinavian languages and so to the
Viking incursions. The English language was practically untainted by

borrowings from Celtic (Forster 1921), suggesting that the two came into contact comparatively little.

The preponderance of place-names from English fitted neatly with an interpretation of the English settlement as a mass migration, and English place-names were seen to have displaced Celtic ones as efficiently as the English peasantry replaced their forebears. During the inter-war and early post-war eras place-name studies accentuated the Englishness of England against its Celtic neighbours and provided important confirmation of the general validity of the 'Guest/Green/Stubbs' view of the English settlement.

This view also found important support in early studies of villages and field systems. A series of monographs certified the close links which were seen to exist between nucleated villages and medieval open fields in England and the very similar phenomena which had been identified in Germany, whence they were generally thought to have been imported by the migrating Anglo-Saxons (Seebohm 1890; Vinogradoff 1892). Even when English studies were subjected to a more regional approach (e.g. Gray 1915), the central assumption remained that the Midland village and the open field should be linked to the arrival of Anglo-Saxons (often termed the '*adventus*') and they were discussed in that context in the first volume of the Oxford History of England (Collingwood and Myres 1936) – a volume which was a milestone in the synthesis of material culled from different disciplines. Such views on villages and open fields were adopted as fact by place-name scholars as well as historians, leading to peculiar perspectives concerning the environmental preferences of different ethnic groups:

> Good farmland was what attracted the Anglian settler, and there is no evidence that the British occupation of the Lakeland hills was seriously challenged till the Norwegians came from Ireland.
>
> (Armstrong *et al.* 1952: xxi)

A migrationary interpretation of the origins of England was also consistent with the early researches of archaeologists who worked on cemeteries in parts of eastern and southern England which were closely paralleled in north-west Germany. Ornaments or sepulchral urns dug out of the earth in England could be placed side by side with continental examples and there could be no doubt that the two groups belonged to the same cultures and, therefore, the same peoples (e.g. Baldwin Brown 1915). As museum collections were augmented, catalogued and studied, so it was possible to trace the artistic development of characteristic ornaments and other artefacts and begin to draw maps, with arrows which represented the direction of cultural influence and therefore the direction taken by Germanic folk during the migration. It was recognized [by the leading scholars] that this was a complex process:

> ... there is ... an archaeological overlap, composed of sporadic parallels, more or less exact, and of a large number of resemblances, not all of

which are of equal value in assessing the time needed for the arts and crafts to resume their natural course of development.

(Leeds 1945: 5)

The starting-point for this approach was necessarily literary – the framework of study was provided by Bede's description of the Anglo-Saxon peoples and their origins (*Historia Ecclesiastica*, 15) and it always suffered from the weakness of a chronology which had no secure start or finish. However, archaeological research focused new attention on objects which had previously been barely acknowledged, and Edward Thurloe Leeds was able to produce the first scholarly synthesis of Anglo-Saxon archaeology. In it he significantly amended the 'culture' map which he had adopted from Bede, and offered a series of what were to be extremely influential conclusions, arguing for example, on the basis of the cemetery sites of southern England, in favour of a riverine immigration as opposed to the use of the Roman roads (Leeds 1913).

That this influx of Germanic peoples was of low status seemed to be confirmed by Leeds's own findings at Cassington near Sutton Courtenay, where over a number of years he was able to carry out salvage excavations as a quarry destroyed a Saxon 'village' (Leeds 1947). The only structures identified in this, the first Anglo-Saxon settlement to be excavated even partially, were thirty-three 'pit-dwellings' which can only have belonged to a group of comparatively low status. The main conclusions drawn from the site by its excavator continued to focus on arrows on the culture-map:

In the main it would seem that the south-westerly advance from East Anglia, by which I have suggested that the Upper Thames came to be occupied in the first instance, halted at the Thames. Beyond it certain bridge-head settlements like Long Wittenham and Sutton Courtenay were established, but farther than that point advance was spasmodic and precarious, encountering almost continuous resistance from a hard core of native opposition, during one of whose attacks the Sutton Courtenay village seems to have been overrun and either exterminated or temporarily put out of action.

(Leeds 1947: 93)

Leeds concentrated on the inhumation cemeteries of southern and central England, leaving aside the examination of the problematical pottery of the 'Anglian' areas. These pots became the life-work of John Nowell Linton Myres. His studies were to provide the basis for a new and even more complex development of the cultural map of the English migrations (Myres 1969), which traced back the groups in England through waves of colonists to tribes on the Continent, among whom German contemporaries were busily demonstrating that extensive cultural intermixing was already occurring. The results suffer from all the problems inherent in a highly subjective area of study but the two hallmarks of Myres's work were the assertion that the Germanic settlement had begun well within the Roman period, and the interpretation of a body of late Roman pottery as evincing Germanic influence in decoration.

In one sense all these studies served to reinforce the Germanist view of the English settlement, yet in another sense there was surprisingly little attempt to test this theory. On the contrary researchers assumed its validity, then sought to reconcile their own work with it. The ethnocentric view of history was accorded by each developing discipline the respect due to a thesis the proof of which was already well established, but outside itself. Cultural influence was measured in terms of the numbers of the two communities interacting and substantial acculturation was deemed necessarily to require a large-scale immigration. When G.M. Trevelyan summarized contemporary opinion in 1926, few would have differed from his view:

> The attempt of the Romans to Latinize the Celtic civilization in Britain broke down because there were too few Romans... The Nordic conquest of England had larger permanent results than any of these conquests, because it was secured on a general displacement of Celtic by Nordic peoples in the richest agricultural districts of the island.
>
> (Trevelyan 1926: 28−9)

It was, therefore, with these messages emanating from place-name studies and archaeology that Sir Frank Stenton in 1943 published what remains the most complete study of Anglo-Saxon history that has ever appeared. He was himself a historian of the front rank, an eminent place-name scholar and in addition well versed in archaeological literature. The English settlement was not central to his brief but in his first chapter he offered an appraisal of the literary evidence which was sympathetic to the veracity of Bede and the *Chronicle* accounts. Turning at a later stage to the peasantry, Stenton (1943: 470 ff.) made it clear that in his view the Anglo-Saxon period witnessed the gradual decline of the status of the English peasantry from an initial state of primitive freedom to economic and personal dependence. His comments are a coherent summation of the Germanist view of early English society, a view which presupposes a large folk migration of German peasant farmers into England.

In the same vein, the possibility of any significant continuity between Roman Britain and Early England was shrugged aside by Professor Dorothy Whitelock in her scholarly and deservedly popular *The Beginnings of English Society* (1952) and less sophisticated Germanist views were about to be confirmed in their general popularity by Sir Winston Churchill (1956−8). The same theme was proffered in a work of considered scholarship by Professor Henry Loyn in his *Anglo-Saxon England and the Norman Conquest* (1962) and has been reiterated on several occasions since. Myres rewrote his earlier (1936) version of the English settlement for the Oxford History of England, the new volume appearing in 1986. The sequel attempted a complex and rarely successful synthesis of the chronicle material with the archaeology and was, if anything, slightly closer to Stubbs's original thesis than his earlier work:

> In the countryside, the landowning classes mostly lost their homes and their estates and were either dead or had fled. Their tenantry will have taken early opportunities of political and social confusion to escape both their legal obligations to their lords and the unwelcome attentions of barbarian raiders. Many of those who survived these experiences may have sought precarious refuge in the towns. Others, particularly in the south-west, would have joined the considerable numbers of displaced persons who made their way overseas to seek a new life in what soon came to be called Brittany. Some farmers... may have sought to maintain the cultivation of enough land to provide a subsistence livelihood...
>
> (Myres 1986: 214)

This volume is out of touch with contemporary historical research, which has found the narratives offered by Bede and the *Anglo-Saxon Chronicle* inadequate as records of the *adventus* (e.g. Sims-Williams 1983a). Yet such extracts demonstrate that the Germanist view of the English settlement remains entrenched. It dominates the popular view of England's origins and has a surprisingly influential following among scholars. Adapted a little and couched in new language, this interpretation remains fundamentally intact.

However, the premises on which it has been based have become progressively less secure. Re-evaluation has proceeded on several fronts, even apart from conventional history.

Perhaps the most spectacular development has been the rise of a new sub-discipline — or interface between several disciplines — landscape history/archaeology. As a subject, it was established by a single, seminal monograph, *The Making of the English Landscape*, published by W.G. Hoskins in 1955, but its roots lay in the studies already under way in archaeology and local history, not only by the author but also by men of the stamp of Arthur Raistrick and O.G.S. Crawford, then by Kenneth St Joseph and Maurice Beresford.

Crawford, then St Joseph, pioneered the archaeological use of aerial photography. The new techniques began to be applied systematically to the problems of settlement identification and this process still continues. The cumulative result has been the recognition that Iron Age and Roman Britain was far more densely settled than had hitherto been imagined. Population estimates leapt upwards from pre-war figures of 300,000 to four or five millions.

This upward re-evaluation has necessarily created problems of interpretation in the early Saxon period. For large-scale population replacement to have occurred, immigration would have had to have been on a scale far greater than had hitherto been envisaged, with half a million or more Germans crossing the North Sea. If the 23 metres long Nydam boat and its complement of around 30 men were typical of the vessels used in the *adventus*, the process has ceased to be credible.

In addition, specific discoveries threatened the entire model of an Anglo-Saxon colonization of Britain's virgin forests. Settlement sites of the Iron Age and Roman period have been regularly identified in many areas which were forest during the medieval period, implying that many of England's Norman and Angevin woodlands were, in fact, not survivors of a steady process of Anglo-Saxon colonization of ancient woodland, but the result of reforestation in the late Anglo-Saxon period or beyond. Under the guidance of Oliver Rackham, the study of medieval woodland has progressed to become a sub-discipline in its own right, with important lessons for those interested in the interface between the Roman and medieval worlds.

In parallel, historians have been increasingly prepared to test their perceptions of the past against the topography. The main progress has been made in the field of Anglo-Saxon charters, many of which have surviving boundary clauses. Their detailed study will always be associated with the name of Professor H.P.R. Finberg, whose painstaking work on estates and territories in Wessex and the south-west led him to initiate the view that Anglo-Saxon charter boundaries might delimit estates which had descended intact from the Roman period (Finberg 1957). A regional synthesis of all charter material from the West Midlands has important implications for our understanding of the mid to late Saxon landscape, and offers insights into what had gone before (Hooke 1981). On the basis of patterns of estate structure which he identified in both Wales and England, Glanville Jones postulated that early land units were organized on a 'multiple estate' system, in which large estates consisting of numerous settlements worked together in an integrated economic system dependant on focal sites of high status (Jones 1976). His ideas have had their critics (e.g. Gregson 1985), but they have at least offered a new route for speculation about early systems of exploitation and social organization.

Arguments in favour of continuity in estate structure were unmatched by the evidence culled from substantial medieval settlements. The first coherent excavation of a deserted medieval village began at Wharram Percy in 1950 and has continued each year since, finishing in 1990. Wharram was the trigger which was eventually to lead to several excavations of deserted or shrunken medieval villages. If these had been founded as organized villages by German migrants in the fifth and sixth centuries, then this should have been comparatively easy to illustrate through the techniques of archaeology. Yet in no instance has it proved possible to trace continuous occupation of a medieval village *per se* back to the middle Saxon period, let alone to the migrations. Although earlier farms might occupy the same sites (as at Wharram) the medieval English village was coming into being during the late Saxon period and thereafter (Beresford and Hurst 1971), when it replaced or amended a pattern of dispersed settlements. Archaeologists have been forced to adopt a far more dynamic model of early medieval settlement, acknowledging the omnipresence of tendencies for settlement shift.

The emergence of archaeological field-walking as a research tool in the last two decades has enabled some progress to be made in the study of the earliest medieval settlement, as a result of which the clear break between Roman settlement patterns and early English settlement has gone (Taylor 1982, 1983). It now seems clear that the farms of the period which witnessed the English migration were closer in style and distribution to those of Roman Britain than to the nucleated settlements of the medieval Midlands.

The antiquity of the open fields has also had to be discarded. Increasingly detailed surveys of documentary and topographical evidence have made it probable that the reorganization of land into a small number of extensive common fields was a phenomenon of the mid to late Saxon and post-Conquest periods, when land was laid out around newly nucleated village communities. That this process involved a revolution of sorts in the countryside remains a defensible view, but it was a change which occurred without any strong link with migration. Links between field systems and ethnicity can be laid to rest without a backward glance, but problems remain in the identification of the fields of the English settlement.

If early Anglo-Saxons did not live in medieval villages, where did they live? In a series of more or less extensive excavations it has been possible to unearth settlement sites of the fifth, sixth and seventh centuries in widely scattered areas of the country, from Northumberland to Sussex and from Staffordshire to Norfolk. The pit-dwellings of Sutton Courtenay told only part of the story. Elsewhere they have regularly been identified in association with substantial timber-framed halls. Such buildings corroborate the vision of the anonymous author of *Beowulf* who described Heorot, the great hall of Hrothgar, King of the Danes. Until the 1950s, parallels with Heorot had been sought in vain inside England. Now the discovery of the remains of such structures is comparatively commonplace (Rahtz 1976; James *et al.* 1984) but marked disparities between the form of settlement in England and in western Germany have led to the suggestion that such buildings owe more to insular traditions of architecture than to the Saxon homelands.

In parallel with these archaeological and topographical developments, a succession of historians have re-examined documents which might be expected to shed some light on England's 'Dark Ages'. In part, this has involved amassing all the relevant material, much of which was in the Celtic languages and unavailable in any modern edition. Works of literature which were largely the results of Celtic historical researches in the period *c.* 800–1200 were pressed into service and woven into a detailed account of the migration period (Chadwick 1969; Morris 1973). These analyses did not satisfy an increasingly critical generation of younger historians, who preferred to err on the side of caution when accepting the value of non-contemporary writings as evidence (Miller 1975a,b; Dumville 1977a,b) and who have since been responsible for a major re-examination of many of the crucial texts (e.g. Lapidge and Dumville 1984; Campbell 1986). Before his untimely death, John Morris put in train a major initiative to publish the principal early sources in new editions (e.g. Winterbottom 1978; Morris 1980).

The documents of the mid to late Saxon period were crucial in the development of the Germanist thesis and the re-examination of law codes, the Tribal Hidage, charters and a variety of others by a succession of scholars (e.g. John 1966; Abels 1988; Bassett (ed.) 1989) has produced a major overhaul of the way we view the social and military structure of the Anglo-Saxons and the emergence of the English kingdoms. Even work on the Domesday Survey has served to change attitudes towards what is likely to have gone before in a manner very reminiscent of the structure of one of the earliest and best monographs on the period (Maitland 1897). Such studies have changed much which had underpinned the 'Stubbsian' view of the English settlement.

Anglo-Saxon cemeteries have always provided the largest single database for archaeological exposition on the migration period and by far the most plentiful source of artefacts suitable for the construction of archaeological typologies. However, this area of research has had more than its share of problems. It was suggested as early as the 1950s that the British practice of inhumation may have influenced Anglo-Saxon mortuary practices (e.g. Lethbridge 1956; Kirk 1956). Few graves, whether inhumations or cremations, can be placed in a stratigraphic context with any other, so that dating can only be attempted by relating the dates of artefacts to each other by reference to typologies of their various classes. This detailed work was begun by Leeds and has continued with major recent contributions by Professor Vera Evison and Sonia Chadwick Hawkes, among several others. The assumptions which underlie typological dating no longer seem as secure as once they were and such dating is at best relative rather than absolute. The dating of an individual grave or even a small group of graves is vulnerable to the presence of comparatively old and/or very new grave furnishings. The dates which can be established are liable to periodic reassessment, as the delicate balance between different typologies is easily upset and can rarely offer a date more precise than within half a century. Even so, they are more accurate than carbon[14] dating has traditionally been. As a result, objective dating techniques have been little used in the study of Anglo-Saxon cemeteries.

The chronology of ornaments and other objects from English cemeteries is necessarily dependent on the dating of artistic developments on the Continent. The inception of the English settlement has oscillated within a time band which encompasses the bulk of the second half of the fourth century and most of the fifth. Dating of the earliest settlement depends on the correlation in Continental cemeteries between ornaments similar to those found in England, and coinage of the late Empire − a correlation which has only proved possible within the more southerly areas of Germany with which English material culture displays close links.

The entire edifice has been seen as a fragile one, the study of which has suffered from the inadequacies of early excavations and publications and the dispersal and loss of grave-groups. The most significant publication of the mid post-war era was a catalogue of cemetery sites (Meaney 1964) but study languished, falling far behind the excellent publication of excavations emanating from West Germany. When a new synthesis of Anglo-Saxon archaeology was published in 1976, ten essays covered every major aspect of the period except pagan cemeteries which were virtually ignored (Wilson (ed) 1976). Cemetery researches were given a much-needed focus by the publication of papers delivered at an Oxford symposium (Rahtz *et al.* 1979) and by a series of new syntheses (e.g. Hills 1979) and regional studies (e.g. Eagles 1979). More recently, the excavation and successive publication of Spong Hill (Norfolk) by Catherine Hills and of Buckland (Dover) by Vera Evison (1987), and the enormous interest generated by the Sutton Hoo Research Project (see the Bulletins of the Research Committee, 1983−90), have done much to re-establish cemetery studies in the eyes of scholars in other disciplines.

Efforts have been made to identify Britons within the English cemeteries (e.g. Faull 1977). However, this has not been markedly successful. Although archaeologists are far less confident now than they were in the 1950s that those buried in the Anglo-Saxon cemeteries were necessarily of German extraction, they have tended to prefer an interpretation of the Anglo-Saxon settlement which leans heavily towards that of Stenton or even Stubbs, adapted but not fundamentally altered to accommodate other information and ideas:

> The quantity of fifth century Germanic material now known from eastern England is considerable. This includes not only moveable objects but also house types and burial rites which have their origins in northern Europe, outside the Roman Empire. This can be explained only in terms of substantial immigration of people who came in sufficient force to retain their religion and way of life − not to become absorbed into existing society but to absorb the remains of that society into their own . . . Intermarriage and political expediency may have resulted in large numbers of the existing population taking on an 'Anglo-Saxon' colouring whatever their antecedents. . . perhaps not all the occupants of 'Anglo-Saxon' graves were of unmixed Germanic blood.
>
> (Hills 1979: 312−13)

The most consistent support for the Germanist interpretation has come from place-name scholars and other philologists. In the 1950s, Kenneth Hurlstone Jackson published his seminal work on the Celtic languages (Jackson 1953), in which he offered his own views of the relationship between language and history in the migration period. He recognized that significant numbers of Britons must necessarily have learnt to speak fluent Anglo-Saxon and his work has enabled other linguists who are not primarily Celticists to begin to tackle the problem of the identification of pre-English elements in English place-names (e.g. Gelling 1976a). However, it is not envisaged that Celtic place-name elements will ever be judged a substantial proportion and the Celtic contribution to the English language as a whole remains tiny. Most place-name scholars have adhered to the view that the English settlement involved the arrival of English-speaking tribesmen in numbers sufficient to overwhelm the local indigenes and swamp or marginalize their languages. The incomers are envisaged as entering a new land heedless of existing communities in occupation of it, in much the same way as European colonists settled in North America:

> Perhaps we should think of small bands, some of them coming together fortuitously somewhere en route. Not all members of a resulting larger band had an identical culture and not all who travelled together necess-arily settled together in one place. Probably most bands included whole families and with them they brought as much as possible of the basic necessities: seed corn, plough-shares, weapons, pots or skins... Some bands settled at the river-mouth and others within a short march of it; but most perforce proceeded upstream to found villages, hamlets or isolated farms beside the stream. Some moved up as far as the source.
>
> (Copley 1986: 19)

Not surprisingly there is now little consensus. Works of synthesis have tended to reflect the particular research specialization of the author. The final judgement of J.N.L. Myres has already been quoted. The opinion of Margaret Gelling has much in common with that view:

> It seems likely that a replacement of the kind which happened after the end of the Roman period... occurs only when the newcomers are farmers rather than, or as well as, overlords.
>
> (Gelling 1976b: 811)

That of Professor Finberg differed from it fundamentally:

> As for British ploughmen and shepherds, a wholesale slaughter of the rural population would be difficult to compass even if it had been desired. Without their labour how could the conquerors make the most of their acquisitions?
>
> (Finberg 1974: 32)

Writing marginally later, Professor Sawyer's remarks harked back to the vestiges of governmental continuity postulated by John Morris:

> ... rulers of the lowlands had certainly acquired significant rights and privileges, some of which survived the turmoil of the fifth and sixth centuries to provide a basis for the authority of English kings.
>
> (Sawyer 1978: 74)

Professor Thompson's views, expressed most forcibly in his work on St Germanus (1984), preferred utter discontinuity resulting from a massive invasion and settlement in eastern Britain in the 440s, which swept away all that then survived of Roman Britain. Yet for Professor Charles Thomas (1981a: 347) and Christopher Taylor (1983: 111), the incomers numbered no more than a few thousand. Christopher Arnold was very sympathetic to an influx on this scale (1984: 122−41) and was happy to envisage Britons in appreciable numbers within 'Anglo-Saxon' cemeteries. Richard Hodges has taken this argument one stage further, placing the inception of Anglo-Saxon England in a European context and highlighting the role of trade and diplomatic contacts with Frankia at the expense of migration *per se* (1989: 22−32).

Several developments in parallel disciplines − or in other sectors of the same disciplines − have played a part in shaping our changing attitudes. Recent writers have been well aware of the collapse of migration as an explanation of cultural change in British prehistory (Clark 1966) and of the developing theories of acculturation which are emerging in the vacuum which that collapse has caused. Theories of the collapse of systems were developed in an archaeological context to explain the sudden fall of civilizations in the Aegean (Renfrew 1979). The characteristics of late Roman and sub-Roman Britain clearly offer scope for an analysis of this type (cf. Tainter 1988), and it is now commonplace for archaeologists to examine the Anglo-Saxon settlement in a prehistoric context.

There has been disquiet at the apparent suddenness of the transition between the two entirely different and quite incompatible systems of Roman Britain and Anglo-Saxon England (Haselgrove 1979). To Richard Reece (1980), the entirety of the fourth and fifth centuries seemed ι period with a unity hitherto unrecognized, during which the high-profile Roman culture progressively gave way to an impoverished Celtic material culture, then an intrusive Germanic one, all within a single continuum.

Professor Colin Renfrew has recently applied himself to an archaeological problem which in many ways parallels the English settlement. In his monograph, *Archaeology and Language* (1987) he argues that the Celts were not a single ethnic people but a group definable solely in terms of a shared language. The cultures archaeology supposedly identifies:

> are simply the result of the taxonomic efforts of the archaeologist: they need not have had any great reality at the time in question.
>
> (Renfrew 1987: 217)

His arguments are unlikely to pass without substantial criticism, but parallel thinking concerning Dark Age Britain might imply that the English were a group defined by language and culture, rather than necessarily by ethnicity, a view already sponsored by Arnold (1984). Such interpretations imply a transfer of language and culture by diffusion rather than migration.

Be that as it may, the problem of the Anglo-Saxon immigration remains. The simple view of a wholesale or near wholesale replacement of a British population with a German one is inconsistent with the evidence which derives from a wide spectrum of research and must either be abandoned or at least massively adapted to the new evidence. Yet the material culture and language of the British lowlands, and the group-identity of the population which emerged, were the property of immigrants. If the mass migration of the Angles, Saxons and Jutes is not in itself a fact, that Bede and his contemporaries believed in it certainly is one. Perhaps these beliefs can be dismissed from the pages of history as myth, but none of the diffusionist explanations which have so far been offered in replacement have satisfied all groups with research interests in the area, let alone the general populace.

Archaeologists have tended in recent years to accentuate the independence of their own discipline and the necessity of reliance on archaeological rather than historical chronologies. While sympathizing with this view, we must beware of launching archaeology on a study of the past without any reference to other disciplines. It is not enough for archaeologists, historians or philologists, to offer their own versions of an explanation, in ignorance or in contradiction one with another. What is needed is for the conclusions of any one discipline or sub-discipline to be tested against research undertaken in others so as to produce a single explanation of the origins of England, however complex that explanation may turn out to be.

To explain the inception of the Anglo-Saxon world we need to examine Roman Britain as well as the Anglo-Saxons. We need to establish the sociological and cultural direction of the Roman world as the province neared its end and the ways these differed from the society which ultimately replaced it. We need to examine the differing experience of different parts of Britain in the fifth century, to assess why the upland or military zone was able to adjust to changing circumstances without massive changes in culture, while the lowland communities suffered a cultural and linguistic collapse and became transformed into Anglo-Saxon England.

This volume explores the possibility that Germanic immigrants comprised only a small proportion of the population of Anglo-Saxon England. To adopt this view can only be valid if the necessary processes of mass cultural and language change can be explained, and the parameters of these processes are therefore explored. In the last resort, it should always be remembered that it is possibilities — occasionally perhaps probabilities — but never certainties, which are under discussion. This volume will not seek to say what happened, since, as Kemble long ago recognized, that is lost. But we can explore the parameters of what might have happened and why.

Does it really matter what happened so long ago? Surely it does, and not just because of its curiosity value. To ask 'Who were the English?' is tantamount to querying the very basis of British national self-identity today. In a multiracial world it surely behoves the English and those who spring from or have been influenced by the English, to debate and seek to understand the make-up of their own particular sense of group identity. Such questions underlie what we think and what we are, and they are relevant far beyond an insular context. The expansion of England, the English people and the English language is one of the principal processes of modern history. It is enough to recall the meaning attached in the New World to the acronym 'WASP' to realize that much of the self-identity of the English has dispersed, with the language and sometimes with the genes, to metamorphose into the group-identity of Americans, Canadians, Australians and many, many more. Such questions matter.

CHAPTER TWO

THE ROMANIZATION OF BRITAIN

Before examining the downfall of Roman Britain, we need to understand the cultural changes that reached Britain as a result of contact with Rome and evaluate the processes which were involved.

Contact, conquest and culture change

Until Caesar's campaigns on both sides of the Channel, Britain lay on the extreme periphery of the Roman world. Even so, a trickle of Mediterranean goods did reach southern Britain, and those who controlled their dispersal obtained considerable political and economic advantages therefrom. Caesar's occupation of the Continental seaboard brought the political and economic system of the Empire to the Atlantic coastline. From there, Caesar launched two exploratory expeditions across the Channel, travelling along seaways by which British communities habitually maintained close contact with their Gallic neighbours.

In AD 43. Roman armies re-entered Britain and Roman forces rapidly occupied the south-east. From there the conquest was gradually pushed outwards towards the north and west until the boundaries of Roman administration reached the western shores of southern Britain during the third quarter of the first century AD. The unpromising lands beyond the Humber and Mersey were long left in the control of Brigantian client rulers but the collapse of Rome's allies there led Roman forces to campaign in the Pennines in the early 70s. Direct rule followed. Thereafter there was no obvious land frontier for Roman territory. Roman governors were faced with the alternatives of total annexation of northern Britain or the establishment of a land frontier. After a series of oscillations across northern England and much of Scotland, the boundary was finally established on the Tyne–Solway isthmus during the next century, with Northumberland and southern Scotland firmly controlled by Roman soldiers. 'Roman Britain' had come into existence.

Imperial authority over the province (later diocese) of Britain did not finally cease until c. AD 410. Indeed, Gildas still expressed himself as a citizen (by implication of an imperial province) several generations later. Britain's Roman history was a long one.

The Roman Empire was a colonial and imperial power which had expanded by the successful use of military force. It was also a cultural and economic system of a specific kind, which had developed within the Mediterranean world, and which Rome exported to the very different environmental and social conditions of transalpine Europe. Provincial communities were subjected to economic and cultural pressures and tended to adopt the cultural and economic habits of *Romanitas* which were reaching them with the armies, administrators and traders of their conquerors. Once arrived, such habits tended to disseminate through existing social hierarchies, downwards from the erstwhile tribal élites.

Although studies of Romanization were already an important part of archaeological research early this century (e.g. Haverfield 1912), the process by which Roman culture influenced the cultures of its provinces and neighbours is currently once again under scrutiny. Scholars of several nationalities have separately examined various sections of the contact zone between Mediterranean and North European cultural systems (e.g. Bartel 1980–81; Wells 1980–1; Brandt and Slofstra 1983; Cunliffe 1988; Barrett *et al.* (eds) 1989; Okun 1989). The ultimate aim of this approach is a greater objectivity, resulting in a better understanding of social and economic processes within indigenous societies under Roman influence. It already offers a welcome counter-balance to the implicitly Rome-orientated, chronological descriptions of Roman Britain which still dominate the literature (e.g. Frere 1978; Salway 1981). In particular, this approach offers valuable insights into the processes of adaptation in Britain to the critical events which begin and end the period: the Conquest and the end of Roman authority. But first, it is important to define the underlying condition of British society at the Conquest, where an expanding economy offered opportunities for cultural and social change.

Growth and its pre-conditions

Britain experienced a rapid rise in population during the centuries immediately before and after Christ (Cunliffe 1978), which was probably both caused and characterized by a decline in mortality rates (Jones 1979). This demographic increase arguably resulted from a concurrence of factors: more sophisticated political and social units emerged in southern England, able to engage in economic specialization and to concentrate and store an agricultural surplus; a climatic regime more conducive to agriculture than any for a millennium (Lamb 1981) provided conditions for crop growth which were near to the optimum in lowland Britain and facilitated the gradual expansion of increasingly intensive agriculture in the north and west, where it had been at a low ebb since the Middle Bronze Age; fewer harvest failures made a shift in the threshold of agrarian viability possible and encouraged agriculturalists to venture on to hitherto marginal land. They colonized such terrain as the wetter, lower terraces of the upper Thames valley (Benson and Miles 1974) and the valley sides of the better drained of the Pennine valleys (**2.2**), where cultivation had hitherto long been uneconomic.

Expansion of production was contemporary with a proliferation of crop species which provided more flexible options for the farmer (Jones 1982) and with improvements in agricultural technology associated with the widespread adoption of iron tools (Rees 1979). The bulk of such improvements in farming equipment had already been widely adopted in the south and east before the Conquest occurred, although iron tools may have remained scarce among the farmers of Wales and Cumbria into the Roman period or even later. In the south, the early centuries AD saw additional improvements in crop-cutting equipment, a proliferation of wells in farmyards and, eventually, a coulter blade and asymmetrical ploughshare which were capable of turning a furrow. Since the spread of earlier elements occurred without apparent check at the English Channel, it is unlikely that the Conquest was a crucial factor in the arrival in Britain of these later products of the Iron Age agricultural revolution.

The conquest of some regions was bloody and may have brought a temporary halt to the growth of the British population. If so, it was one which seems to have been too slight or too brief to be detected today through the blunt instruments of settlement or pollen studies. All have produced results consistent with continuing and rapid population growth in the first century AD.

If the Conquest made a positive contribution to demographic expansion, then it was in the suppression thereafter of tribal warfare. This would have been significant only if raiding was a widespread problem. The deployment of tribal manpower in the summer months for war rather than harvesting, or the fear that arable fields would be dangerously vulnerable to raids may, hitherto, have artificially constrained the spread of agriculture. Livestock were more easily removed to safety than near-ripe corn. It is possible that those areas with marked concentrations of hillforts (Dorset or the Welsh and Scottish Marches) may have been zones where slave raiding was prevalent (Cunliffe 1983; Higham 1987a). Communities elsewhere probably lost no more from raiding than their children were to pay to Rome in taxes. Indeed, some had necessarily benefited, and inter-tribal hegemonies probably reduced warfare to a low level. That taxation stimulated agricultural production in early Roman Britain is a poorly founded view still too rarely challenged, but rising levels of cultivation can only have increased tax revenues.

The origins and causes of the linked demographic and economic expansion were, therefore, environmental, technological and organizational. They owed little to the Roman invasion, even though expansion arguably continued well beyond the Conquest and Romanization certainly encouraged specialization and production for the market. When expansion peaked is a matter for conjecture. The collation of palaeobotanical evidence indicates a relatively long plateau of maintained clearance which might indicate that the population stopped rising soon after the Conquest (perhaps in the second century) and then held more or less steady for a considerable period. The total reached is unknown and, in absolute terms, unknowable. However, it was clearly the greatest population density that this island had experienced hitherto.

Since the Second World War, site discovery has led to an exponential increase in most areas of England in the numbers of settlement sites known, so that population estimates for Roman Britain have been successively uprated from the *c.* 300,000 of the pre-war era. A total in excess of the Domesday population of 1.5−2.5 millions now seems certain, although levels closer to the suggested estimates of 4−5 million of *c.* AD 1300 remain contentious. Significant technological differences separate the Roman and high medieval communities with consequences for productivity. It has as yet proved impossible to establish for any region outside the Fens a density of Romano-British settlement which compares numerically with that of *c.* 1300, but we might still expect the population of the province to have reached 3−4 millions.

Population increase and expanding land-use resulted in an episode of rigorous woodland clearance for pasture and arable. This has been identified in most locations where it has been possible to test suitable deposits. Its origins were non-synchronous, occurring earlier in the milder and drier parts of the country and spreading thence to the north and west and to the uplands, where, for technical reasons, it has been most extensively recorded (e.g. Turner 1981a). To give just two examples from many, pollen analysis of peat at Rishworth in West Yorkshire established that, at a horizon centred on 1 BC to AD 140, herbaceous pollen rose steeply to *c.* 50 per cent of the total pollen count, while arboreal pollen fell to *c.* 20 per cent (Bartley 1975). At Featherbed Moss, Derbyshire, pollen representative of trees and shrubs was reduced in favour of herbaceous plants; the latter reached 60 per cent of the total pollen counted and cereal pollen began to appear. A date of 155 BC to AD 25 was derived by carbon-dating a sample from early in this episode (Tallis and Switzur 1973).

Exceptions to this expansionary picture have been identified on Arran (Robinson and Dickson 1988) and in south-west Ireland (Lynch 1981), and agrarian expansion reached the core of the Lake District only comparatively late in the Roman period (Pennington 1970). However, these instances should probably be attributed to the marked oceanity of local climatic conditions. A general climatic shift elsewhere towards a more Continental type of climate created conditions suitable for agricultural expansion and rising population levels required larger stocks of grazing animals.

Late Iron Age and Romano-British farmsteads were typically enclosed yards defined by bank and ditch, fence or wall, within which more or less numerous round houses provided the bulk of the covered accommodation, used both for human living space and for a variety of other functions (**2.1**).

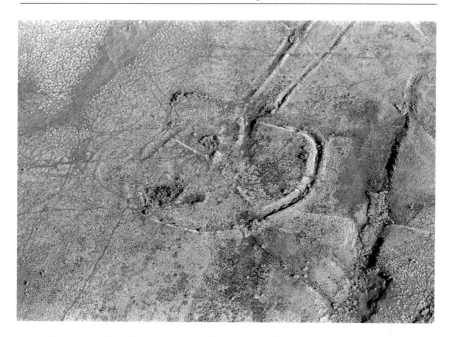

2.1 The unusually well-preserved earthworks of a farmstead almost certainly occupied in the Roman period, part of a complex of farms and fields on Aughertree Fell, Cumbria (copyright G.D.B. Jones and the author).

Many settlements were associated with enclosure systems, also defined by a variety of means but predominantly by ditches and banks along which hedges were probably planted and maintained (e.g. Robinson 1978). In many instances these field systems were small agglomerations associated with only one or a handful of settlements; such systems always predominated in the north and west (e.g. Bowen and Fowler 1978 *passim*; Gates 1981; Higham 1986a).

However, farmers were exploiting the land available to them with increasing rigour and to increasing effect. The tendency for ever more numerous generations to follow one another over several centuries created growing pressure on limited territorial resources. Where most heavily affected − in parts of the south and east − regional communities had recourse to defining and therefore defending individual or group rights by wholesale enclosure of vast tracts of their land. Some of these enclosure systems display an impressive degree of regularity over vast areas, implying that they were the work of social groups rather than individuals.

In parts of East Anglia, some systems clearly predate the Roman roads (Rodwell 1978; Williamson 1984, 1988). It is in this region that such field complexes have been most widely researched and their component parts categorized. Comparable systems are a dominant landscape feature in northern and eastern Kent, where they have received far less attention.

Similar systems were laid out on land reclaimed from the sea during the Roman period on the Wetlooge Levels on the Welsh side of the Bristol Channel (Allen and Fulford 1986). In all these instances the basic fabric of the system still exists, despite the post-war agricultural revolution which has caused massive losses among hedges and field-tracks in eastern England.

Although surviving only as crop-marks, similar systems have been identified and in part dated as pre-Roman and Roman in the north-east Midlands and south Yorkshire (Riley 1980) and across much of the Fenlands (Philips 1970; Hall 1987). Similar but more restricted evidence has been identified at Brockworth in Gloucestershire (Rawes 1981), where it was suggested that wholesale replacement of one rectilinear and aligned system by another occurred during the Roman period.

Standing enclosure systems which are still visible as earthworks are widespread on the lower slopes of the limestone Pennines, in Wharfedale, around Settle and in the valleys of the Doe and Lune, to give a handful of the more obvious examples (2.2). On downland in southern England 'celtic' field systems were a commonplace before modern arable destruction. Most have been presumed prehistoric and some seem to have been out of use before the Conquest but recent research on the Berkshire Downs has established that, there at least, much of this field creation post-dated the advent of Rome: 87 per cent of the boundaries sampled originated during the Roman period, implying a major intensification of land-use and the widespread conversion of old pasture to regulated and enclosed arable (Ford *et al.* 1988).

These examples are by no means exhaustive but they do indicate that complex enclosure systems were a widespread phenomenon in the Iron Age on both sides of the Roman intervention in Britain. Little of this was entirely novel. Communities a millennium earlier had similarly used 'co-axial' field systems, for example on Dartmoor. However, the later Iron Age witnessed a widespread expansion of enclosure. Centuriation (the characteristically Roman grid of roads and fields) may have occurred around one or more of the *coloniae* but its impact was geographically very limited and little evidence can now be identified (e.g. Gloucester, see Wacher 1974a: 154). Elsewhere it is unnecessary to look to specifically Roman systems of landscape management to explain the available evidence, although enclosure and re-enclosure continued to occur during the Roman period. Some later Roman farms and villas were clearly equipped with new trackways, paddocks and field systems, but such were no more than representative of a continuing process of agricultural enclosure or even re-enclosure, the roots of which were firmly planted in pre-Roman Britain.

This investment in enclosure systems was internally resourced by communities or individuals who expected a social and economic return. Enclosure gave cultivators and graziers alike greater control over land-use, enabling standing crops to be defended from foraging herds. It facilitated the selective livestock breeding which protected strains of sheep imported

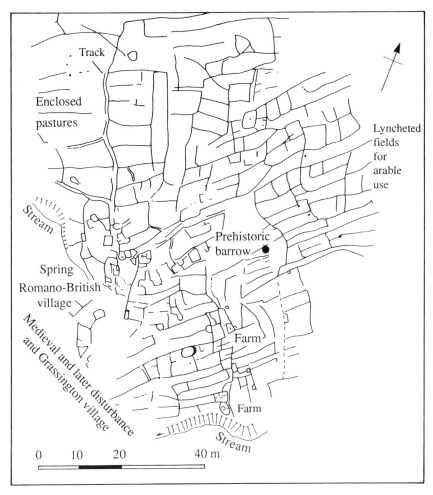

2.2   Iron Age and Roman period fields at Grassington (Wharfedale). This detail from the extensive field system on the lower limestone fells at Grassington is typical of numerous examples which were in use during the Roman period and abandoned at some point during the following millennium. Fields on steeply sloping ground (as here) tend to be smaller than those laid out on comparatively flat terrain, but pronounced lynchets on parts of the system demonstrate that it was used for arable cultivation. Soil erosion in the course of its use may have been an important factor in the abandonment of the system which was ultimately replaced by strip lynchets of typical medieval form on the lower slopes of the valley.

in the late Iron Age or Roman period, from reversion to indigenous types (Wild 1982; Ryder 1984) and enabled stockmen to breed cattle of a superior size. Across the landscape, increasing human pressure reduced stocks of wildlife and thereby reduced the incidence of crop losses from deer and other animals, the hunting of which re-emerged as a popular, aristocratic pursuit in the Roman period. Provided the necessary technological and organizational skills could be deployed to maintain fertility, the community could expect increases both in total production and in productivity, whether measured per unit area or per unit of labour.

The integration of Britain into the Empire began when this demographic and agrarian expansion was in full flood, and presumably benefited from its continuation across the early generations of Roman Britain. It meant that those who had access to the agrarian surplus collectively enjoyed an income which was buoyant or rising and unusually predictable at the very time when they were presented with a series of cultural options by the colonial power. Who controlled that surplus and how did they exercise their options?

The Romanization of Britain

The social hierarchy
In the early post-Conquest period, military garrisons in the south and east of England provided local communities with a limited acquaintance with Roman culture. The commerce which was attracted to the fort gates provided a more effective network of market facilities than had existed before and attracted traders and artificers from the Continent as well as the hinterland. Within a generation the soldiers moved on leaving tribal communities already in the process of social change, as tribal élites began to adopt a more Romanized role for themselves, translating their existing local dominance into forms which conformed ever more closely to imported ideas, fashions and social systems.

Archaeological evidence and classical ethnography are mutually supportive in indicating that many tribal societies in Celtic western Europe were hierarchically organized when the Conquest occurred (e.g. Nash 1981). Southern Britain was no exception (Haselgrove 1984). Social control was expressed through a mesh of vertical relationships which Roman writers equated with the patron–client system of the Classical world.

The Conquest smashed the inter-tribal hegemonies of the Catuvellauni, the Brigantes and others but it left internal tribal hierarchies largely intact. It was presumably members of the leading families of tribal societies who emerged from the late first century onwards as the Roman-style magistrates (*curiales*) of the newly self-administering tribal territories (*civitates*). To serve was both an honour and a considerable expense. The competitiveness which had been a characteristic of tribal society was now diverted into more Romanized channels: investment in the urban infrastructure of *basilica*, baths, bridges and water supply, or the provision of entertainments. Only those with a large purse could afford to enter office. The magistracies of the *civitates* probably circulated exclusively among those who controlled the surplus from agrarian production.

A settlement hierarchy in the Roman countryside is shown by the contrasts between comparatively Romanized sites such as villas, and other farms. This hierarchy began to emerge within the first century, when a few villa-palaces and large numbers of modest Roman-style farms were constructed. By the third century, the hierarchy was entrenched. The consensus view is that villa owners consisted predominantly of those with control of significant amounts of land or the surplus therefrom — that is, the indigenous landed gentry and aristocracy.

In the few cases where excavation has strayed beyond the residential apartments of *villae rusticae*, evidence of agricultural buildings and corn-dryers suggests that home farms were often attached, the produce of which was owned by the proprietor. The curial classes were, therefore, characteristically in direct control of land. Their enterprises were many-headed, large-scale agrarian enterprises which used the best technology available and produced a large surplus, beyond what could be consumed on the estate, for sale in the market-place. Villas were part of the cash economy and tended to congregate around some but not all urban markets (Hodder and Millett 1980).

However, the villa owners were more than just large-scale farmers. The social status of the curial class is probably better defined through its relationship with the farming population than with the land itself.

At the Conquest, weapon-carrying tribesmen were a large and important component of the population, albeit in the more advanced societies of the south and east associated with individual tribal leaders in a form of social dependency involving reciprocal but unequal services. As inhabitants of Rome's new province, these tribesmen lost their military role to soldiers who were full-time professionals. The erstwhile tribesmen were disarmed and henceforth prohibited from owning or using weapons. They were 'civilianized' and 'detribalized'. The change in their social standing was fundamental: they were converted from tribal farmers into peasants — traditional farmers operating within and at the base of a complex state society.

The sociology of peasant farming in the Roman Low Countries has been explored by Slofstra (1983) and her conclusions are generally applicable to lowland Roman Britain. Such a peasant society operated an economy which was small in scale and family-based, with individual families linked laterally through ties of kinship. It worked with traditional technologies, skills and organizational practices to produce yields consumed primarily in subsistence. The bulk of whatever surplus there was went in compulsory outgoings which left only marginal amounts for family members to use in exchange or social interactions. They were, therefore, able to participate in few of the material or cultural aspects of Romanization.

Within the Empire, peasant societies were typical in hinterland situations and dominated both by a complex state apparatus and by a social élite whose roots were local but whose culture, economic behaviour and self-perception were more or less extraneous and Roman. Both élite and peasantry descended from the tribal communities of the Conquest period and it has been cogently argued in the context of northern Gaul that tribal relations of dependency were transformed as a consequence of the Conquest into a patron—client relationship on the Roman model.

The adoption of this model for Roman Britain would confer the role of patron on the villa owner and that of client on their peasant neighbours, and define the relationship between them primarily within these roles. Clients would look to the patron for support within the local community and its courts, and as an intermediary *vis-à-vis* the state, as represented by the taxman, recruiting officer or judge. In return, their 'gifts' would supplement the income of the patron and their presence would, on occasion, swell his entourage (Saller 1982).

The peasant farms of Roman Britain were, characteristically, dispersed holdings, visible on a wide variety of different types of soil and terrain. Most were of a size to be family farms and evidence from excavation and fieldwork has been generally consistent with this model. Pottery from field walking such sites is far less in quantity, diversity and quality than derives from villa sites, and coinage is poorly represented. The architecture was relatively conservative, with investment in Roman styles of architecture slight and late, where it occurred at all. Such farmsteads were numerically dominant within the lower levels of the settlement hierarchy in the countryside of Roman Britain.

In contrast, particularly at their peak after *c.* AD 280, villas were centres of highly Romanized modes of consumption, as exhibited in their architecture, ornamentation and plan. To take mosaics as just one indicator among many, renewed investment by villa owners in the late third and early fourth centuries typically led proprietors to commission schemes dominated by Classical iconography. Such mosaics betray a widespread traditional Roman education among the local gentry and, to an extent, even among the mosaicists (Stupperich 1980; Cookson 1984). The evidence of wall-paintings is directly comparable. If the gentry of Roman Britain were availing themselves of the standard Roman education of Vergil, Latin grammar and rhetoric, then they were alienating themselves from anything which was distinctly British in their history in favour of the traditions of the Imperial power. They were also fitting themselves for a public life of a peculiarly Roman kind, within a Romanized *civitas* administration.

Some peasant farms have been identified in nucleated groups, some immediately adjacent to substantial villas. One such example was under excavation at Raunds (Northants) in 1989 and others are known at Chalton, Nettleton Scrubb, Grassington, Grandford, Thistleton Dyer and, perhaps, Hibaldstow. Such groups are reminiscent of medieval manorial villages and may imply that some villa owners obtained a significant income as landlords (Rivet 1964; Percival 1976).

Tenant farmers known as *coloni* were a typical component of Imperial estates in Italy and elsewhere by the first century AD, paying rents in cash and produce, supplemented, from Trajan's reign onwards, by annual labour services. Imperial estates were probably widespread in Britain throughout the Roman period, some being agricultural and some associated with mineral exploitation, and the same status may have been introduced at an early stage and spread to other estates. It is possible that some peasants were tenants of villa owners from early in the Roman period, whether their settlements were nucleated or dispersed.

If these arguments are accepted, then the curial classes had available to them three methods of drawing off the agrarian surplus: by direct cultivation of a small proportion of the land surface; by the proceeds of tenancies, potentially of larger areas; and by the profits of a patronage system which could extend far beyond land over which the villa owner had any pro-prietorial claim to include groups of peasants, small towns or rural artisans who were unattached to any particular estate. Such a system of patronage probably developed from pre-existing associations within tribe and kinship group but rapidly developed characteristics which were more Roman than British.

The system of land tenure practised in Roman Britain is poorly evidenced. Attempts to apply the principles of medieval Welsh tenure by kinship groups have tended to dominate recent discussion (Stevens 1947, 1966; Jones 1972; Percival 1976). The identification of numerous villas in Britain and north Gaul with two or more accommodation units (the 'unit-system') has encouraged the suggestion that tenure even among the gentry was centred within the kinship rather than the individual or stem family (Smith 1978, 1985). Although challenged as an interpretation of specific sites (e.g. Webster and Smith 1987), this view has been remarkably persistent as a guiding principle.

Notwithstanding the general trend of recent argument, the case for kinship tenure of villas is inconsistent with the status, capital accumulation and aspirations of an élite who had adopted the language, education, life-style and culture of Rome. Such an élite is unlikely to have allowed itself to be constrained by pre-existing tribal systems of tenure. Parallels with the Edwardian conquest of Wales, for example, suggest that tenure systems can replace one another with relative ease when the local élite find attractive an alternative offered by the colonial power. The sole surviving land sale document from Roman Britain (from Chew Stoke) uses Roman civil law (Turner 1956). The comparatively strong view of private property that characterized Roman law had obvious advantages for those capable of asserting proprietorial rights over land. Multiple units of habitation on villa sites are as easily explicable via the Roman practices of 'universal successors', of the division of property of the intestate, or even by the dower house principle, as by medieval Welsh law. The occurrence of hall-type villas —

dominated by a single large room – may imply that architecture was influenced by social pressures from within the family, but the type is not common in Britain.

There were several mechanisms by which Roman land law can have become familiar in Britain: through the expropriation and administration of land for Imperial estates; through the acquisition of land by Continental aristocrats; or by the training of local gentry in Roman law as one element in a multifaceted process of acculturation. All provincials were in any case Roman citizens from Caracalla's reign onwards and technically subject to Roman courts. While certainty remains beyond our grasp, it seems likely that the villa-owning class did adopt Roman land law during the Roman period. Tribal tenure systems survived among the peasant tenants of villa estates, groups of free peasants within systems of clientage, and among the communities of the north and west. In practice, land tenure probably provides another means of comparison between a Romanizing élite and the embedded culture of the ex-tribal peasantry.

One area in which there was plentiful scope for the exercise of patronage lay in the administration of taxation, by which the peasantry were expected to contribute substantially towards the Roman system of government and the army. Under the early Empire, taxes consisted of three elements: tax on the capital value of land (*tributum soli*); a poll-tax (*tributum capitis*); and various indirect taxes. The last were collected initially by *publicani*, then by procurators, the remainder by the magistrates of each *civitas*. The system required that the peasantry exchanged goods for coin in which to pay their taxes. The tax system provided, therefore, an important stimulus for interaction between the peasantry, who grew and sold their produce, the urban markets which enabled them to exchange their produce for cash, and the social élite who distributed the burden and had it collected on behalf of the state. Taxes were normally collected in cash and the grain needed by the army was purchased, at least until the collapse in the value of the currency led Diocletian, in the late third century, to replace taxes in coin with taxation in grain and other types of produce. Before the reign of Diocletian, grain was not obtained directly by taxation but was requisitioned at a fixed, and generally acceptable price (Mann 1985).

Urbanism

Urban life was the key to Roman civilization. Indeed, for the purposes of local government, the Empire could be defined as a network of self-administering towns, each the focus of its own territorial unit. Tacitus was accurately reflecting the expectations of Roman colonial administrators when he recorded his father-in-law's putative efforts to urbanize the British tribal aristocracies (*Agricola* 21). According to his account, the indigenous élite adapted themselves relatively quickly to a civilized life-style which was necessarily urban.

The earliest British towns had in fact already been imposed from above.

These were the several *coloniae* (initially Colchester, Gloucester and Lincoln), communities of high status, probably planted on *territoria* commandeered by the state, within which existing land-use rights were disestablished. Built by soldiers, they were principally but not exclusively communities of retired veterans enjoying land grants (Wacher 1974a; Salway 1981). If they provided a bond between Britain and the Empire it was at the expense of considerable hostility, which found an outlet in the Boudiccan rebellion.

By the Flavian period, tribal societies in the south and east had begun to metamorphose into a network of self-administering *civitates*. Since some of these administrative units were apparently new-fashioned, it seems probable that the provincial government played a leading role in their spatial organization (**2.3, 2.4**).

Under the gaze of this same officialdom, the new *civitates* developed urban centres which served them as local capitals. These new urban foundations characteristically focused on an integrated block of public facilities composed of a forum and basilica, baths and other amenities, laid out probably with official help to a Roman blue-print, with streets on a grid plan and near square *insulae* between. Many were sited on the recently evacuated fort sites (e.g. Exeter: Bidwell 1979) and they rapidly succeeded the early *vici* as the principal regional centres. They performed a variety of functions as centres of administration, jurisdiction and distribution. Within them, new temples sited, built and ornamented with statuary in the Roman mode provided a spiritual expression of local corporate identity. The concentration of cultural and leisure amenities provided an environment well suited to the new preoccupations of the tribal élite, who could indulge in recreation and social intercourse on the Roman model in intervals between the management of their business interests and client systems.

During the first half of the second century, the tribal élite appear to have concentrated their resources on constructing public buildings in the larger towns. Perhaps with subsidies from the state, these were built in stone from a comparatively early stage. Around them was erected a miscellaneous group of timber-framed private buildings, apparently designed as shops and workshops as well as residential premises. Among them, the homes of the élite are not conspicuous, perhaps owing to the heavy commitments of their owners to public building and to repaying the money-lenders who facilitated much of the early investment.

After the mid-second century, the timber-framed buildings tended to give way to far less closely spaced, stone-built town houses, which often, like those so well represented at Verulamium, had wings arranged around a courtyard, mosaic floors, plastered walls, painted frescoes and hypocausts (summarized in Wacher 1974). The construction of such houses involved a substantial private investment and it is generally agreed that they represent the normal residences of the curial classes in the later second and third

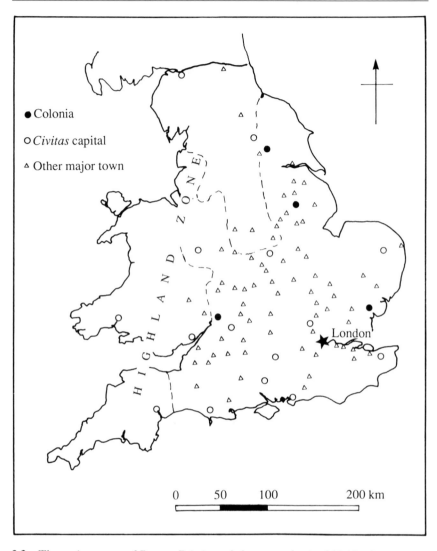

2.3 The major towns of Roman Britain and the non-urbanized highland zone: significant towns were concentrated in southern and central Britain, and tended to avoid the Fens and the Weald. They were almost entirely absent from the hill country of the west and north, where isolated *civitas* capitals and *vici* represent the limits of urbanization and Romanization, beyond which local communities probably remained organized as *pagi*.

centuries, whose rural residences were probably rarely occupied other than by estate managers. The tribal élite were, at this stage, predominantly town dwellers.

Until the late third century, towns witnessed the major concentration of investment in both public and private buildings. By comparison with Italy

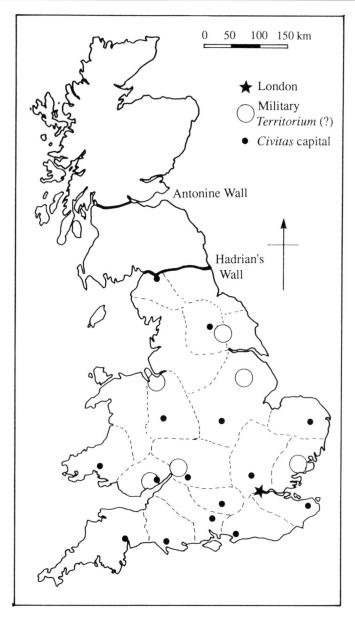

2.4 The legionary fortresses and the *civitates* of Roman Britain: only those territories containing a capital town are known to have been *civitates peregrini*. Within the province, all tribal boundaries are necessarily speculative.

or Provence, levels of investment were generally modest. Less prestigious classes of amenity, such as the public water supply, seem to have been provided with singular parsimony. However, the relative success and extent of the urban network imply the adoption of Roman culture, life-style and economics by numerically significant sections of the population, led by the local aristocracy.

The urban élite clearly spoke Latin and were presumably educated in it. It was to this community that Carausius addressed himself when he inscribed one of his coin issues with a quotation from Vergil. The extent of Latin among other sections of the urban community is a matter of guesswork, but late second-century Latin graffiti on the walls of a derelict house at Leicester (Wright 1964) are just one of many indications that provincial Latin was the *lingua franca* of the towns. In Gaul, Latin eventually supplanted the indigenous Celtic language, even in the countryside, and this process may have at least begun to occur in parts of lowland Britain.

Towns were a vehicle for Romanization, where the Empire and the local community met and interacted. The process was a complex one, Romanization occurring through the filter of a hierarchical social system. It is certain that, however it be measured, integration into the Roman cultural system was far more complete in the towns — and there particularly in the households of the rich — than in the hinterland.

Between and beside these larger towns there developed a network of smaller urban or quasi-urban centres. Commercial factors were probably crucial in the evolution of many small towns, which grew up at coastal or riverine transhipment points, river crossings, at route junctions and at comparatively regular intervals along major and much-used routes (Finch Smith 1987). Others developed as *vici* outside the gates of the forts along the frontier or at boundaries between one tribal territory and another (Hodder 1975) or between a tribal territory and the territory of a major army unit, particularly a legion (*prata legionis*, as at Heronbridge: Mason 1988). Many depended heavily on a single commodity or service: such included the social and religious centres at Springhead and Bath, salt extraction at Nantwich and Droitwich, and the redistribution of locally manufactured pottery at Chesterton and Mancetter (Todd 1970).

At such sites the narrow street-fronting houses and workshops of artisans and shopkeepers predominated, suggesting that low-status dwellings, small-scale manufacture and redistributing were important functions. Houses with rooms linked by a corridor which closely parallel small rustic villas may have housed substantial farmers or the owners of small estates. Other inhabitants may have worked as agricultural labourers in the surrounding countryside, implying that some small towns may have been little more than estate villages.

Few small towns ever enjoyed many of the amenities of Roman town life (e.g. Alexander 1975) and, with the exception of ever-fashionable Bath, small towns were far less élitist than were the *coloniae* and *civitas* capitals.

The city which received most stimulus from the movement of goods was London. Resources of all sorts reached the armies on the north-western frontiers from the Mediterranean via a tax and trade conduit up the Rhône to the Rhineland and thence to Britain. London was the north-western terminal of this movement of goods. By AD 100, at the latest, it had become the provincial capital and was by far the largest and most densely populated urban centre in Britain, with bustling commerce and warehousing focused on wharfs and quays on the waterside. From the town gates radiated the provincial road system of the second century along which residential and commercial activity spilled over into suburbs, such as Southwark. London's civic and, perhaps, its private buildings were orna-mented with a wealth of imported marbles and porphyry from southern Gaul, Italy, the Greek islands, Turkey and Egypt (Pritchard 1986), which far exceeded the supply of such exotica to other Roman sites in Britain.

With the exception of London, which belongs in a separate class, the towns of Britain were modestly successful specimens of transalpine urban-ization. The larger examples came to consist first and foremost of the residences of the local élite, grouped around the recreational, cultural, religious and commercial facilities which they patronized, and the admin-istration which they oversaw. The broad outline of the geography of most towns was established between c. AD 90 and 120. The size and shape of most was to change little over the next century and a half and it was essentially the town as existing in c. AD 120 that was walled in the late second or third centuries (Crickmore 1984).

Burial practice and religious beliefs

On the Yorkshire Wolds, late Iron Age communities practised furnished inhumation under barrows. Apart from a thin scatter of similar burials in other parts of Britain, most regions entered the Conquest period with methods of corpse disposal which are not archaeologically discernible. The same is true of some Rhineland communities (e.g. Willems 1983).

Caesar's conquests carried Roman sepulchral practices to Brittany and Normandy in the 50s BC. Some members of the British community pre-empted the Claudian invasion by several generations, adopting cremation from c. 40 BC, and the practice spread over the next 80 to 90 years throughout the south-east. The occurrence of primary burials with satellites and differential grave-goods may indicate social hierarchies and varying social status (Black 1986).

After the Conquest, cremation cemeteries of characteristic Roman type proliferated, sited (as required under Roman law) outside the boundaries of Roman forts and towns. By the later second century, the rite of cremation was giving way to inhumation throughout the western Empire, including Britain, with the result that different rites occurred in the same cemeteries, with inhumation slowly replacing cremation.

Since inhumation, like cremation, was viewed as the threshold of the afterlife, the burial party did what they could to expedite the departed on their journey, burying them clothed and with grave-goods which might include coins for their passage and talismen or amulets for protection. Presumably for the same reason, graves were often laid out on a specific orientation, the commonest being north−south, although east−west or west−east orientations are common, particularly in the *civitas* of the Regnenses, in Sussex.

These changes in mortuary practice were neither precisely contemporary with, nor caused by, the Roman Conquest: the fundamental change-over to cremation began almost a century before the Claudian Conquest; the shift from cremation to inhumation gathered pace over a century later. Invasion is, therefore, an inadequate explanation of these changes, which must be attributed to more complex processes of cultural contact and cultural change. Burial rites were a comparatively unstable part of British culture, prone to oscillation under a variety of stimuli from across the Channel.

Although numerous Roman-period cemeteries and burials are known, there is a danger that they are unrepresentative of the total provincial community. The vast majority lie immediately outside towns and forts. However, the urban and military population was never more than *c.* 20 per cent of the total. What of the cemeteries of countryfolk? The villa-owning classes are probably represented within urban cemeteries as well as in the small but prestigious mausolea which occur near some villas. In contrast, peasant burials are rarely identified, excepting a scatter of burials within rural settlements, most of which are infant burials and some of which may be foundation deposits. Urban cemeteries are not so large that they are likely to contain large numbers even of those peasant families who lived and died in the immediate vicinity. Indeed, they rarely seem sufficiently large to accommodate the estimated urban population.

There is some evidence for very different burial rites in the Roman countryside. These include poorly furnished barrow burials, many of which were secondary insertions into prehistoric mounds. Examples have been found as far afield as Northumberland and East Anglia (Lawson *et al.* 1981), where some (e.g. Eastlow Hill, Rougham) were comparatively sophisticated, with cremations in glass jars deposited in wooden coffins or in a tile-built burial chamber. Other examples were surrounded by multiple square ditches. The rural shrine at Lancing Ring, Sussex, was associated with cremation burials dated as late as AD 200, at the end of a sequence which begins with a Bronze Age urn.

These examples are exceptional but they do suggest attempts by the indigenes to reconcile insular mortuary practices with those of the intrusive culture. The more sophisticated, at least, are unlikely to represent peasant burials. It is tempting to think that the mortuary practices of the rural peasantry of Roman Britain were normally as archaeologically obscure as those of their pre-Conquest ancestors; indeed, they may have continued those same traditions throughout the Roman occupation and beyond.

If so, Romanized burial customs failed to penetrate the lower reaches of the social hierarchy. Such a view is consistent with that of numerous other indicators, and further reinforces the view that a cultural gulf existed between urban and élite communities and the rural peasantry.

Religious observance was also an important area of interaction between Roman and British ideas. Julio-Claudian colonial governors initially antagonized the newly conquered tribes by the establishment of an Imperial cult at Colchester, then the provincial capital. However, by the last decades of the first century, increasingly Romanized and urbanized élites were investing in stone temples, sited in Roman fashion in major towns. Roman and Celtic religions were similarly polytheistic and lacking in overall organization. Synthesis of the two was comparatively painless. Urbanization established a network of new cult centres which enjoyed the patronage of the social élite, who readily adapted imported gods from Continental pantheons to their own needs, and adopted the fashion for anthropomorphic representation. By the late second century, such changes were well established, and urban priesthoods and the management of urban temples were probably integral to the administrative structure of the *civitas*.

Outside the major towns, local religious observance was focused on rural shrines, many of which flourished during the Roman period, accepting some influences from Roman religious practices but retaining much that was British, and continuing to attract funds and devotees from locals and travellers alike (Blagg 1986). Late pre-Roman structures were replaced with so-called Romano-Celtic temples, which translated insular architectural forms − for example, at Heathrow − into new materials (Wilson 1975; Muckelroy 1976). If their architectural conservatism reflected a stable ritual, then most temples in the small towns or in the countryside of Roman Britain housed cults which were indigenous, served by rites which were traditional. Even extensively Romanized cults retained pre-existing locations and compromised over the presiding deities.

At one extreme, such cults included highly Romanized cult centres such as that which 'twinned' the local deity Sulis with the Roman Minerva, in a large and Roman-style temple at Bath (Cunliffe and Davenport 1985), or the crowd-pulling temple and theatre complex at Gosbecks (Dunnett 1971). At the other end of the scale, a shrine within the Iron Age hillfort at Chanctonbury Ring (Sussex) attracted offerings from the mid-first century at least until the late fourth, focused on a flint-walled *cella* with three side walls and an east-facing entrance, ornamented with painted wall-plaster and a tessellated pavement (Bedwin 1980).

Religious customs in Roman Britain were characterized by their diversity of form and focus. There was much that remained predominantly Celtic, much that demonstrated a compromise between local cults and Roman practices, and a further spectrum of cults imported *in toto*, by soldiers and civilians, from the Continent or further afield. The latter tended to be the preserve of specialists − townsfolk, soldiers, administrators or other members of the 'international' community. Elsewhere, independent, local and traditional cults continued to flourish, strongly supported by numerous votive deposits.

Cultural frontiers and the periphery of Roman Britain

The provincial frontiers were barely permeable barriers to the movement of manufactured goods. Roman products reached southern Scotland during the Antonine period, but rarely before or thereafter (Robertson 1970; Macinnes 1989). Few Roman goods reached Ireland before the eventual breakdown of the frontier system. Comparison between the finds from excavations in Northumberland and those in Durham and Cumbria imply that the deposition of artefacts of all kinds is far greater on farmsteads within the province than without, and the local élite controlled the dispersal of Romanized goods outside the province. On present evidence, the provincial frontiers of Britain were zones of military and diplomatic activity, across which there was only a severely inhibited exchange of material culture.

However, the geographical limits of the province were not the frontiers between a fully integrated Roman system within, and a barbarian society without. As characterized by the twin institutions of civilian towns and villas, the Romanization of Britain fell far short of its western or northern frontiers. Neither type of settlement is regularly found in the proximity of forts with contemporary occupation levels, nor in marginal terrain.

Only five villas have been identified among the *Dumnonii* of the south-west, four lying close to their probable eastern boundary, in the vicinity of Ilchester. In south Wales, Carmarthen and Caerwent achieved *civitas* status long after most southern and eastern centres, probably in the Hadrianic period. Few villas occurred in Silurian territory excepting second- and third-century examples, clustered on the narrow coastal plain (Robinson 1988; **2.5**). No such Romanization occurred in north Wales, where Wroxeter represented the western limit of urbanism and Chester retained its primarily military character throughout most of the period. In the north, the *civitas Brigantum* focused on Aldborough and was another second-century creation, associated with no more than a thin scatter of unspectacular villas and very few small towns. This northern outpost was reinforced, perhaps as late as the third century, by the establishment of the villa-less *civitas* of the *Carvetii* based on Carlisle. With this uncharacteristic exception, the extension of the network of Romanized towns and country houses had ceased by midway through the second century. A rough line drawn from Exeter through Caerwent and Wroxeter to Lincoln and Aldborough would leave only Carmarthen and Carlisle on the wrong side of a cultural frontier which was internal to the province, separating the comparatively Romanized south and east from the less Romanized north and west. It is a commonplace to divide Roman Britain in this fashion into civil and military zones, and to describe them in separate terms, or describe only one while virtually

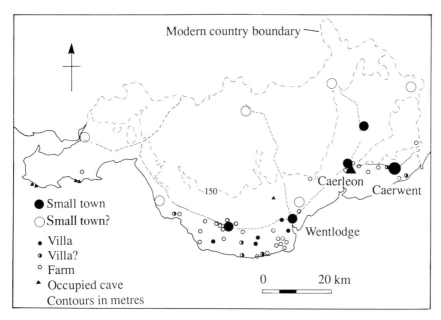

Modern country boundary —

Small town
Small town?
Villa
Villa?
Farm
Occupied cave
Contours in metres

Caerleon
Caerwent
Wentlodge

—150—

0   20 km

2.5 Romanization on the periphery: settlement hierarchies and the structure of Roman period settlement in south-east Wales (based on Robinson 1988).

ignoring the other. However, these zones are not of themselves a product of the Roman period: the concept of a distinctive archaeology of the highland *vis-à-vis* the lowland zone was an important exploratory model in the 1970s (e.g. Evans *et al.* 1975; Limbrey and Evans 1978) and remains valid today.

Since the Anglo-Saxon settlement was predominantly a southern and eastern phenomenon, this chapter has concentrated on interpreting the Romanized social system in southern and eastern Britain. However, both zones were part of Roman Britain and both were affected, if in different ways, by the arrival and eventual departure of Roman culture. In many respects, their experiences of Romanization during the occupation equipped them in very different ways for the challenges posed by its end. It is that which justifies here a brief review of the cardinal characteristics of Roman Britain's military zone.

The north and west have a near monopoly of Britain's high ground, rain which far exceeds the needs of the arable farmer, and soils which are severely leached or impermeable (**2.6**). Like many Roman frontier regions, upland Britain produced little food and represented the edge of the European temperate climatic zone.

Much of the high ground was already permanently cleared long before the Roman period and subject to peat growth. However, renewed clearance was characteristic of the centuries on either side of Christ in much of

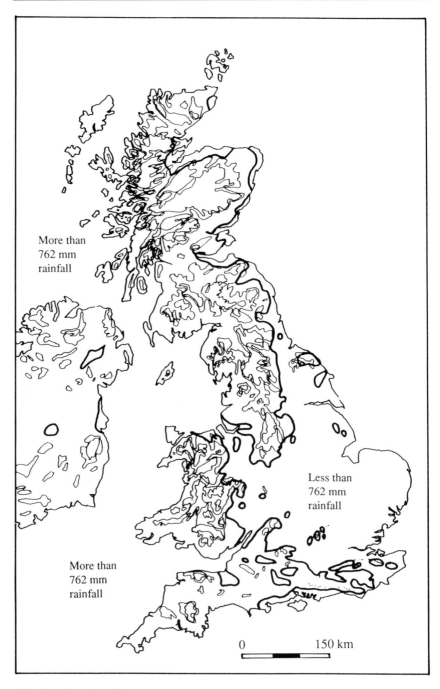

More than
762 mm
rainfall

Less than
762 mm
rainfall

More than
762 mm
rainfall

0   150 km

2.6 Relief and rainfall: a geographical definition of the upland/lowland divide.
Contours are at 123 and 246 m (400 and 800 ft). Rainfall is below 762 mm (30 in) in
eastern England, rising to two and three times this level in the north and west.

Wales and in the north-east of England, implying improving climatic conditions, rising population and an expanding rural economy. Although extensive field systems are scarce, cultivation was widespread – it seems now impossible to excavate the banks of the *vallum* beside Hadrian's Wall without finding evidence of cultivation beneath, much of which probably belongs to this period.

The north

By AD 100, almost all the *c.* 40,000 men who comprised the provincial army were stationed in the north and west. In the 120s the Emperor Hadrian evacuated Wales and concentrated the bulk of them in the north and there most of the slowly dwindling auxiliary units remained, excepting only a minority who were redeployed to new forts such as Reculver and Brancaster on the Channel coast in the 250s or 260s.

In the first century, the army was a major vehicle of Romanization. However, this stimulus declined during the second century, by the end of which most auxiliaries on the northern frontier were probably Britons (Mann and Mann 1973), from low-status and comparatively un-Romanized backgrounds, whose first language and outlook were Celtic. Much recruitment was probably local, particularly after the Severan division of Britain into two provinces, and army service offered members of the local community their only obvious means of advancement. During the third century, many soldiers had families with them and presumably established widespread links of kinship with local families living in the *vici* or on the land. As a consequence, the division between soldier and civilian which characterizes the civil province was gradually eroded in the military zone and substantial links forged between them.

One effect of the garrisons was to create a powerful demand for foodstuffs, raw materials, equipment and manufactured goods of all kinds, which was met by taxation, compulsory purchase and trade. The result must have been a net inflow of wealth to the frontier zone from the south and east and, until the Severan period, from the Continent. One of the primary functions of the *vici* outside the gates of many forts was the provision of trade-goods to the soldiers. Merchants and carriers were attracted to the area from far and near by official contracts and by the regular pay of the troops. Limited manufacturing occurred locally, but most was abandoned during the second century in favour of imports of better quality. Although there is ample evidence of metalworking in the *vici* and military depots of Lancashire and Cheshire, there was no industrial revolution in the countryside of the Roman north.

In the military zone, the wages of the garrisons brought cash which entered the economy through their purchases in the *vici*, but few coins were lost on local farmsteads. There was a vast gulf between the rate of deposition of coins and other artefacts in the forts and *vici*, and in local farms. The latter display none of the evidence for social hierarchies so characteristic of the areas where villas were common, and it is difficult to identify any mechanism for collecting the rural surplus so as to sell it to agents of the military.

Although an influential case has been made for local provisioning of the army (Manning 1975), it is unlikely that northern communities ever produced sufficient corn to feed the troops stationed among them, or sold a substantial surplus for cash. Requisitioning from farms which grew coarse grains in small quantities would have been at best tedious, at worst uneconomic.

The sameness of the farmsteads of the frontier zones suggests horizontal organization of the local community through kinship groups, comparable perhaps to that of the Belgic tribes in Gaul on the eve of the Roman Conquest (Roymans 1983). They probably retained pre-Roman systems of land tenure and other tribal characteristics throughout the Roman period. Landscape studies imply a family-based settlement system with individual or small groups of settlements associated with clusters of fields, the whole surrounded by unenclosed pasture. Cultivation of crops is unlikely to have risen much above subsistence levels and most of the land surface was probably given over to cattle rearing.

Hidden subsidies helped to neutralize, for government agencies, potentially adverse effects from the length of the supply lines which brought bulk produce to the soldiers, so local provisioning may have been less important than has been supposed. Even so, the absence of coin from farmsteads leaves the problem of tax payments by the northern community. If the example of Frisia is relevant, local farmers may have been allowed to pay their taxes in cattle. Alternatively they may have sold produce in the *vici* for the cash with which they paid their taxes, then exchanged whatever loose change remained for goods before returning home. A trickle of bangles and pottery onto farm sites identified archaeologically may favour the latter interpretation.

The upland communities were disarmed, and to that extent reduced to civilian status and even peasantized, but the absence of a Romanizing aristocracy made them less vulnerable than their peers in the lowlands to a drop in status and they made few concessions to Romanity: unless they deposited their dead in the cemeteries outside the *vici*, their burial practices are obscure.

The west

By the end of the first century, the West Country was already self-administering, with a *civitas* capital at Exeter (Isca). However, Romanization made little impact on the settlements of the Dumnonii, despite signs that levels of population and agrarian land-use were rising. Except for a single example near Illogan, villa construction died out close to the eastern borders of the *civitas*, with the handful of small Romanized farmhouses such as Holcombe (Pollard 1974). Elsewhere, settlement was not obviously hierarchical. Enclosed settlements, termed 'rounds', existed prior to the Conquest or were, like Trethurgy (Quinnell 1986), constructed during the Roman period. In some areas, rounds are so numerous that they leave little room for other settlement types. Elsewhere, unenclosed settlements were contemporary with them and differences in size, defensive circuits and artefacts may reflect a primitive social hierarchy.

The Hadrianic evacuation of Wales coincided with successful attempts to integrate south Wales into the civil province. The result was a localized settlement hierarchy which compares with many parts of the lowland zone, with Roman-style towns as social, religious and administrative centres, and a countryside exhibiting small towns, villas and farmsteads (**2.6**). Outside these southern islands of Romanization, the settlement structure of Wales was closer to that of the south-west.

The lowlands of Pembrokeshire were characterized by a type of enclosed settlement similar to the Cornish round, locally termed a 'rath' (Williams 1985). That at Walesland was certainly occupied in the Roman period, and circular structures were abandoned in favour of a rectangular building more than 9 m × 3.5 m, and located adjacent to the Iron Age entrance (Wainwright 1971).

Further north, there is even less to distinguish Roman period settlements from their Iron Age precursors. Hillforts such as Tre'r Ceiri were either continuously occupied or reoccupied during the Roman period, but most settlements were small, either enclosed or unenclosed farmsteads, with buildngs which departed little from the Iron Age circular design. Most were sited on cultivable land (Johnson 1978) and many were associated with lyncheted fields. Romanization is conspicuously absent from this countryside, although small quantities of low-status artefacts reached some settlements. At others, the dating of occupation causes problems almost as severe as those in Northumberland and carbon 14 dating has proved an essential method of fitting settlements into even a crude chronological context.

Frontiers and the local people

With the exception of marginal areas such as southern Wales (which moved from the military to the civil zone, then back again), all parts of the upland zone exhibit broad cultural similarities during the Roman period. All shared in the common expansion of population and land-use, and were probably characterized by subsistence agriculture combined with stock rearing on a scale capable of a surplus. They appear to have had no use for coin before, and little during the Roman period. There is a low level of settlement hierarchy and a tendency towards large numbers of broadly similar settlements; all exhibit a low level of institutional or architectural Romanization.

The picture which emerges in all areas is of a generally peaceful but thoroughly un-Romanized society, which had made few concessions to the colonial power and remained embedded in a social structure and economy which was, to all intents and purposes, that of the pre-Roman world. The reasons for this are complex and not well understood. Any explanation must take account of the comparatively low levels of population and productivity which were typical of these communities. Both factors must have inhibited development of a Romanized social hierarchy. It must also take account of the role of government and of the military in siphoning off large amounts of land and other resources for their own use. Parallels for such un-Romanized zones are common enough in other frontier provinces. However, these are not, on their own, adequate explanations.

Their apparent immunity to Roman culture owes much to the social structure of these communities. They were distant from the cross-Channel trade routes that had stimulated the foundation of pre-Roman chieftainships and tribal kingships in the south and east. When Roman frontiers moved nearer, they did so with a speed which prohibited complex social change. A client kingdom existed for a single generation in the north and its rulers constructed the massive *oppidum* at Stanwick, but there is little evidence for the rapid development of social hierarchies elsewhere in Brigantia. When the kingship of Venutius was swept away, it left a scatter of communities without extended social hierarchies. The leading Welsh tribes resisted Rome with an obstinacy which implies that they made no sudden changes to internal social structures, successively adopting Caratacus, an outsider from the Catuvellauni in south-east England and therefore removed from tribal hierarchies, as their military leader.

Most of the north and west probably entered the Roman province with tribal societies within which there was little stratification, with tribal systems of land tenure and undifferentiated (and unknown) mortuary practices. The signs are that they retained these broad social or cultural characteristics into the later Roman period. In contrast, the tribes of the south and east were led into the provincial system by a self-interested and self-motivating élite who had traditionally sought and competed for imported culture in its various forms. Such an élite had not developed in the north and west and changes wrought by the Conquest naturally favoured social stability and the status quo. Free tribesmen linked to one another by ties of kinship coped with the pressures of Roman culture from a position of approximate economic equality one with another. From this starting-point very few were able to progress towards a fully Romanized life-style.

Without the resources which the gentry of the lowlands drew from their clients, tenants and demesne lands, the tribal leaders of the upland zone did little more than flirt with Romanization. Their households remained in the countryside, habituated to social intercourse conducted in Celtic and to residences which gave little indication that they occupied even a far western corner of the Roman Empire.

CHAPTER THREE

BRITAIN AND THE LATE ROMAN STATE

Crisis and response: the later Roman Empire in the West

The Empire was subjected to successive political, military and economic pressures in the third century. The constitutional trauma began in AD 238, when, in all, five Emperors were variously deposed in fewer months. Military usurpations destroyed any hope of peaceful succession to the leadership of the Empire as rival army commanders and armies fought for control of the central system of patronage. Armies on campaign within the Empire impoverished the communities on whom they were billeted or from whom they requisitioned supplies. Barbarian peoples invaded and did widespread damage to the economy and social fabric of both town and country.

The first indications of a monetary crisis preceded even the political collapse. The Severan emperors raised army pay and numbers and, to fund it, reduced the silver content of the denarius from *c.* 70 per cent to 45 per cent. Thereafter, successive governments diluted the precious metal content of the currency, producing a coinage of cheap alloy with only 5 per cent silver content, with debasement at its most extreme around AD 270. Prices rose between the 190s and 260s by a factor little short of a 1000 per cent, and continued to rise, if less dramatically, into the fourth century. Whereas requisitioned supplies had, in the past, been purchased for cash, escalating needs, declining discipline and a moribund currency meant that requisitioning was progressively transformed into a species of taxation.

In many respects, centripetal administrative and cultural forces peaked in the second century, both in Britain and in the Rhineland (Bloemers 1983). With Emperors distracted by events in the East and on the Danube, the disgruntled soldiery in Gaul raised Postumus to the purple in AD 259 and he was acknowledged by the British and Spanish provinces. The so-called Gallic Emperors retained a semblance of central control over the western frontiers, until their territory was reunited with the remainder of the Empire under Aurelian in AD 274.

Even thereafter, Gaul and its neighbours were expected to raise sufficient resources and recruits to maintain their own armies and their own administration. Rising governmental demands fell on a reduced and impoverished civilian population. Much land had been abandoned in vulnerable areas behind the Rhine frontier. German cultural influence was flooding into the Gallic frontier provinces as the Roman system declined, but Roman administrations sought to reconstruct their tax revenues and defend the prefecture.

A succession of capable, Illyrian soldier-Emperors retrieved the political unity and geographical integrity of the Roman world in the decades after AD 268. Building on their achievements, Diocletian and Constantine I reconstructed the body politic of the Empire in line with the changed military, administrative and fiscal conditions of the early fourth century.

The state that emerged from their reforms in the mid-fourth century was very different from the Rome of Hadrian or Marcus Aurelius. Indeed, the succession of Diocletian has been seen by some scholars as representing the break between the ancient and medieval world systems, so marked were the several new departures which he instituted.

Within the new polity, the division of the role of the Emperor among several individuals became a normal constitutional stratagem. Imperial absolutism became far more blatant; provincial government was divorced from military command and the number of provinces virtually doubled; the Empire was reconstructed with a hierarchy of province, diocese and prefecture; the administration was reformed and increased markedly in size; the civil population was regimented in a command society – organized in hereditary classes by occupation, each of which was compelled to meet the needs of the state for goods and services instead of responding freely, for cash incentives, to market forces.

The army was also changed out of all recognition: the number of army units was substantially increased and a new hierarchy established in which the frontier forces (*limitanei* or *limitatenses*), under *duces* ('dukes'), lost status, influence and resources to field armies (of *palatini* and *comitatenses*), under the command of *comites* ('counts'). Cavalry were given a much higher profile and barbarian soldiers tended to dominate the élite units. The field army grew rapidly in size, incorporating the more effective of the old-style legions and auxiliary cohorts as well as new recruits, and was divided into several regional forces. Field army units were not regularly attached to forts but were billeted in towns on the main route network in the hinterland of the Empire. Army commanders were no longer the amateurish aristocratic careerists who were hitherto so common but professional soldiers, many of whom had risen from the ranks. As a result, soldiers from the periphery or men born outside the Empire became increasingly common at all levels of the career structure within the Roman army, and the way was open for the rise of figures such as Stilicho, guardian of the Emperor Honorius. At the end of the fourth century, the person of the Emperor represented a vital link between military and civilian hierarchies and the demise of the tradition of warrior emperors was critical to the cohesion of the Empire.

After the extreme debasement of the silver coinage, restoration of the currency was a pre-condition of economic reconstruction, of sound administration and flexible taxation. By the death of Diocletian, in AD 337, the Empire had a much sounder coinage than for several generations, in gold, silver and copper denominations, and under far stricter central control than hitherto. Throughout the fourth century, coinage (particularly bronze coinage) proved a key vehicle for Imperial propaganda and was carefully controlled by Imperial administrations.

To pay for renewed state expenditure on an enlarged army and administration, and on an enthusiastic programme of public building, Diocletian effected a thorough reform of taxation. Governmental salaries were being paid in the late third century in food and fodder, to protect the civil service from the effects of rapid inflation. To provide for the basic needs of army and administration without recourse to the market, Diocletian established state factories for strategic goods and replaced the much devalued taxes in coin with taxation in kind, based on the productive value of agricultural land (measured in *iuga* – yokes) and of labour (in *capita*). Taxation and its destination fell under the control of the several praetorian prefects.

Collection remained the responsibility of the municipal oligarchies, who bore collective responsibility for any shortfall in the tax burden of the entire community. The wealth of the curial classes was threatened by the increasing demands of the state, as well as by recent barbarian raids. The administration recognized that municipal office was now a burden and used compulsion to maintain the co-operation of the *decuriones*: they were incorporated and given collective responsibilities for various services (*munera patrimonii*), and the property qualification for membership was lowered to as little as twenty-five *iuga*. Even so, in many areas, the aristocracy withdrew to their estates, or sold them and took refuge in flight. Anyone who was able to disguise the extent of his wealth or removed himself from the lists of civic membership. Suppression of pagan temples under Constantine I was to reduce further the ability of *decuriones* to finance municipal government, and many took refuge in the tax-exempt status of the Christian Church.

All but slaves and, perhaps, *coloni* (*Cod. Theod.* XI.14) were individually responsible for their taxes to the local administration. Most tax obligations were tied to land and passed, with that land, from one owner to another. Where land fell out of use, the tax burden on other members of the community was automatically increased, thus tending to create spiralling abandonment where the agrarian economy was weak. City administrations were thereby forced to seek new cultivators for all abandoned land.

Where those with access to Imperial patronage gained the privilege of tax exemption, their share of the tax burden was similarly spread across the remainder of the community. Many wealthy landowners eventually obtained the privilege of commuting payments to cash (*Cod. Theod.* X.25,1;

XI.20,6) and so avoided the often onerous cost of the delivery of tax in kind, but this was resisted by successive governments through the fourth century. By the reign of Majorian (457−61), land taxes were regularly commuted at two gold *solidi* on the *iugum*.

Taxes in kind never entirely replaced exactions in coin, which were still required for a variety of purposes, and were collected in gold and silver from the trading classes. Kent (1956) argued that renewed fiscal reform took place under Valentinian I, after which taxes paid to the Imperial household were accepted only in the form of bullion bars, derived from melting down coinage extracted as tax from the *civitates*, at government treasuries. From them fresh coins were struck at the convenience of the Emperors' officers, by what amounted to a travelling mint. His case has since been widely endorsed (e.g. by Casey 1979b). However, although important changes undoubtedly occurred at this date, it would be a mistake to assume that these changes encompassed all forms of taxation and civil obligation. More or less regular issues from a number of Continental mints seem to have continued. Garrison troops and post stations were still clearly in regular receipt of taxation in kind long after 367 (*Cod. Theod.* XI. *passim*) and it is doubtful if taxation in precious metal made much headway in replacing taxes in produce or services before the loss of Britain.

This unwieldy and burdensome tax system was integrated with a command economy: groups of traders, artisans and other specialists were formed into gilds which enjoyed exclusive rights within their own specialism but had to bear much-increased obligations to the state. Such gilds were hereditary and membership was compulsory. They were held liable collectively to the labour or service imposts of the state, and compulsion replaced the market incentives of the early Empire (Williams 1985).

All but persons of illustrious rank were required to undertake public duties of a menial nature, on demand. These might be the provisioning of public services, constructing or maintaining public and sacred buildings, roads and bridges, or finding the expenses of delegates or tax gatherers. Even Aurelian's walls around Rome were constructed with conscript labour. In addition, provincial communities were expected to provide recruits for the army, or payment in commutation (*Cod. Theod.* XI.16,15; Ammianus XXXI. 4).

The proliferation of social controls required an army of bureaucrats, informers and overseers and it is clear that the late Roman economy suffered from all the drawbacks of a command economy: economic stagnation and the suppression of enterprise; corruption and injustice, and scarce resources wasted on the maintenance of an administration boosted numerically by men in search of its privileges and with ample opportunities for venality. The result was an oppressive inflexibility. Faced by tax nonpayment, the state apparatus could make no exceptions for harvest fluctuations or changes in the productivity of land. It sent troops to collect the outstanding taxes, where necessary stripping peasant farmers of their capital equipment. Those who did not flee were forced into debt. Debts, contracted within the patronage system or by the non-payment of rent, necessarily weakened the position of the smallholder or tenant *vis-à-vis* the gentry and that of the gentry *vis-à-vis* the great aristocracy: many hitherto free peasant communities passed in the fourth century into a form of servitude — *coloni* — and became tied to the land.

The opportunities created by successive political proscriptions, the partiality of Imperial patronage and Imperial concern at the abandonment of land encouraged the rise of an Empirewide aristocracy, the most successful of whom held vast landed interests which spanned the land mass of the entire Empire. These *possessiones* were the natural allies of the state, trading the collection of taxes and army recruits for increased authority over tenants and clients alike.

The search for a state religion
By the late third century, Roman religion was exhibiting pronounced signs of syncretism, attempting to unite different faiths. A series of Emperors recognized the social and governmental advantages of a state religion and experimented widely with the Roman Pantheon, the Sun-God and, ultimately, with Christianity. Constantine was personally sympathetic to Christianity and subjected it to the ultimate test on the field of battle in AD 312 at the Milvian Bridge. Continuing success thereafter encouraged him to give Christianity preferential treatment, by massively endowing its churches, by adding his authority to its councils and by adopting it as something not far short of a state religion. Despite Julian's patronage of Neoplatonism, Christianity became increasingly dominant among the élite of the Empire and in its towns throughout the remainder of the century. In the West, Christianity had been of little significance in the third century, but it now spread through the governing classes, within the patronage system, along trade routes and among urban communities. In most areas of the Empire, Christianity had come to stay. For the future, the Emperor and his officials would attempt to control what people did. His bishops told them what to believe, and the Christianity of the late Empire became an integral part of the command society, the religious structure mirroring that of the secular world.

Britain and the Empire

Unlike Gaul, Britain was little affected by the political and military turmoil of the third century. Indeed, this was probably the most prosperous and peaceful century of Roman Britain. However, the insular provinces and their populations were substantially affected by wider economic forces, and by the military, social and fiscal reorganization of the state under Diocletian.

The armed services

The Severan campaigns in Scotland re-established the credibility of Roman arms among the tribal communities of the far north. The long peace that ensued facilitated widespread troop reductions. At least ten of the Wall forts were partially or totally abandoned during parts of the third century, along with many others in the northern hinterland.

Even so, most forts along the Wall retained a military presence, but garrisons were much reduced in numbers. After his defeat of Allectus at the end of the century, Constantius set in train a programme of structural renewal, which is still visible at several of the Wall forts, such as Housesteads. Pre-existing barracks were demolished and replaced with terraces of close-set but free-standing 'chalets' (e.g. Daniels 1980). The capacity of the new-style housing was no more than 15 per cent of that which it replaced, implying the presence of much smaller garrisons, now occupying 'married' quarters. Although widely distributed, the northern command of the *Dux Britanniorum* may have been no larger than *c.* 5000 men, all of whom consisted of the lower-paid frontier troops.

During the second half of the third century, some troops were redeployed to the south coast, where civilian communities had seen few soldiers for two centuries. Britain was protected by the Channel from the bulk of the German attacks across the Rhine. The *classis Britannica* (the Roman fleet operating in the Channel) remained operative from its principal bases at Boulogne at least until *c.* AD 240 and Dover until *c.* AD 210 (Cleere 1989).

The fleet was probably effective in containing Germanic piracy to the north of the narrow seas between Kent and the Pas de Calais. The communities of the south Scandinavian and German coasts numbered trading, piracy and raiding among their economic strategies throughout the period. However, their traffic seems to have been coastal and there is no evidence that their sail-less ships had the capacity to raid Britain across the breadth of the North Sea. Roman maritime supremacy in the Channel, therefore, protected the whole of Britain and Gaul from Continental raiders. The Dover–Boulogne narrows served as a maritime *limes*, or frontier, where a Roman fleet controlled the passage of craft towards all the shores of the Empire.

Along with other regional fleets, the *classis Britannica* either fell into decay or was disbanded in the middle of the third century. Its functions were reallocated on an *ad hoc* basis to army units, some of which had previous experience of shore defence. New bases were provided for the purpose, sited so as to defend harbours, which may have been used as bases for offensive action on the Channel. In Britain, these are known as the Forts of the Saxon Shore (3.1), but the title is evidenced no earlier than the *Notitia Dignitatum*, in which a series of coastal garrisons comprised the separate command of a *comes*. Before the late fourth century, there is no evidence that they constituted a system: they were not built in a single episode but probably as piecemeal responses to several stimuli, including

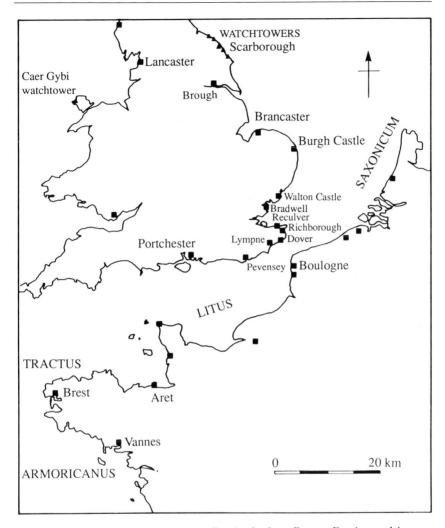

3.1 The defences of the Atlantic coastline in the later Roman Empire, and its command structure.

pirate attack; in architectural style they reflect successive developments in military design from the middle to the end of the century or even beyond (Cunliffe 1975; Johnson 1976, 1989; Johnston 1977).

In response to growing threats from Scotland and Ireland, maritime defences were provided on other vulnerable British coasts during the fourth century, and these continued in use long enough for Theodosian coins to reach many sites. Forts comparable to those on the Saxon Shore were built in the west, for example at Cardiff, at Burrow Walls and at the Wery Wall, Lancaster. The later Empire clearly had a marine capability in the Bristol Channel and in the waters around Anglesey and Cumbria to guard against the Irish. Watchtowers flanked the western end of Hadrian's Wall, and the north-east coast at least as far south as Scarborough and Filey. They were most probably used in combination with ships to deter Pictish raids from travelling southwards down the coast to attack eastern or southern Britain. The civilian inhabitants of the decommissioned fort at South Shields were joined during the first quarter of the fourth century by *numerus barcarorium Tigrisiensium*, a unit of bargemen from the Tigris who were specialists in estuarine defence work, and a similar unit has been identified defending the Lune near Lancaster (Shotter 1973).

These new dispositions emphasize the continuing professionalism of the provincial army and its commanders, its social and functional segregation from the remainder of society and its responsiveness to the shifting pattern of the threats by which it was confronted. It is a story of adaptation, achieved despite falling numbers and declining status, by an insular army which never became a peasant militia.

In the second century approximately an eighth of the Roman army was stationed in Britain. During the third century, British garrisons were used as a reservoir of manpower by successive commanders on the Continent. As a consequence this fraction was reduced in the fourth century to about a thirtieth. The legions were changed beyond recognition: troopers of *VI Victrix* probably still occupied the partially refurbished fortress at York but Caerleon was all but deserted by AD 300; at Chester, barracks fell out of use in the same period and *legio XX* may have been permanently withdrawn, although the large theatre and administrative buildings continued into the mid century. The last documentary reference to a legionary commander, in the *Notitia*, identifies *II Augusta* at the much smaller but coin-rich fort at Richborough, where only a fraction of the old-style legion could have been accommodated. Yet troop withdrawals continued, even into the last years of the century, as Magnus Maximus attempted to establish himself as Augustus in the West, and Stilicho sought to stave off military collapse in north Italy. One recent estimate (James 1984) argues for insular troop levels as low as 12,000 in the late fourth century, including the newly created diocesan field army of, perhaps, 5500 men. If the latter were billeted in the towns, there is little evidence of their presence, bar the graves at Lankhills (Winchester) and Dorchester (which may not, in any case, equate with these troops) and the lead-weighted throwing darts found at Wroxeter.

Now that Romano-Saxon pottery has been discredited as an indicator of Germanic soldiers (Gillam 1979; Roberts 1982), there is little evidence that the Roman garrison in Britain was reinforced by the granting of land rights to barbarian *laeti* or *foederati*. The arrival of several groups of barbarians was documented by Roman writers, but all were probably drafts for Roman-style military units and few are archaeologically identifiable. None are Saxons. At Housesteads, epigraphic evidence reveals the presence of the *numerus Hnaudifridi* and other Frisian soldiers (e.g. RIB. 1576), who left behind them fragments of their own distinctive pottery (Jobey 1979). Compared with imports to the region, this was poor in quality but its cheapness and ready availability may help to explain its acquisition by troops at Chesterholm and Birdoswald. An Alamannic King, Crocus, helped Constantine to seize the purple in AD 306 at York, but it requires very special pleading to establish him as the leader of a settlement of *laeti* in Yorkshire (as proposed by Myres 1986) and he probably sailed with Constantine, whose army in AD 311 consisted of troops from among the barbarians he had conquered – Germans, Gauls and men collected from Britain (Zosimus II.15). Similarly, a certain Fraomar was sent to Britain in AD 372 to take command of Alamannic troops but these were a regular army unit (Ammianus Marcellinus XXIX. 4,7), rather than colonists settled under terms. Contemporary writers expected any barbarians who were settled within the provinces rapidly to become Romanized, 'giving up their savagery' (*Pan. Lat. Vet.* VI (VII) V, 3, referring to Constantius and the Franks). Such settlers are not easily identified by the archaeologist.

The late Roman army within Britain was generally successful in guarding its frontiers, but, by the mid-fourth century, it faced attacks from barbarian neighbours who were less fragmented and so more dangerous than hitherto. The newly unified Picts and the Scots broke their treaties with Rome and took offensive action in AD 360 (Ammianus Marcellinus XXI. 1), necessitating an expedition from Gaul in mid-winter. Ammianus described ever more serious raids which occurred in AD 365 and 367 (XXVII. 8), when the barbarians overran the defences of the provinces, killed the *comes* and raided widely in the south-east, while Saxons and Franks hit Atlantic Gaul.

Ammianus's full description of this episode owes much to its suppression by the elder Theodosius, father of the Emperor in power when he was writing. His account is clearly unbalanced by this factor, and gone are the days when every later fourth-century bonfire on the site of the fort or villa can be ascribed to raiders in 367. Theodosius was able to restore order with a tiny expeditionary force, but 367 does seem to have been the prelude to renewed building in the northern forts (summarized in Higham 1986a). Subsequent troop withdrawals left the northern frontier thinly manned and vulnerable to barbarian action.

Economy and society

The shrinking manpower of the post-Severan British army had implications for the insular economy. The provincial army of the early Empire sucked in coin, goods and services to the island, and from the south and east to the north and west, where most troops were stationed. Army pay declined in real terms in the third century and the pay of the low-status British *limitanei* never recovered its purchasing power. The combination of a drastic fall in numbers and declining pay *per capita* imply a significant downturn in the demand side of the state sector of the insular economy, with important consequences for both the military and civil zones. Late Roman governments exploited this downturn to extract labour and supplies from the insular economy for the Rhine frontier. Britain became a net exporter of taxes in kind and in services (see, for example, Ammianus Marcellinus XVIII.2). This compulsory outflow may help explain the willingness of the several British provincial élites to support separatist governments in Britain.

Allied to chaotic conditions in Gaul, these processes contributed to the rapid decline of long-distance trade in the third century. A consequence was the disappearance of a wide variety of goods from British markets, of which the best known archaeological indicator is Gaulish Samian pottery. Provincial industries responded to the challenge, producing new ranges of fine wares, including several red-coated types directly reminiscent of Samian. Third-century Britain was nearer self-sufficiency in manufactured goods than had been the case in the recent past and manufacturing gave employment to numerous rural artisans.

London was probably the greatest victim of these changes. The water-fronts of the capital had been the main entry point for imports to Britain and had experienced an economic boom in consequence. At some point between AD 190 and AD 217, the metropolis was furnished on its landward sides with walls of Kentish ragstone, some 3.2 km long, fronted by a V-shaped ditch. Within this wall, at least one magnificent public building seems to have been erected during the third century in the south-west corner of the city, but elsewhere the widespread buildings attested archaeologically in the mid-second century were not renewed but were overlain with the dark earth which has caused so many interpretative problems in later Roman towns (Vince 1990). At such sites, the rate of deposition of artefacts declined dramatically and never recovered. For whatever reason, by the mid-third century the character of London had gone through a process of radical change. For the remainder of the Roman period, the city was little more than a walled enceinte containing a basilica and forum, an amphitheatre, several baths and a scatter of large stone buildings – offices and the residences of the governor of Britannia Superior (later Maxima Caesariensis), and of the vicar of the diocese.

While these official establishments guaranteed the survival of the town and may have given it a semblance of prosperity, London never recovered as an entrepôt and its wharfs were probably used henceforth largely to send taxes in kind to the Rhineland. The degree of retrenchment in suburbs like Southwark is a matter of debate but the presence there of late Roman graves in what had been house-plots must imply a contraction of settlement.

Decline in the economic demands of the British garrisons was offset by exponential increases in the administration. Division of the British province

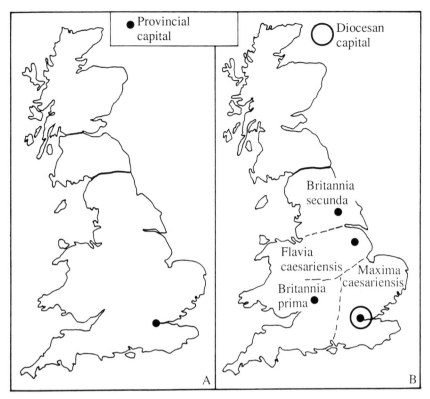

3.2 The structure of Roman Britain: (A) the second century; (B) the fourth century.

and its troops occurred under Severus with the creation of a northern province (*Britannia Inferior*) based on York, and separate from the territory administered from London. The two were further subdivided under Diocletian into four provinces, within an insular diocesan structure forming a part of the Gallic Prefecture (**3.2**). A possible fifth province was created under Valentinian (Valentia), although its location remains a mystery.

Each province had its own administration, governor and council, creating a rapid escalation in the number of administrative posts to be supported. The separation of civil and military command structures and high levels of recruitment to the bureaucracy further extended the payroll, as well as insulating the aristocracy and army commanders from one another. The result was an episodic but persisting escalation in the number of non-combatants within the Imperial establishment in later Roman Britain. They were certainly numbered in hundreds and probably in thousands and many had the right to wear official uniforms and to draw pay in cash and in kind. Belt fittings from their uniforms are a not unusual find from late Roman towns and villas. Such finds need not reflect the presence of army units, let alone German soldiers; they may, alternatively, point to the presence of men who had gained the tax privileges that went with employment within the state bureaucracy.

By the mid-fourth century, there are signs that the trade system was faltering. Along the Wall, pottery from East Yorkshire had driven out black-burnished wares from the south (Gillam 1973) and pottery imports to the west coast had practically ceased. The East Yorkshire wares were of poor quality but had a shorter distance to travel than southern vessels, and they probably benefited from the flow of bulk agricultural produce from Yorkshire to the Wall as taxes in kind, which may have enabled them to be transported at a subsidized rate. Exactly when this supply ceased is unclear but it was artistically moribund by the 370s, by which time the northern *vici* had been abandoned, implying a significant decline in the market facilities serving the frontier forces.

Elsewhere, other pottery industries were showing signs of stress. New Forest pottery exhibited its last datable change in fabric and form *c.* AD 375 (Fulford 1975) and Oxford wares *c.* AD 350 (Young 1977), although both were still in production at the turn of the century, as was the Alice Holt industry at Farnham (Millett 1979). Even at their height, these regional industries were probably staffed by seasonal workers who were also farmers and the like. In the New Forest, they seem to have declined numerically during the second half of the century, perhaps drawn away by landowners and administrators desperate to cultivate land which was liable for tax. Local hand-made pottery increasingly supplanted more technically advanced products in the south-east in the last decades of the century, offering an alternative that was probably cheaper and more readily available, if technically inferior. Elsewhere, no alternative was proffered and pottery use was reduced.

Why did this decline occur? One suggestion has been that middle value goods such as ceramics lost out in the market place. Many artisans had, in the past, worked for the public sector. The needs of the state in the fourth century were met by forced labour, most of which was unskilled, and paid work for the skilled evaporated. The impact of conscripted labour on tradesmen was to drive them out of the market — where they were vulnerable to loss of earnings — towards the land where they could at least expect to feed themselves and their families. The loss of whole sections of the coin-earning community had a major impact on markets for ceramics and other mass-produced commodities.

Other factors contributed to this decline. The aristocracy preferred more valuable vessels of silver or glass, the bulk of which were probably imported. Barbarian raids in the 360s can only have damaged suppliers, carriers and markets, and the dwindling of many urban populations seriously damaged both marketing mechanisms and consumption. The middle classes of late Roman Britain were locked into a decline from which only fundamental social change could have saved them, but the demands of the state were forcing society into a mould entirely inconsistent with their survival. During the last decades of the century the gradient of decline steepened and the condition of the entire system became critical, with the economy becoming more and more localized.

The élite: town and country

The second and third century tribal gentry of Roman Britain were successful converts to the Roman habit of town life. Few towns were defended with walls before the late second century — the principal exceptions being the *coloniae*. At that stage a minority of urban communities (e.g. at Caerwent, Cirencester, Silchester and Verulamium) set about constructing masonry gateways and continuous circuits of earthwork defences. Many sites were properly walled during the early third century or soon thereafter.

Excepting London and York, it was probably the local élite, through their role as *curiales*, who raised the resources necessary to carry out these leisurely programmes of construction. In Britain, the walled area of most towns approximated to the layout of the second-century towns, in contrast with Gaul, where walls were commonly constructed in the last quarter of the century around a small urban core. Unlike Gallic examples, the gradual and unsynchronized development of British town walls implies that they were generally not built against a specific military threat. They were, therefore, probably intended to lend status to the urban community and to the magistrates who commissioned them, in which case, town walls are yet one more example of aristocratic investment in the towns in which they lived and worked.

The way in which wealthy men spent their surplus resources was broadly consistent from the late first to the late third century; most of it was derived from the countryside but recycled to the towns in the form of private and civic expenditure. The exact nature of this changed over time, beginning with the construction of public buildings (late first and early second centuries), then turning to private houses (later second century) and finally to walls (very late second, predominantly third, century).

After *c.* AD 280, this pattern ceased abruptly. There was very little fresh construction of public buildings, and work on town walls changed in nature, with the adoption of a very different style of walling associated with the deployment of engines and presumably of soldiers. Walls of this kind are less clearly the product of expenditure by the *civitates* and their magistrates, except when under orders from the state, wherein lay the command of whatever troops were present. They were probably constructed in large measure by the use of forced labour.

Walls were often reconstructed in the later fourth century around small towns (e.g. Horncastle, Mildenhall) or refurbished by the construction of external towers and the widening of ditches but, of the major sites, only London received completely new defences and its first riverside wall (Hill 1977), but this has recently been redated to the late third century (Brigham

1990). Walls around the diocesan capital were presumably constructed on the orders of the *vicarius*. Given that they contained large quantities of sepulchral stonework (Evans and Pierpoint 1986), it is clear that this was done with minimum expense, using material extracted from the cemeteries nearby, probably again erected by conscripted labourers.

In many towns, the major buildings survived to the last quarter of the century, but many were poorly maintained or converted to uses inconsistent with their initial purpose. At Silchester, for example, the *basilica* remained in use long enough to attract Theodosian coins and may have survived into the early fifth century, but it had been converted to industrial use (Fulford 1985). Baths and theatres generally remained in commission, but they rarely required much input of resources; the theatre at Canterbury was sufficiently well built to remain standing to the Norman Conquest. At Lincoln, the *principia* and forum remained in use throughout the bulk of the fourth century, but rubbish accumulating in the later period implies falling standards of civic control (Jones and Gilmour 1980). At Wroxeter, the main buildings of the town burnt down early in the fourth century and were not replaced.

Most fourth-century *coloniae* or *civitas* capitals continued to consist largely of town houses and it is not difficult to find examples of fourth-century refurbishment of high-status dwellings, in towns such as Gloucester. However, Verulamium apart, new building in stone is rarely evidenced. For example, in *insula VIII* at Gloucester, a stone building was deliberately demolished in the second half of the fourth century and replaced by a timber butcher's shop (Heighway and Garrod 1980) which fell out of use *c.* AD 390. The abandonment of stone footings or stone walls is one of many indications that Romanization was in retreat in the latter half of the century, when the élite were probably only rarely occupying their urban property. It is likely that farms were operating from within the refurbished and updated walls of late Roman Cirencester and Verulamium (Wacher 1974b), in which case magistrates may have been attempting to obtain a tax yield from agriculture to compensate for the decline of more conventional urban taxes. Such signs in two of Britain's most prominent, peaceful and affluent towns bode ill for town life in the rest of the Roman period.

The continuing vitality of urban communities and markets is much debated (e.g. Reece 1980; Brooks 1986). Fine-ware pottery may have continued to be distributed via urban markets and high-status services, such as mosaic-making, may have been centred in specific towns, although there is little hard evidence for this common assumption. However, it has been suggested that coarse wares were distributed directly from the site of manufacture (Esmonde Cleary 1989). The volume of trade passing through urban markets may have been small and the surplus produce of villa estates was probably an important component. The steady deposition of small change continued but that may represent an increasing proportion of coin in circulation as surfaces were less regularly cleaned at the end of the period.

British towns exhibit a rate of coin loss in the fourth century which is significantly higher than that of contemporary Gaul or Italy, with the official coinage enhanced during periodic shortages by counterfeiting on such a scale and of such quality that it may have been officially sanctioned (Reece 1973; Ryan 1988). Coin use remained an urban phenomenon into the later fourth century, buoyed up, perhaps, by the wages of local administrators and field army units, and the general need to convert some produce into coin for the purposes of taxation.

As elements of a Romanized cultural system, towns entered a period of decay which in many instances had become terminal by the end of the third quarter of the century. A major causal factor was probably the withdrawal of aristocratic expenditure such as had hitherto flowed from the presence of the landowning élite, who had customarily spent resources derived from the countryside in the towns. They left urban communities with a diminished economic base, with little industry and with commerce tending to decline in volume and value as markets shrank, the whole exposed to pressures of taxation and forced labour from the state.

The last two generations of Roman Britain had to contend with an accelerating decline in economic specialization and in exchange, which eventually reduced the technological base of society to pre-Roman levels, even among the luxury trades. After *c.* AD 370, few, if any, new villas were built, few new mosaics were laid in those which remained, and repairs to existing examples were unskilled. New masonry is conspicuously absent and on those sites where new buildings can be identified, timber-framed buildings replaced stone-founded architecture.

The archaeologically accredited influx of investment to villas in some parts of Britain in the period *c.* AD 280−350 indicates that the British aristocracy had sought to distance themselves from the more onerous demands of government by dispersing into the countryside. They did this whether within or without the territories where they were enrolled as *curiales* is unclear, but the possibility that they attempted to leave their own *civitates* should certainly be borne in mind.

Rich householders and their households occupied, refurbished and massively extended many villas and built new ones from scratch. To take a well-known example, the villa at Bignor was initially constructed as a modest dwelling *c.* AD 200 but was massively extended around a large courtyard after *c.* AD 290 (period IIIA) and reached its most ornate and extensive form thereafter (IIIB; Frere 1982; **3.3**). The villa at West Park (Rockbourne, Hants) started as a simple three-room range in the late first century, on the site of a native farm. In the early fourth century, it grew to become the largest establishment in the area, with forty rooms and farm buildings around three sides of a west-facing courtyard. Heated floors complemented painted wall-plaster and mosaic pavements and two bath

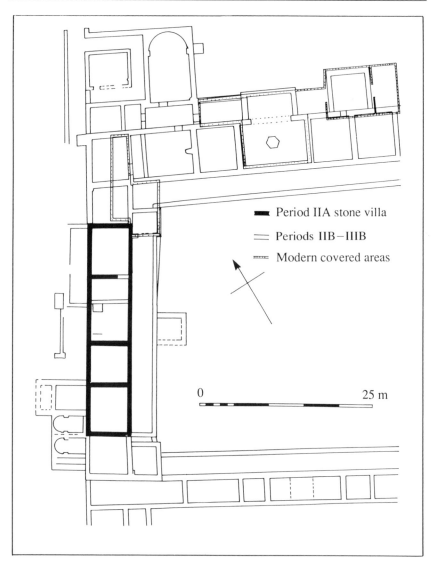

3.3 Bignor: the development of a Roman villa (simplified, after Frere 1982).

suites may imply the existence of a separate household or guest suite in one of the wings (RCHM 1983).

Although many town houses were maintained and were presumably occupied when their owners were serving as magistrates or present on business, there can be little doubt that many of the provincial élite had forsaken the towns as their normal place of residence, in favour of the countryside where landowners could expect to minimize their overheads.

Villa sites are numerous and changes within them reflect a widespread and important shift in patterns of settlement and spending among the élite. However, not all villas long enjoyed this Indian summer of Romanization. Piddington (Northants) had ceased to act as a high-status residence by the late third century. Continuing coin deposition was associated with agricultural use of the erstwhile residential structure (Friendship-Taylor, 1989; **3.4**). At Honeyditches (Devon), fourth-century occupation was not accompanied by expansion and the buildings remained modest (Miles 1977). In the south-east, villas always had a patchy distribution and may have been actively discouraged by the presence of the Saxon Shore garrisons in the fourth century (Black 1987). The small and probably early villa at Cromwell (Notts) was replaced at an unknown date by a bewildering array of linear boundaries and enclosures associated with two large post-built rectangular structures (RCHM 1989).

More extravagant types of villa tend to group, being identified most densely at a distance from the bulk of the armed forces, in Britannia Prima, particularly on the Cotswolds, around Cirencester and the Bristol Channel, where mosaicists and muralists found many of their richest commissions during the early fourth century. This grouping of the more affluent villas may imply the presence of renegade aristocratic households from the eastern provinces of Britain or from Gaul, who then lived on the profits, provided largely in coin, by their agents managing estates elsewhere. Villas such as Chedworth were probably sited on aesthetic grounds rather than economic ones, and need not have been associated with large estates in the immediate vicinity.

Growing differentials between the more successful villas and the remainder may imply that the aristocracy were numerically shrinking, with increasing numbers of villas owned by a few wealthy families. The suppression of insular rebellion in the 270s (Zosimus I.66) and in AD 296 may have been occasions for a proscription of the supporters of the failed regimes. After the fall of Magnentius, in AD 354, Paul 'the Chain' was reputed to have carried out a savage proscription among the propertied class in Britain (Ammianus XIV.5,6). The high-status accommodation at villas like Boxmoor, Northchurch and Park Street was abandoned, but the sites continued to function as agrarian centres, the change coming in the 350s (Neale 1978). Many other villas failed to survive to the mid-century, as at Whitton (S. Glam.), where a site occupied continuously since the Iron Age was abandoned *c.* 340 (Jarrett and Wrathmell 1981).

If large tracts of land fell to the Emperor, they may, thereafter, have been either leased or granted away to those with access to Imperial patronage. Britons barely featured among this imperial élite and it is probable that many British estates fell into the hands of wealthy but absentee outsiders, like Probus (Ammianus XXVII.9,11) or Melania the Younger, who rarely if ever visited the diocese. Perpetual non-residence may have encouraged such owners to decommission the villa residences,

3.4 Detail of the fourth century 'corn' drying oven inserted into a villa-structure which had already been abandoned for residential purposes, at Piddington, Northants. Spelt wheat came from the immediate vicinity, and peas were also present (courtesy of Roy Friendship-Taylor).

while others may have suffered from engrossment of several estates into a single but larger unit, leaving erstwhile villa sites as dependent centres for the management of farm produce.

If active members of the aristocracy were fewer, then systems of patronage were probably more extensive, and focused on wealthier patrons whose power was enhanced. Alongside other western provinces, Britain probably witnessed a progressive shift of governmental functions from public to private hands (Matthews 1975), with increasing control vested in an aristocracy which had relocated to the countryside.

The presence of this élite may have had important consequences for the peasantry, whose interests were now less likely to be under the protection of independent local gentry. One result may have been increased nucleation of settlement within the countryside. There is some evidence that 'villages' became more common in the fourth century and some surviving roadside settlements and small towns may have consisted largely of peasant farms.

Our knowledge of the development of the dispersed farm system depends heavily on field walking and the analysis of pottery scatters. In many areas (e.g. south-east Suffolk, Newman 1988) numerous dispersed farms continued to produce Roman pottery, while some new sites were established and others were abandoned, consistent with a continuing pattern of occasional mobility. However, continuing artefact deposition may hide important functional changes. For example, what had started as a farm site at Werrington (Cambs) had already become part of a pastoral estate system by the late second century. In the early fourth century it was a non-residential element within a beef production unit, yet still producing pottery (Mackreth 1988).

While living standards were rising on some villa sites, there are indications of agricultural stagnation or recession. Improved ploughing equipment appeared in Britain in the fourth century but has been found almost exclusively on high-status sites, admittedly largely within hoards which need not reflect their distribution when in use (Rees 1979; 3.5). Peasants are unlikely to have had the capital to take up new technologies which might have freed them from debt, and the flow of technological innovation so characteristic of the first two centuries AD had virtually ceased. On the Berkshire Downs a 70 per cent decrease in pottery deposition on the surface of arable fields may imply a decline in cultivation in favour of pasture (Gaffney and Tingle 1989), or a decline in the quantities of pottery reaching the farms supplying manure. A recession in agriculture is implicit at Eller Beck and Waitby (Cumb), possibly as a result of soil erosion and exhaustion; irregular fields probably intended for stock replaced regular enclosures within the life of the Romano-British farms from which the land had hitherto been cultivated. The best evidenced export of fourth-century Britain was not grain but cloth (*Edictum Diocletiani* XIX.28, 29, 48); a specialist government-run, cloth-making and wool-weaving centre existed at *Venta* (Winchester or Caistor-by-Norwich), manufacturing cheap and nasty military uniforms for the army (Wild 1982).

Peasants paid their taxes in produce and labour. The latter was used as directed by the representatives of the state. That this may have occurred at a distance is made abundantly clear by building inscriptions on Hadrian's Wall which recall the work of men from several southern *civitates*. More normally, the local community was expected to maintain and repair roads and bridges and provide draught animals and drivers for governmental purposes.

3.5 An iron plough coulter from Great Witcombe, Gloucestershire. Although this example is unprovenanced, it belongs typologically to a group of later Roman agricultural equipment generally thought to represent the use of a plough capable of turning a furrow. There is little evidence that such equipment was in use in the early Anglo-Saxon period. Length approx. 70 cm (reproduced by courtesy of the Trustees of the British Museum).

Taxes in kind were owed in the first place to the tribal *curiales* but there is no evidence that urban granaries were ever built to accommodate them. Taxpayers were responsible for the delivery of their foodstuffs direct to the point of consumption. For most British communities, the bulk may still have gone to the forts which were equipped with large granaries, to the post-houses and to the private homes of the urban bureaucracies. Such payments were necessarily grouped for transporting, and grain was probably collected centrally at specific sites in the countryside, for carriage to the point of consumption, or to markets to procure gold coins to pay taxes in cash.

The unique, fortified 'villa' site at Gatcombe may have been one such collecting point (Branigan 1977; Esmond Cleary 1989). However, such sites need not have been so distinctive as Gatcombe. In central and eastern England, there were numerous large barns, often aisled, built during the late third and fourth centuries. Some, like the examples at Rivenhall (Rodwell and Rodwell 1986), Shavards Farm (King 1988) and Bignor, were associated with Roman villas. Others succeeded earlier settlements, such as the successive aisled buildings at Beddington (Adkins 1986, 1987). Styles varied but many were extremely large, modelled, perhaps, on the granaries of the military (Morris 1979).

Of those which were not used for accommodation, it might be suggested that such structures bear comparison with the tithe barns of later medieval England. They seem far larger and more numerous than was necessary for the cultivation of home farms associated with villas. If it be accepted that they acted as storehouses for tax in kind, their presence emphasizes the power of the major landowners over the rural communities, through the bonds of clientship, of debt, of tenure and of tax payment. The fourth-century élite of the lowlands of Roman Britain had become *de facto* seigneurs, exercising both private and public jurisdiction over men, and expanding their control over the land of their inferiors within an increasingly oppressive and unequal system of patronage, guaranteed by the armed forces of the state.

In the process, one might speculate that a revolution was under way in the structure of landholding. Hitherto, ring-fence estates had probably existed only as a result of the predatory activities of Imperial authority. Outside such estates, patron—client linkages were at least as important to the aristocracy as direct control of land, and probably accounted for the bulk of the land surface of the lowland zone. Yet the landscape had long been divided into units for agricultural purposes, and these had implications for land tenure: peasant communities with customary tenure seem to have enjoyed various rights of use within one or more blocks of the countryside. In the last century of Roman Britain, all this came under new pressure: the intrusion of 'foreign' landowners, tax dependence, debt and the conflation of client with tenant served to raise the profile of lordship and to transfer rights in land from free peasant communities to the aristocracy. It may be that we should envisage this as the period when aristocracies first established proprietorial (as opposed to patronal) control over blocks of land containing entire agrarian systems, which were henceforth to function both as economic units and as estates. The developments at which we can guess in the late Roman period are likely to have further distanced patron from client, élite from peasantry, *possessiones* from *coloni*, in a society which had polarized at the very time when the middle classes were suffering terminal decline.

Religion in late Roman Britain

The progress of Christianity in Roman Britain was not dissimilar to that in other northern and western provinces, with the proviso that it was probably a weaker force before *c.* AD 300 than in southern Gaul or Spain. There is negligible Christian archaeology in Britain before Constantine, excepting a handful of graffiti on highly mobile artefacts. Gildas named only three British martyrs, all of whom were probably pre-Diocletian; there is no way of knowing whether he knew the names or locations of any others. The cult of St Alban seems to have been well established by the 420s, when St Germanus visited the shrine (Constantius, XVI) and cults of Aaron and Julius may have existed at or near Caerleon or Caerwent in the fourth century (Stephens 1985). Before Constantine, Christianity was probably confined to urban and commercial communities, but a diocesan structure existed at latest by AD 314 when three bishops, a priest and a deacon attended a Church Council at Arles. The bishoprics or metropolitans they represented are assumed to have paralleled the secular administration of the four provinces.

After Constantine, Christianity gradually came to occupy the position of a state religion. Imperial patronage provided important taxation immunities and encouraged those who were active either politically or intellectually to give serious consideration to membership. Christianity became identified with many changes in patterns of worship and burial in the second half of the century.

In Britain, the progress of Christianity was characteristic of all other elements of the initial Romanization of the province and of subsequent responses to Roman cultural change. It disseminated through the social and political hierarchy and was centred at sites of administrative activity in the towns and in the households of the élite. Christianity was the last major element of Romanized culture to spread through the West, arriving when many other aspects of Romanization (such as urbanism and trade) were in retreat. Its apparent success owed much to the extensive and centralized administrative hierarchy that characterized the Roman state during the period. This monotheistic, intolerant and hierarchically organized religion was a natural partner to the absolutist monarchy and intrusive despotism of the secular state.

Certain examples of churches are few in number, although this may be because many pre-existing buildings were converted from earlier uses. Most have long been known and have been widely discussed (e.g. Ralegh Radford 1971). The least controversial remains the example excavated by Sir Ian Richmond in 1961 at Silchester (Frere 1975) which was a basilican structure built at some stage between the mid-third and mid- to late fourth centuries, and probably at the latter end of this period. A strong case has also been made for a church and baptistry at Richborough (Brown 1971), and at Icklingham (West 1976). Elsewhere, a handful of buildings may have been used as churches and a scatter of lead cisterns, many inscribed with the chi—rho monogram, probably represent baptismal fonts (Guy 1981).

Opinions vary concerning the probable proliferation of churches and congregations. An optimal view (Thomas 1981a) would expect churches of the Theodosian period to be numerous, particularly in the towns, but much depends on the state of the towns by this stage, which may have had populations inadequate to support congregational churches. The alternative view of a numerically weak but episcopal church may at this stage be closer to the evidence (e.g. Frend 1982).

The strongest evidence for widespread Christianity derives from the homes and possessions of the aristocracy, who patronized the mosaicists responsible for the Christian motifs at Hinton St Mary and Frampton, the artists who painted the Lullingstone chi−rho and the silversmiths responsible for the numerous late platters and spoons bearing the chi−rho monogram. No instance of a villa-church is yet entirely convincing, but the use of Christian iconography is certainly evidence that villa owners recognized the new status of Christianity and were sympathetic to it at least as a political and cultural force. However, we should not overemphasize the significance of this Christian influence. Christian motifs were incorporated into the artistic and ideological stock-in-trade of smiths and mosaicists, rather than replacing it. Other elements remained conservative and classical in inspiration, and these were numerically dominant. The work of mosaicists reflects the processes of religious syncretism and the growth of monotheism, rather than committed Christianity, and much silversmithing in the second half of the Roman period continued to use motifs which were both traditional and pagan, as exemplified in the Mildenhall Dish (3.6).

Despite the influx of Christianity, pagan cult-sites were far more numerous than churches throughout the fourth century. Many long-established indigenous cults continued, with few signs of crisis, at least into the last decades. These included many prominent centres such as the spring-based cult at Bath, which was newly walled during the fourth century, the temple associated with healing is dedicated to Nodens and the more modest well of Coventina at Carrawburgh, on Hadrian's Wall. Although new shrines are uncommon they do occur, as at Great Dunmow, Essex (Wickenden 1988), and their scarcity may be a factor of the adequacy of existing provision rather than any decline in their attractions.

A minority of pagan shrines may have been converted to Christian use; a case has been made for Ivy Champs, Witham (Turner 1982), and pagan votive material was removed from West Hill, Uley soon after AD 400 when major structural change occurred on the site, which might imply conversion to Christian use (Ellison 1980; Woodward and Leach 1990).

Despite these exceptional cases, there is plentiful evidence that British paganism was in excellent health at the end of the fourth century. It seems likely that Christianity did not make significant progress among the peasantry of the lowland zone, or among society at large in the north and west, but was confined to a social veneer − the upper ranks of the field army, commercial classes in the towns, and sections of the landowning élite, such as St Patrick's grandfather, the gentleman-priest Potitus.

The extent of Christian influence over late Romano-British burial practices remains a matter of debate. Orientated inhumation was already dominant by the mid- to late third century, and at cemeteries such as Lankhills, Winchester, unaccompanied burial with the head to the west was customary by *c.* AD 310 (Clarke 1979), without any necessity to invoke Christianity as a causal factor. At Ospringe, adoption of this orientation may reflect Christian influence. Burials there which reject the newly

3.6   The great dish from the Mildenhall treasure. Manufactured presumably for a client of high status, this is one item from the many late Romano-British hoards which were deposited in the ground and not subsequently recovered (reproduced by courtesy of the Trustees of the British Museum).

dominant alignment may be pagan, but burial with head to the south remained dominant throughout the period at the provincial and diocesan capital of Cirencester, where one might expect Christian influence to have been concentrated (discussed in Black 1986). More certain Christian influence may be detected among the chalk-filled graves in the highly ordered cemetery at Poundbury, Dorchester (Green 1982; **3.7**) and the mausolea, lead coffins and ossuaria which are scattered unevenly across lowland Britain.

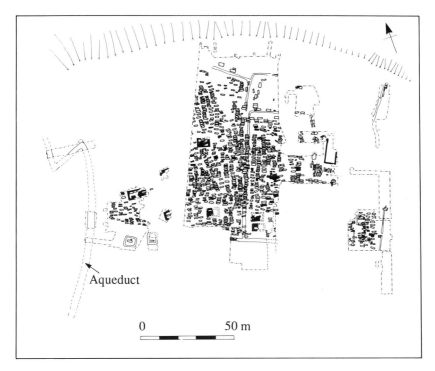

3.7   Poundbury: a late Roman suburban cemetery (after Green 1982).

The major caveat to this discussion is the problem of distinguishing evidence of active Christianity from the general trend of late Roman mortuary practices. The bulk of the evidence provided by burials falls into this trap. Prominent British communities had concurred with Roman cemetery etiquette for three centuries before the legalization of Christianity, without necessarily holding or even being acquainted with the religious ideas which underlay such practices. By the late fourth century, their descendants were burying their dead after a fashion which was similarly imported from the core of the Empire. The fashion was Christian only by adoption and may simply have been used by or for anyone who preferred to conform with the socially dominant tradition on a highly public occasion.

CHAPTER FOUR

BRITAIN WITHOUT ROME

The fall of Roman Britain

Between 385 and 411, Britain was ruled by Emperors in control of Italy for only eight years, with Magnus Maximus in charge for a further five and Constantine for four years. Legitimate authority was, therefore, a matter of debate and inclined to be intermittent, with the insular diocese of Britain in particular and the Gallic Prefecture in general tending to follow a different political road from the remainder of the Empire. After 411, Britain was never again administered as part of the Gallic Prefecture. For the historian this break in governmental authority signals the end of Roman Britain. The break itself resulted from a series of factors, some deliberate, some accidental, concerning the historicity of which there is, at present, a lively debate (e.g. Thompson 1977, 1979, 1982a; Bartholomew 1982; Jones and Casey 1988; Burgess 1990).

As a result of this controversy, several archaeologists have lost patience with the historical approach and denied that the literary sources have any value at all. However, the events of 406 to 411 rank among the most vividly described in the history of Roman Britain. As such, the relevant writings necessarily command attention, if not uncritical acceptance.

Although himself a distant observer in both time and space, Zosimus drew heavily for this part of his narrative on the generally more critical (but lost) history of the period 407 to 425 by Olympiadorus of Thebes, whose work was also quarried by Sozomen in the mid fifth century for his *Ecclesiastical History*. Zosimus's copying is careless in detail and his entries concerning the usurpation of Constantine III are neither systematic nor entirely consistent. However, the general drift of his account of events finds support in the references to British events in the two Gallic Chronicles (known after their last entries as 452 and 511), the chronological and contextual reliability of which has survived much recent criticism virtually intact (Burgess 1990), and in Germanus's visit to Britain in 429, as recounted by Constantius in his late fifth-century *Life of St Germanus*, but also by Prosper in a newer contemporary chronicle. Where their testimonies overlap these sources are mutually consistent.

These writings can be usefully examined alongside the changes that were occurring in the supply of coin to Britain. Excepting the usurpations, no coins were minted at London after *c.* 326 and the island was dependent for its coinage on Continental mints, at Trier, Arles, Lyons and in Italy. The supply of coin to the diocese depended entirely on state expenditure and could be interrupted by political events. The provision of small change dwindled after *c.* 392 and stopped *c.* 402. The supply of gold coins died away within the next decade. To the extent that the insular economy was coin-using, it was, thereafter, dependent on the dwindling supply of coins already in circulation. The large number of hoards of precious metals including coins deposited after (and probably soon after) the supply had ceased, that is in the period *c.* 402–20 (Archer 1979), suggests that coin-use finished comparatively abruptly, with precious metals deposited for safe-keeping pending the re-establishment of proper authority. Coin-use was in steep decline by the late 380s outside the towns, where civil servants and the *comitatenses* continued to received some of their pay in cash as long as any was available (Ryan 1988). Prominent sites were not necessarily the greater towns or *civitas* capitals; Dorchester and Alchester show high levels of loss of the last major issue of 388 to 392, suggesting that officials or army units were present at both. The pattern of government may have already been shifting in Britain a generation before the collapse of the state.

That early fifth-century officialdom did not have recourse to copying implies either that they had less need of coin, or that they found die-cutters more difficult to come by. Given that the field army was away in Europe from 407, and that the Gallic mints were in steep decline, both conditions may well have been fulfilled. That part of the frontier army and bureaucracy which still remained in position was no longer paid in cash.

Without fresh coin since 402, and presumably unpaid, British garrisons had good cause by 406 to mutiny. That year was auspicious in the annals of British insurrections since it was the centenary of Constantine's elevation to the rank of Emperor at York. This was the only long-term success among numerous rebellions which had originated in Britain, and tales of the benefits Constantine had conferred on his supporters are unlikely to have lost much in the telling.

In 406, the British troops rebelled and enthroned one Marcus, replacing him after an unspecified time by a civil magistrate with the politically significant name of Gratian (legitimate Emperor in the West, killed 383), only to replace this candidate in turn, after four months, with the more aptly named Constantine (henceforth Constantine III). He was described (Zosimus VI.2; IX.11; Orosius VII.40,4) as a common soldier, but he clearly had some political flair. He made capital of his own name and those of his sons, whom he named (or renamed) Constans and Julian, the latter presumably intended to rally pagan support alongside the Christian appeal of his own name. His initial rank may have been understated: Procopius later described Constantine as a man of no mean station (*History of the Wars* III. ii.31).

On 31 December 406, a barbarian horde of Vandals, Suevi and Alans breached the Rhineland frontier and began to devastate Gaul. Constantine III crossed to Gaul early in 407, apparently to stem the tide and to take his opportunity to seize the Gallic Prefecture as the logical next stage in his challenge for the purple. He seems to have consciously emulated the strategy of Magnus Maximus, securing Spain and establishing himself at Arles whence he negotiated with Honorius with such success that the latter recognized him as an Emperor. But Constantine's bold strategy backfired. His armies were extremely small and he was unable to press home his single recorded success against the barbarians who remained within the prefecture. The bulk of his soldiers were sent into Spain to destroy the forces of Honorius's relatives. His general there, the British soldier Gerontius, allied himself with the raiders and rebelled, trapping the erstwhile aspirant to the purple at Arles where he eventually met his death.

Up to this point, Constantine's story had been unexceptional and the provincials of Britain could reasonably expect the re-emergence of strong authority within a very few years, whether Constantine succeeded or not. However, his activities were only one of several conflicts generating chaos in the West. The administration of the young Emperor Honorius was competing for pre-eminence with that of his brother at Constantinople, while trying to fend off Attalus, a puppet of Alaric the Goth, and had neither money nor troops to tackle the problems of insurrection and barbarian raids beyond the Alps. Barbarians were on the loose in unprecedented numbers, and in several different groups, throughout the West.

The collapse of Constantine's cause left a power vacuum in Gaul, with widespread revolt along the Atlantic coasts. It was not until the mid-420s that a concerted effort was made by Aetius-to re-establish Imperial control in northern Gaul, and success even then was only partial, leaving government very largely in the hands of powerful territorial magnates; the tax taken into Roman coffers never recovered; barbarian kingdoms came into being the connivance of Roman officials and were recognized by Roman Emperors. Armies led by generals as diverse as Constantine and Gerontius, Jovinus, Aëtius and Aegidius, relied heavily on the barbarians for their manpower. Defence of the towns fell to bishops like Sidonius Apollinaris at Clermont, and 'loyal' Roman communities such as his were given over to barbarian kings in the by-play of Imperial politics. The Gallic Prefecture was in no condition to re-establish Roman control over its insular diocese; indeed, Roman generals were hard put to control even southern Gaul consistently.

In Constantine's absence, raiders struck at the Channel coasts:

> They [referring back to the barbarians from over the Rhine] reduced
> the inhabitants of Britain and some of the Gallic peoples to such straits
> that they revolted from the Roman Empire, no longer submitted to

Roman law, and reverted to their native customs. The Britons, therefore, armed themselves and ran many risks to ensure their own safety and to free their cities from the attacking barbarians. The whole of Armorica and other Gallic provinces, in imitation of the Britons, freed themselves in the same way by expelling the Roman magistrates and establishing the government they wanted.

(Zosimus VI.5, trans. Ridley 1982)

In a masterful and influential article, Thompson (1977) argued that this amounted to a rebellion aimed at securing both independence from Rome and social reform. However, his crucial interpretation of rebellion in maritime Gaul as an outbreak of the social revolution known as the bacaudic revolts, documented in Brittany in the 430s and thereafter, has not been universally accepted (Bartholomew 1982), and recent reinterpretation of the *bacaudae* has undermined Thompson's hypotheses in this respect (Drinkwater 1989). Zosimus and his sources were at their least well informed when reporting on events within areas which would henceforth be independent. While his information about Constantine in Gaul, and Spain seems well founded, we should not perhaps take too literally his comments on events in Britain post-407. It may be significant that his description of the final split with Rome neatly shifts responsibility for it from Rome to Britain, but it must also be noted that he represents the British as taking action only as a result of insupportable barbarian raids. His testimony does not overtly describe a revolution. The act of Britain's leaders in arming their own dependents to confront the raiders necessitated the rejection of the critically important Roman law (*Lex Iulia de vi publica*) which denied weapons to the populace. Procopius made no mention of revolutions, recording merely that the Romans never succeeded in recovering Britain, which was henceforth ruled by 'tyrants' (Procopius *Wars* III.2,38). Roman administrations long continued to act as if they controlled the destiny of Britain, with Belisarius, Justinian's general, reputedly offering to exchange it with Gothic rulers for Sicily (Procopius *Wars* VI.2,28), and, according to the *Secret History* of the same author, Justinian himself supposedly even sending cash to its barbarian kings. The interventions of St Germanus can be plausibly interpreted as a part of official Imperial policy, concerning 2 diocese over which control had lapsed only temporarily.

If the social element in Zosimus's revolt is discredited, an incursion from Germany is confirmed by the Gallic Chronicles, although that confirmation is clearly weakened by the apparent grouping disasters around the sack of Rome. There is no reason to interpret Zosimus's Germans as Constantine's garrison troops (*contra* Bartholomew 1982), given his assertion that the attacks occurred due to Constantine's carelessness, rather than as a result of a rebellion. Faced by barbarian raiders, a rush to arms by the rural proletariat is incredible, if only because they had none. Even the most tentative effort at military action from within the civil population would have relied upon the patronage system of the great landowners, some of whom did display the capacity to raise forces in the western Empire during precisely this period — Honorius's relatives in Spain fought against Constantine III, for example. Veterans and surviving units of the frontier army could have provided the nucleus of a British force adequate to chase out barbarians who had come to pillage rather than to fight.

Nor did German raids threaten the cities. Few facts are better documented for this period than the incompetence of German irregulars when faced by walls and Thompson is surely right to prefer the sense of *civitates* as a translation for Zosimus's πολειϭ. The Saxons raided the countryside. If the raiders were repulsed, it was by whatever forces could be put into the field by the British aristocracy, perhaps including the last generation of the Roman army in Britain, the survival of whom remains plausible to this point, if unknown to Zosimus. If not, it can be assumed that they simply went home when they had finished, under their own steam.

In these circumstances, a British revolt against Constantine is credible and seems to be confirmed by a further passage of Zosimus (VI.6). By 410, his cause was lost and it was no more than good sense for those not irretrievably committed to him to expel his administration and appeal to Honorius to send a new *vicarius*, governors and military high command, with the troops necessary to replace Constantine's lost *comitatenses*.

In a passage which has aroused much contention, Zosimus recorded that: 'Honorius sent letters to the cities in Britain, urging them to fend for themselves...' (IV.10; trans. Ridley 1982). This entry is sandwiched between passages relating to the actions of Alaric and Honorius's payment of his soldiers, all of which occurred in Italy, and it has often been suggested that this is one of Zosimus's errors, substituting Britain (*Brettania*) for Bruttium (*Brettia*). Even so, communication between the British aristocracy and Ravenna at this stage is consistent with the remainder of Zosimus's account and might be expected. Sozomen (IX.15,2) noted that parts of Constantine's territories returned to their allegiance to Honorius. Previous experience would have alerted the Britons to anticipate an imperial expedition within the near future. That Britain would not be reoccupied was surely unthinkable after 370 years of Roman rule.

Gildas, writing in southern Britain about a century later (p. 161), offered retrospective view of the late fourth and early fifth centuries in which appeals to Rome featured prominently. Like his account of the building of the walls (Higham, 1991), this part of his 'historical introduction' is fictional, but the appeal to Aëtius, which ends his sequence, is probably historical, implying that such an appeal in *c.* 410 is a distinct possibility. Honorius had already found it necessary to encourage provincials to undertake their own defence (*Cod. Theod.* VII.xiii. 16−17) and his relatives in Spain had attempted precisely that against Constantine. We should, therefore, be prepared to give the so-called 'Honorian rescript' the benefit of some doubt (Thompson 1982a).

These events left the British diocese in obedience to Honorius but lacking representatives of his authority. Those parts of the diocesan and provincial governments which were staffed by Britons could have continued to function for a time and there must have been precedents for the administration of either during a temporary vacancy at the head, caused by death in service or similar mishap. Government by committee and without the back-up of regular army units would probably have been comparatively weak and participants inclined to adopt self-serving policies, particularly as the interregnum lengthened, although the expectation of a resumption of Imperial control may have long delayed further usurpations.

The lack of evidence is such that the political structure of Britain *c.* 410–30 is beyond recall. In perhaps the most stimulating recent thesis, Professor Thompson (1984) argued that government of southern Britain was, in 429, in the hands of the slaves, peasants and *coloni* who had taken control (in his interpretation) two decades earlier. The small amount of detail which Prosper and Constantius separately offer concerning St Germanus's visit is incompatible with this interpretation: Germanus was sent by central Roman authorities in response to an appeal from Britain, which is hardly likely to have come from revolutionaries; the heretics (followers of Pelagius) with whom St Germanus supposedly disputed were richly dressed and well-attended; Elafius, whom he met on his second visit, had a Greek name (Constantius rendered it in Latin), which was unlikely to have been given to a man of peasant stock, yet he was the chief man of his district. Government by what was, in effect, the Worker's Revolutionary Party of late Roman Britain must, regrettably, be set aside. Effective control of Britain in the 420s was in the hands of the land-owning classes, who may well have taken the opportunity offered by the collapse of Imperial power to tighten their grip on society. Whether they continued to co-operate provincial government is impossible to determine but there are indications that the four fourth-century provinces were more enduring than has generally been allowed. In the very early seventh century, Britain was divided between four 'overkingships', operating in the north (Æthelfrith), the northern and central Midlands (the Mercian, King Cearl), the south (Æthelberht) and the west (the kings of Gwynedd). Although these are not identical with the territories of the fourth-century provinces (as, for example, Cirencester's removal to the southern 'over-kingship'), the similarity may be more than coincidence, and the 'over-kingship' of the west, at least, can be pushed back with confidence to the late fifth century (Higham, 1992).

The collapse of Imperial authority brought an end to taxation in gold. Nor could new coin be minted, since to do so would have been provocative and proscription was, on past experience, already too likely. It was, though, very much in the interests of the land-holding classes that Roman law be maintained, and courts seem to have survived. St Germanus was implementing in Britain laws against Pelagius's followers created by Honorius only after Britain was lost to central authority, and Gildas's education a generation or so later was the traditional training for the lawcourts of the Roman provinces (Lapidge 1984). The jurisdiction of Roman-style courts was subject to the geography of the Roman provinces and *civitates* and would probably have tended to perpetuate them. A *provincia* was referred to in the *Life of St Germanus*, although it has been suggested that this allusion should not be taken literally (Thompson 1984).

What emerges from these shreds of evidence is a diocesan community which continued to be organized in a traditional fashion, but one which was changing rapidly along lines already visible in the fourth century. The land-holding aristocracy were consolidating their comparative immunity from the demands of the state and their control of the peasantry, and expanding their property rights to incorporate the lands of erstwhile free clients. If they needed an umbrella by which to protect themselves from further demands from provincial governments, the Christian Church, with its traditions of tax privileges, offered the ideal mechanism. The tenure of Church office by Patrick's father and grandfather and by Gildas implies an interest in the Church as a tax haven. In such circumstances, it seems likely that the decentrallization of power already visible in the rise of the villa reached its logical conclusion under the sub-Roman aristocracy. The term 'region' (*regio*) was used as a description within which important political or military events might occur, in the *Life of St Germanus*, in the *De Excidio*, and later by Bede. In the early fifth century it may have designated the expanded estates of one aristocratic family, who were well on their way to usurping many of the prerogatives of empire.

It is doubtful whether much remained of the British army by 410. Most commentators have assumed that the diocesan field army provided the core of Constantine's expeditionary force. It consisted of units drafted from the Gallic *comitatenses*, not Britons, and never returned. Troop levels on the northern frontier were low already by the 380s and later coin losses no more than intermittent. Coin finds indicate that the tower on Holyhead Mountain (Anglesey) and the coastal towers in Yorkshire were manned by paid soldiers in the 390s (e.g. Boon 1986) and occasional finds of the coins of Magnus Maximus and of the house of Theodosius in Cumbria and at Lancaster indicate garrison payments there until the end of the century, on however reduced a scale (Jones and Shotter 1988; Shotter 1989).

Whatever troops remained thereafter were non-coin-using. Their basic needs could still have been met via taxation in kind within the diocese but the collapse of the diocesan government meant the end of the military commissariat. Without direction from the administration, it is highly un- likely that southern landowners would have continued to supply the soldiers on the periphery of the province with the produce or recruits which they drew from their tenants. The tax yield on which the garrisons could continue to rely was presumably limited to those areas over which they could exercise duress. Most forts were probably abandoned. Elsewhere, for example at Catterick, a thin haul of finds may indicate continuity of occupation from the late Roman to the English periods but not of a regular army unit. The discovery, in 1989, that timber-framed buildings were constructed on the site of the granaries at Birdoswald in the coinless fifth century is the first indication that some northern garrisons survived into the post-Constantinian era, though interpretation of this important discovery must await full publication. The Birdoswald garrison was well placed in the fertile Irthing valley to levy supplies from peasant neighbours or to feed itself. The difficulties of identifying such archaeological levels make it possible that examples were missed in the decades before Barker's excavations at Wroxeter established new standards of excavation above Roman masonry structures. Even so, it seems unlikely that garrisons at highland forts such as Housesteads long survived the disruption to the tax flow which accompanied the fall of Constantine III. The cessation of the flow of pottery from Yorkshire probably reflects the collapse of the transit of taxation in kind from the most productive corner of *Britannia Secunda* to the Wall.

The exceptionally high rate of coin loss at Richborough was probably due to the bulk passage of coinage through the port for reminting on the Continent. Five coins of Constantine III and coins of the first half of the reign of Honorius end the sequence. Reports on the coinage suggest that the site was no longer garrisoned after 413 and the evidence of insular military equipment is not at variance with this view (Cunliffe 1968). Occupation continued at Portchester at least until coinage ceased, and metalwork finds indicate that this occupation included a military component, even if only intermittently, on a site which the excavator diagnosed as 'disordered' (Cunliffe 1975).

Birdoswald apart, there remains no evidence that a regular army survived in Britain into the 420s, and all that we know about the period argues against it. The force assembled in some part of the south in 429 to combat a barbarian incursion, supposedly of Saxons and Picts, was small and unprofessional, not a regular army unit. If the 'Halleluiah Victory' described by Constantius actually occurred, it was probably the achievement of the clients and household of a member of the local aristocracy, who had not yet evolved the full-blown warrior kingship censored by Gildas in Wales several generations later. With neither an army under centralized control nor a diocesan administration, it ceases to be valid to speak of Roman Britain and, in the eyes of historians and archaeologists alike, a new era had begun. However, without the aid of hindsight, those who were born in the two decades centred on 400 may have had a great deal more difficulty in recognizing these symptoms as the end of Roman Britain. For them, continuity with the recent past was probably of far greater importance, bound up as they were in a dynastic, social and economic continuum. Their expectations of the future adjusted only gradually, as the prospect of reoccupation by Roman forces receded and other events successively altered the parameters of the world in which they lived.

Crisis and response: British society without Rome

The archaeological evidence from Britain in the fifth century is a catalogue of interpretational problems: the decay and collapse of all the more easily identified manufacturing activities, the collapse of the coinage, and problems in identifying or dating settlements and burials contrast with signs that the occupation and use of land continued across the bulk of the lowlands at levels not markedly different from that of the previous century. Adherence to one or other side of this radically contrasting picture has led to interpretations of the period which oscillate widely from fundamental continuity to a discontinuity which is near total. The several elements will here be discussed separately, in order to explore the light which they shed on the whole.

Population and environment

Demographic trends in the fifth and sixth centuries have been much debated. Early scholarship, from Bede to Bishop Stubbs, followed Gildas's apocalyptic view of a population in rapid decline under the pressure of famine and hostile raids, and such a picture would be consistent with recent models of systems collapse (e.g. Renfrew 1979).

Part of the responsibility for population decline was placed on the severe plague epidemics which are documented in the Mediterranean in the reign of Justinian, which the Spanish chronicler, Hydatius, stated 'spread to the whole world' (*Continuatio chronicorum Hieronymianorum*, 442). Whether or not such epidemics reached Britain is a matter of speculation from which the present generation has been warned away (e.g. Todd 1977). If they did, they might have caused population decline as extreme as that which occurred in the fourteenth century, when between a third and a half of the population died and many settlements were abandoned. Settlement abandonment was certainly widespread in the post-Roman era, but British literature which has been thought to corroborate plague death should not be burdened with this interpretation. There is currently no method of establishing the relevance of such parallels to the Dark Ages.

If we cannot reconstruct demographic processes directly, we can hope to approach them tangentially via pollen analysis, since the balance between different types of land cover might be expected to shadow crudely movements in the size of the population. Such processes lie behind all reconstructions of demographic change as undertaken by prehistorians and they have some currency in this later if all but prehistoric period, although the results are necessarily approximate in the extreme.

Comparison between selected pollen diagrams from the highland zone has revealed widespread woodland regeneration soon after the Roman period, with major episodes identified at numerous sites in north England and Scotland (Turner 1981b, 1983) and on Exmoor (Merryfield and Moore 1974). There are some parallels from the lowland zone, for example from Essex (Wilkinson 1988). Pervasive though this evidence is, however, it now appears characteristic only in areas of marginal land-use. Elsewhere, a growing number of palaeoenvironmental studies have failed to identify significant woodland regeneration. These instances are becoming numerous in the lowlands, where an undated study of Buckingham Mere (Godwin 1968) and current and dated work at Shotover Forest, Oxfordshire (Day 1990) supports the evidence from the Durham lowlands (Bartley *et al.* 1976) and from the Winchester area that land-use continued at Roman levels into the fifth and sixth centuries, without a check. Research at Hockham Mere suggested that pasture land tended to replace the extensive arable of the Roman period during the second third of the millennium, but this trend was reversed in the seventh and eighth centuries (Jones 1986). At Tatton (Cheshire), a major agricultural phase occurred in later prehistory which was followed successively by localized woodland regeneration carbon-dated to the Roman period, then by clearance associated with the cultivation of rye and wheat, dated to 430−670, probably associated with occupation on the Tatton village site close by (Chambers 1991). Similar oscillations in the balance between arable, pasture and woodland have been observed in Sussex, Berkshire and Dorset, but in no instance do these confirm large-scale woodland regeneration in the fifth century (Bell 1989). The end of Roman government in Britain appears to have occurred without any discernible fracture in the processes of land-use and the maintenance of clearance. Recent reinterpretations of faunal remains are similarly unsympathetic to a major reforestation in the fifth century, suggesting a continuum of pastoral farming in a comparatively unaltered landscape from late prehistory into the mid Saxon period (Biddick 1984).

Clearly, no single generalization is applicable across the whole country, except, perhaps, to deny that there was any very general reforestation in the fifth and sixth centuries. Patterns of land-use certainly altered, but in varying ways and to varying degrees, and the pattern which emerges is a localized one. Even where woodland regeneration has been identified, tree pollen rarely attained a higher proportion of the total than had been the case locally in later prehistory, suggesting that population levels fell only to the still comparatively high levels of the later centuries BC. Hallowell Moss (Durham) provides the obvious exception, where population appears to have crashed. Woodland regeneration occurred abruptly and arboreal pollen reached 96 per cent of the total, but this was identified at a horizon dated as late as 640−75 (Donaldson and Turner 1977).

The conclusions which emerge from this survey are highly speculative, because the relationship between population levels and vegetation should not be construed as a simple one. Within a densely populated community, steep demographic decline need have had little impact on the balance between woodland and human activities in open country, yet losses of comparable proportions in a landscape which was initially less densely peopled might dramatically alter such a balance. Indeed, such considerations may explain the tendency for reforestation to be identified in marginal upland areas, where existing population levels were lower.

That said, it does seem likely that population levels declined from *c*. 300 to 700, but this was relative to the exceptionally high population levels of the central Roman period. The geography of demographic decline was erratic, and the levels reached were probably still high by the standards of prehistory.

That medieval woodland eventually covered areas of Roman farming is certain, but the date of this regeneration is rarely known. Some demonstrably occurred under seigneurial pressure in the late Saxon period or thereafter. Settlement in well-wooded or afforested areas was commonplace in medieval England and was probably as common earlier, when rural settlement was generally less nucleated. The identification of Iron Age, Romano-British or early medieval settlements in areas which were later wooded is not, therefore, a sound basis for assuming massive woodland regeneration in the fifth or sixth centuries.

Considerable woodlands had survived the Roman period intact, the best researched example being Epping Forest (Baker *et al.* 1978) but other candidates include the Weald, the Lyme and Inglewood Forest (Higham 1986b). Belts of woodland had survived best on poor land where local population densities were comparatively low — hence the long-lived woodlands with Celtic names (Arden, Lyme) which probably retained substantial tree cover throughout the prehistoric and Roman periods.

Population was arguably as buoyant as in the late Middle Ages, if not more so, particularly on that terrain best suited to farming, predominantly in the south and east of Britain. Site desertion was commonplace but the desertion of landscapes less common, occurring principally in marginal areas, or in places with special problems like the fenlands of East Anglia and Humberside, where marine incursions were occurring (Potter 1981; Hall *et al.* 1988).

If a single factor be sought to explain both population decline and changes in land-use, climatic change remains the best candidate. Improvements in climate appear to have been influential in the demographic and economic expansion of the Iron Age and early Roman periods, just as they enabled a shift northwards of the ranges of a variety of living things from vines to bugs. Decline away from the climatic optimum during the fifth and sixth centuries threw these processes into reverse. Whether or not volcanic eruptions were ultimately responsible for climatic change (Burgess 1989; Baillie 1989), it does seem probable that climatic deterioration accompanied the collapse of Roman Britain, and it may have been an important causal factor. Indeed, research on glaciers within the polar region and across the globe implies that a steep climatic trough occurred across the entire northern hemisphere between *c.* 250 and 450, with the greatest implications for human activity in areas like Britain on the edge of the temperate zone (Grove 1988). Climatic changes led to agrarian recession and a crisis in the resourcing of the western Empire, which culminated in the downfall of the intricate and resource-greedy system of centralized government, with its professional bureaucracy and army. After their demise, the markets which they had sustained collapsed, leaving the civil aristocracy without a mechanism for exchanging their agrarian surplus for other types of goods and services.

The demise of the specialist

The Roman system was based on role specialization: professional soldiers protected the entire community and manufacturers supplied all who could afford their wares. The first half of the fifth century witnessed the end of the distinctive material culture of Roman Britain, and, for the archaeologist, heralds the gateway between Roman Britain and the so-called 'Dark Ages'. At the same time, the process signifies the contraction of specialization in most sectors of the community accessible to archaeology.

Many of Britain's pottery industries were still in production when Constantine III crossed the Channel. Given the static styles by then prevalent and the absence of coin-dating, no precise dates can be given for their eventual demise (e.g. Millett 1979). Evidence from Rhineland graves implies a growing shortage there of wheel-turned pottery by *c.* 420, and Britain's experience was probably similar (Fulford 1979). Estimates vary from region to region: Buckland (1980) favoured a date prior to 400 at Cantley in south Yorkshire and the East Riding industry ceased soon after, but all others who have been sufficiently incautious to offer an opinion have opted for the period 410–20 (e.g. Young 1977). It remains possible that such estimates are over-pessimistic and that some Roman-style pottery industries continued well into the second quarter of the century, but the case is as yet unproven.

In the late fourth and very early fifth centuries, small quantities of pottery had been imported to Richborough, London and the south-east from the Rhineland (Fulford and Bird 1975). This, too, now ceased and there is no evidence of Roman-style pottery being imported to Britain until the revival of small-scale contact between the Mediterranean and western Britain in the later fifth century (Thomas 1976, 1981b; Fulford 1989). Wheel-turned pottery was not to reappear in eastern Britain until Frankish imports reached Saxon Kent.

Hand-manufactured pottery similar in form to Belgic types was already widespread in Kent and southern England in the late fourth century. This also seems to have ceased production, implying that it, too, was a specialist area of manufacturing dependent on distribution via the market, or that it was driven out by a preference for incoming German industries. After *c.* 430, excluding the occasional import, those parts of Britain which were under British control were not only coinless but also increasingly aceramic (without pottery), with pottery production reduced to locally made grass-tempered vessels, the sherds from which are comparatively friable and survive only poorly in ploughsoil.

The collapse of pottery manufacturing is mirrored by the disappearance or near-disappearance of most other consumer durables at approximately the same time. Smithing proved the most durable of the craft skills for which we have evidence. Most of the belt-buckles used by troops and officials in the last few decades of the Roman period were imported through the commissariat from state factories in Pannonia or Illyricum (Simpson 1976). Such importation could not be expected to outlive Roman control, but new examples were manufactured during the early fifth century in Britain. Smiths trained within a late Roman milieu made pennanular and quoit brooches, although production sites have not been identified. Although they found their best markets in the Severn Basin, their wares achieved a wide distribution in western Britain in the fifth and sixth centuries, but the total number recovered remains extremely small (Dickinson 1982), while most examples from eastern England have come from Anglo-Saxon cemeteries (**4.1**). Hanging-bowls and enamel working

4.1 A silver quoit brooch from the Anglo-Saxon cemetery at Sarre (Kent), part gilded and decorated with applied birds and engraved friezes of animals (reproduced by courtesy of the Trustees of the British Museum).

similarly grew out of the metalworking traditions of Roman Britain (Longley 1975; Bateson 1981), and some of this production passed out of British hands into aristocratic Anglo-Saxon society, perhaps as tribute. Even so, the material evidence of craft continuity from sub-Roman Britain to either Celtic Britain or Anglo-Saxon England remains small in quantity, if only because British aristocracies retained the custom of unfurnished and unaccompanied burial.

Town life was also coming to an end. Most public buildings still in use in the 370s became derelict in the period *c.* 390 to 410. Although occupation of some sort can be traced into the mid-century within many Roman towns, urban life gradually ceased. The literary sources which have been cited for continuing town life in the fifth century do not support this: the life of St Germanus notes a man of high status (of tribunician power), but he need not be a townsman, and the vitality of the shrine of St Alban tells us nothing of the life of the Roman town beside it (Constantius XV.16); the contentious Honorian rescript implies no more than that the government at Ravenna was unwilling to recognize any insular government above the level of the *civitates*; Gildas, who interpreted the deserted Wall forts as towns (*De Excidio* XVIII.2), is not a reliable guide to the state of Britain before the English settlement. On his own admission, towns were gone by the time he was born, probably in the second half of the century. His blaming of the Saxons smacks of fitting an unsolved crime to a known criminal (XXIV.3).

The possibility that occupation continued in some form or other within the walls of some Roman towns was championed by a succession of eminent urban archaeologists during the 1960s and 1970s (Frere 1966; Wacher 1974a; Biddle 1976). However, their expectations have not in general been supported by subsequent discoveries. The most substantial evidence for late occupation in the Roman tradition is still that from Verulamium, where the masonry building XXVII/2, constructed *c.* 380, fell out of use during the second quarter of the century, after having corn dryers inserted within it. It was replaced by a building which Frere (1983) interpreted as a barn, and the whole context could have been that of an urban farm. This building was, in turn, cut across by a well-crafted pipeline which implies the survival of the town aqueduct. It is difficult to envisage an abandonment of occupation on this site before the 480s, but until it becomes apparent what sort of establishment was served by the water pipe it will remain impossible to determine whether this aceramic occupation had any other characteristics of Roman town life.

Structural evidence at several other towns suggests activity of some sort stretching into the mid fifth-century (e.g. Gloucester, Silchester, Cirencester) but while some may indicate continuing use of specific boundaries or territory, it is only Canterbury and Wroxeter that have provided sufficient evidence to pursue the issue of urban occupation beyond *c.* 450 (see below, pp. 104–5, 114).

Continuity and the pressures for change

The end of specialization in economic and social functions had critical consequences for British communities. If British society was to survive in a world without professional armies it would have to adopt new mechanisms for its own protection. As Roman troops failed to materialize after 411, so defence became an ever more critical issue. Without government oversight, it seems likely that the élite initially took the opportunity to enhance their own interests to the detriment of weaker neighbours (as suggested for Gaul, Wood 1987), so establishing themselves as *de facto* rulers of larger territories, with influence or even authority over entire regions through manipulation of existing systems of social control.

This élite seems to have continued to perform the role of local civil government and, as expectation of an Imperial expedition receded, it eventually took upon itself the organization of civil defence. The British leaders in the 420s naturally still turned to the Imperial Church for support against what they perceived (or chose to portray) as an outbreak of Pelagianism. This heresy developed from the teaching of Pelagius, a British lawyer who moved to Rome in the very late fourth century to further his education and there began to preach. There is no evidence that his teachings reached Britain until the arrival of the Pelagian Agricola, son of a Continental bishop, during the 420s. It was this action which triggered the British appeal, and St Germanus's first visit to Britain was the result. Pelagianism and its élitist and sectarian Christian culture had attracted considerable support among the aristocracy at Rome before the sack of 410 (Brown 1968), but was threatened by an alliance between St Augustine's universalist view of the Church and Imperial desires to achieve Christian unity. In 417/18, Pelagianism was condemned. Its leaders were already dispersed but there is no evidence that either its (originally British) founder or any of his principal lieutenants sought a refuge in Britain. Even so, insular Christianity in the 420s probably had much in common with Pelagianism, being essentially élitist and aristocratic in character, and Pelagian literature and refugees may have found a warm welcome among a provincial élite eager to ape the culture of far-off Italy. In Gaul it was St Martin who began to provide the antidote to élitism within the Christian establishment, by his wholesale missionary activities. There is no evidence of similar 'universalism' within the fifth-century British Church. Gildas appears to have been unable to distinguish between orthodox and Pelagian writings, which presumably, therefore, did circulate in Britain. If Pelagian views gained any whole-hearted converts, then Britain may have seen members of its aristocracy divesting themselves of family estates and wealth to give the proceeds to the poor, after the fashion which Pelagius prescribed. However, the hagiography of Constantius is a poor foundation on which to base any such conclusions (Thompson 1984) and it has long been recognized that the apparently corroborative evidence offered by the *Historia Brittonum* is of negligible historicity.

There are other indications that a form of Romanized government persisted down to the end of the century. The juxtaposition of the terms *rectores* and *speculatores* by Gildas (I.14) may imply that the roles of 'civil governor' and 'watchman' were distinguishable in his own lifetime. The same writer's 'proud tyrant' and his councillors imply the existence of this same government role, with the tyrant performing functions hitherto undertaken by the Emperor or his representative. His own Classical education and familiarity with Vergil is a clear indication that Romanized education and law courts persisted to the later fifth century. Indeed, Gildas referred to what can only be Roman law in his complaints concerning the tyrants (XXVII). Such indications imply that a civil government continued, if only at the level of the *civitas* or *regio*, whatever that may have been. The Roman army of Britain, however, could not be reformed so easily.

Britain was threatened by several barbarian neighbours. These enemies were tribal, practising comparatively little functional specialization within their own societies. Their aristocracies supplied war-leaders, and the possession of weapons was a privilege, even an obligation for the free man. These were communities of generalists — in contrast to the rigidly defined Roman specialists — and overflowing with individuals eager to profit from their proficiency in the use of arms. They posed a severe threat to the unguarded diocese.

The Saxon raid on Britain in *c.* 410 was probably merely one among many. Barbarian raiding was to be a major problem over much of the following two generations and came from every direction. St Patrick's account of his capture by Irish raiders implies that this was an everyday risk in the second quarter of the fifth century. Although his home near the otherwise unrecorded *Bannavem Taburniae* is generally placed in western Britain, if one recalls the capacity of later Scandinavian raiders for travelling across England there is no logical reason to envisage the Irish threat being confined to the west. *Taburniae* may imply a military *vicus* but *Banna* was a common place-name element in Roman Britain, occurring in a civil context in Lincolnshire and Northamptonshire. Options remain open and a lowland homeplace for Patrick is in many ways more attractive, given his upbringing in a Christian, *villula*-occupying, Latin-speaking and slave-owning household within a civilian *civitas*. If the catastrophe of 367 resulted in Pictish or Irish raids in the extreme south-east corner of Britain, there are no obvious barriers to Irish raiders anywhere in the diocese in the fifth century.

Gildas wrote of endemic raiding by the Picts and Scots, against which the Britons were initially powerless. His account is factually incorrect and this section of the *De Excidio* contains inventions: he has, for example, both Roman walls constructed after the death of Magnus Maximus. Gildas was highly subjective in the task he set himself and his approach has more in common with the role of an Old Testament prophet than of a historian. However, it may be significant that while blaming British misfortunes on the cowardice and immorality of his countrymen (XIX.2), he also recognized the lack of military expertise and equipment which characterized the provincial population (XIV). To leap the gap from unarmed provincial civilians to the semi-professional war-bands of his own day, he constructed a fictional account of Romans advising and training the British to take up arms and assume responsibility for the defence of their own property and families (XVIII.1). There is very little archaeological evidence of destruction by raiders (e.g. Darling 1987), but the Gallic Chronicles and perhaps even the putative experiences of St Germanus confirm that raiding was a serious problem, and also make it clear that Saxons were as much responsible for this as Picts (for whom there is the least evidence) and Scots.

However, the amount of Roman gold and silver reaching Scotland (Robertson 1970) and Ireland is far from impressive as a record of successful raiding over several decades, even supposing that most was subsequently reworked by local craftsmen. In Ireland, fourth- and fifth-century material is concentrated on the north and east coasts, with some, in addition, scattered inland in the south. The Balinrees hoard takes pride of place, deposited after 410 at Coleraine, Londonderry (**4.2**). However, this hoard is exceptional and is as likely to have been a diplomatic gift as booty from raiding. Other finds include copper coins with little intrinsic value and hoards which may have been diplomatic payments to barbarian leaders (Bateson 1973, 1976). The archaeological evidence seems to imply as much peaceful as violent contact, and may indicate the presence in

4.2 The Balinrees silver hoard (Coleraine, Londonderry). The coins indicate a date of deposition after *c*. 410. The tendency for pieces to approximate to a specific weight might imply either that it represented a diplomatic payment or that it was loot which it was intended to share out (reproduced by courtesy of the trustees of the British Museum).

Ireland of refugees from the Empire, who may have been the Christians to whom Pope Celestine dispatched a bishop in 431. There is little evidence that precious metal was in circulation in Britain after *c.* 420, and accessible to raiders.

If it was not precious metals with which their boats were typically loaded most Irish booty was presumably in the form of perishables such as clothing, livestock or humans. Given the problems of ferrying a herd of cattle aboard a boat of the type used in the Brendan voyage (Severin 1978), slaves were probably the most important of Britain's exports. Within the predator community, slaves could be sold on to more distant communities in the hinterland, as were St Patrick and the Irish captives of Coroticus. The result was wealth and elevated status for the captor, and increased production and, therefore, wealth and leisure for the owner.

Raiding brought slave workers to the estates controlled by their captors or purchasers. Migration was an alternative, which brought the captors to the workforce *in situ*. In terms of the effort involved, migration was obviously the more economic of these alternatives, but the risks and the upheaval might be greater.

Settlement within the old Empire was clearly an option which attracted many of its neighbours, who were drawn to its apparently unlimited wealth, its extensive agricultural lands and its well-disciplined cohorts of peasants. Whether it was the land they sought or the tax revenues (Goffart 1980) is an academic question, since most immigrants would presumably expect to acquire a workforce with their new land, and rent and tax were by this stage indissolubly linked.

Both forms of aggression were threats to which the local societies of Roman Britain needed to respond. Their success in so doing was very variable. In those parts of Britain where Romanization had been slight, competent military leadership and a warrior class evolved comparatively quickly. Where Romanization had been more successful, there is far less evidence that British societies successfully adapted themselves to the new realities. Local aristocracies attempted to maintain their fundamentally civilian role, and copied contemporary Roman practice in Gaul by employing barbarians as military specialists. By so doing, they, as a class, inadvertently signed their own death warrants, leaving Gildas, himself clearly from that class, to pronounce their epitaph in the process of haranguing their more adaptive neighbours in the highland zone. Those who were the butt of his invective were successful in re-establishing the capacity to defend themselves and the societies which they headed, and sloughing off the impediment of their own incipient Romanization.

Adaptable societies: the north and west

Communities within the old military parts of the province adapted comparatively successfully to the changing circumstances of the fifth century.

Although most eventually fell under Anglo-Saxon control, this did not occur until two centuries or more had elapsed since the fall of Constantine III, in an era which saw the rise of a minority of English kingdoms to levels of military and political power unheard of in the mid-fifth century. The most successful area − Wales − retained its indigenous ruling classes, its characteristic culture and its language into the later medieval period.

In the wider context this is surprising, given that the military zone was the least prosperous part of the province, with lower population densities and lower levels of output than much of southern and eastern England. In these respects, the area was less well equipped to survive the stresses of the fifth century with an indigenous culture immune from drastic outside pressures. Success may be explained by several factors: local societies had made few concessions to Romanization; they had not evolved a complex social hierarchy, headed by a small élite of extremely powerful and highly Romanized villa-occupying landowners; they had the shortest distance to travel to regain a military capability, with the capacity to recruit and re-equip warriors from the large middle ranks of the tribal population; such communities were reinforced by a cultural unity expressed through the use of a single language at all levels and by the poor penetration of Romanized market economics within the community; 'peasantization' had made few inroads, despite the disarming of the tribes; Romanized religious cults, including Christianity, had arguably made little impact. Some communities may have gained some advantage from the presence of whatever remained of the military expertise and equipment of the frontier army.

British communities between the Hadrianic and Antonine Walls, ruled from York, fell within the outer orbit of *Britannia Secunda*, where Romanization amounted to no more in material terms than the acquisition of a handful of Roman manufactures: building styles and settlement architecture remained untouched by Roman fashions into the fifth century. Sited across Britain's only land frontier, this community was particularly vulnerable to Pictish raids and may have been left under Pictish control after operations against raiders within the province instigated by Stilicho in 398 (Claudian, *de consulatu Stilichonis* II.250−5). The hoard of silver work at Traprain Law implies either booty from the Empire or a diplomatic payment by the Roman authorities to potentially dangerous barbarians in command of the old tribal *oppidum* of the Votadini, but whether or not these were Pictish is unclear.

However, the region did not become Pictish but remained one of Brythonic speakers under local British leadership. There is no evidence of successful Pictish settlement anywhere in the old diocese, although Irish settlement occurred in Argyll in the decades around 500, in what had presumably been Pictish territory, establishing there a linguistically distinctive and self-governing Irish community. Successful British war-lords established tribal dynasties which emerged into the historical dawn of the sixth and seventh centuries, at Edinburgh, Dumbarton Rock, the Mote of Mark, and elsewhere. Behind them, small kingdoms came into existence in what had been the north and west of *Britannia Secunda*, temporarily free of the threat of immigration.

Gildas saw raids from the Celtic periphery as an overriding threat to Britain during the early sub-Roman period (XXII.1). Whatever the veracity of his remarks, immigration did occur in the west, although the evidence of Irish activity is limited in scope, depending on Gaelic elements in place-names, late fifth- and sixth-century inscriptions in ogam and a small corpus of literary sources (Nash-Williams 1950; Richards 1960). This material is concentrated in south-west Wales, in what became Dyfed, and may be consistent with the establishment there of an Irish dynasty (**4.3**). However, the extent to which this represents a folk movement, as opposed to a warrior take-over, is quite unclear. Ogam inscriptions include numerous Roman or Romanized names such as Victor and Pompeius and many inscriptions are in both Latin and ogam, implying the presence of an influential sector of society which was literate but unable to read ogam. Bilinguality was probably common, rapidly diluting the cultural and ethnic separateness of these immigrants, although their success locally may have encouraged many of the indigenes to adopt Gaelic. Late literary sources recorded the coming to Britain of the Desi of Munster but confusion may have arisen out of the meaning of this tribal name ('unfree'), given that the Irish saw Britain at this stage as a pool of potential slave labour. It would be a rash observer who equated the evidence of Gaelic speech in western Britain with mass migration from Ireland.

Irish settlement has also been claimed in north-east Cornwall and west Devon (Thomas 1973–4) and in Somerset (Rahtz 1976b) but, although late Irish texts identified Glastonbury, for example, as an Irish stronghold, such settlements are of dubious historicity. The presence of Irish inscriptions demonstrates little more than frequent intercourse across the Irish Sea, and the presence of Irish exiles or clerics, who are known to have been inveterate travellers.

Outside these enclaves of the Gaelic language, the communities of western Britain were predominantly speakers of Brythonic languages and were ruled by families who, whatever their origins, give every appearance of being indigenous. Over several centuries, Gaelic was driven out by indigenous languages and died away. In contrast, Gaelic survived as the language of Dalriada, in Argyll, where a Scottish dynasty and aristocracy retained its internal identity, although often under Pictish or English overlordship, over the next few centuries.

Tribal identity and kinship systems had probably remained strong in the upland zone throughout the Roman period. Where kindred groups remained a powerful political force, their leaders – and particularly their newly emerging war-leaders – were in a position to take power, in what must have appeared to be a long drawn-out crisis of local security. Each may have established himself as an independent ruler – a parochial emperor –

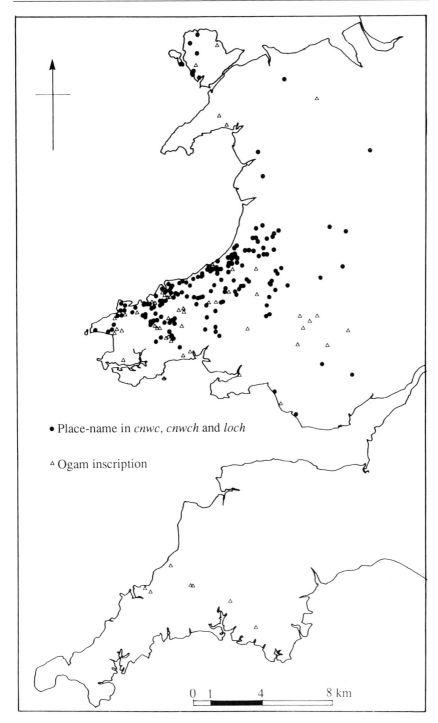

• Place-name in *cnwc, cnwch* and *loch*

△ Ogam inscription

0 1 4 8 km

4.3 Irish settlement and cultural influence in western Britain in the fifth and sixth centuries.

supported by control of the Imperial fisc, erstwhile government taxation of the tribal community, and the perquisites of landholding and patronage already under his control or handy for his acquisition. With this income in kind, petty kings recruited and supported war-bands with which they sought to protect their own lands, raid or conquer their neighbours, and secure the inheritance of their positions by their own families.

The kingdoms which emerged probably focused on a core of people — and the land over which they exercised rights of exploitation — secured to the dynasty by self-interest and kinship, surrounded by a mesh of subordinate communities attached by variable ties and with their own aristocracies. Of their origins we know very little, since the re-emergence of the historical Celtic kingdoms in the lifetime of Gildas post-dated much consolidation and conquest, but royal families had by then certainly established their exclusive rights to leadership, and not uncommonly bolstered their positions by recourse to Roman-style titles such as 'Protector'. They shared with the late fourth-century Imperial court a taste for praise-poetry, although all insular survivals are in the vernacular.

There eventually re-emerged from the fifth century several large polities which mirrored and may have continued the tribal *civitates* of Roman Britain — hence the Demetae, Gododdin and the Dumnonii of both the south-west and Strathclyde. However, much of later Celtic Britain was organized in tribal kingdoms which bore no known relationship to the Roman system. This apparent discontinuity may be an accident of our ignorance, since we are peculiarly ill-informed about political structures in the Roman period in the west and north. None the less, name changes were occurring. The Carvetii, for example, probably re-emerged as Rheged (Cumbria) and the *civitas* of the Brigantes had no straightforward Dark Age successor: its peoples re-formed into what may have been underlying tribal identities, Elmet in the south and the north-easternmost territory of Deira to the north, around Catterick. There are no known Romano-British precursors for Bernicia — an area badly neglected by Ptolemy — but the core of Deira must lie in what had been the territory of the Parisi. Such territorial divisions and name-changing may mean little: after all, there is some evidence that tribal name-changing was an intentional stratagem in later prehistory (Higham 1987a). The Dark Age kingdoms probably represent a compromise between the powers of kingly coercion, partible inheritance and the internal tribal loyalties of British communities within and beneath the structure of an erstwhile Romanized local government system of which we are lamentably ignorant.

The *civitas* of the Dumnonii (in England) either survived intact or, like the *civitas* of the Silures, was brought back to a degree of unity by successful warrior-kings. It became a kingdom, taking in the entirety of the south-west peninsula, but the *civitas* capital at Exeter was abandoned as a political centre and at some stage reused as an inhumation cemetery. Underlying political continuity was no guarantee of a static society. Widespread changes occurred in the countryside. The enclosed farming settlement or 'round' at Trethurgy continued into the fifth century with two or three stone-founded, oval houses covered by a ridged roof (Quinnell 1986; **4.4**). Thereafter, and probably still within the fifth century, this and other rounds were abandoned. Unenclosed, dispersed settlements had always been a significant element in the settlement pattern of the Roman period and these now became characteristic of the region. All this implies a comprehensive dislocation of existing settlement, stemming from the

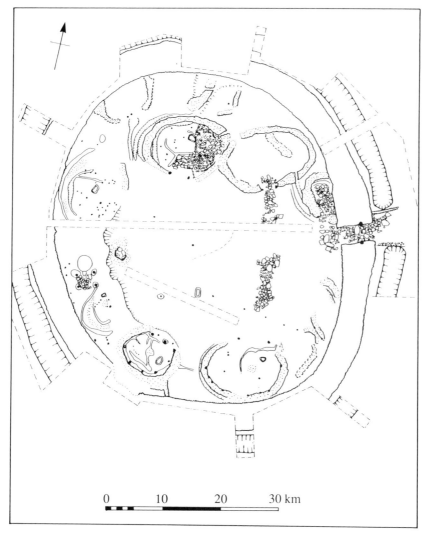

4.4 Trethurgy: a Cornish round near St Austell, showing late Roman layers (after Miles and Miles 1973).

collapse of the Roman economic and political system, as newly released political and social pressures rapidly moulded local society in new directions.

Reorganization seems to have centred on the creation of territorial units (the *keverang*) comparable to the Anglo-Saxon hundred, each consisting of about 100 settlements (*trefs*), apparently as the basis for the organization of military service. There is evidence that trefs were carefully planned with a near standard amount of arable land of 3 *modii* (a late Roman measure: see Preston-Jones and Rose 1986 for discussion and full references) though the chronology of their development is unclear.

At the apex of Dumnonian society were sites of larger size and higher status, so far identified at Tintagel (Thomas 1988), and perhaps Bantham Ham and High Peak, and distinguished from the later fifth century onwards by the presence of relatively large quantities of ceramics imported from the Mediterranean or southern Gaul (Thomas 1981b). Such sites invite comparisons with the high-status entrepôt sites characteristic of the late pre-Roman Iron Age and indicate the restoration of a social and economic structure with much in common with that period. Continuing excavations at Tintagel are likely to establish that site as the western British end of trading links with the Mediterranean, where tin was exchanged for exotic consumer goods at a site under direct royal control, and where the kings of Dumnonia were frequently resident (C.D. Morris, personal communication).

In neighbouring south-east Wales, analysis of the Llandaff charters suggests that large estates termed *agri* continued in use until the early eighth century. At this stage, a process of widespread land division brought about the dissolution of the sub-Roman pattern of landownership, in favour of small, single focus estates which, unlike the *agri*, are traceable in the modern settlement pattern (Davies 1978a). The *agri* were arguably Roman in origin, and may have been estates associated with the territories of the area's numerous villas. Although the latter appear to have been abandoned before the end of the Roman period, the tenurial and social structures, physical boundaries and agricultural systems with which they had been associated may well have continued thereafter, with settlement of groups of varying status shifting within them, as the community adjusted to an economy closer to subsistence and a military system internal to the social hierarchy.

In these instances, changes in site use and social organization were fundamental. Settlement mobility was widespread, despite the high degree of ethnic continuity. Throughout the old diocese, settlement instability is the best evidenced characteristic of the post-Roman era, and occurred apparently irrespective of the presence or absence of immigrants.

In the west, the form of kingship which emerged was described in scathing terms by Gildas (XXVII–XXXVI). It was first and foremost a warrior kingship, supported by military companions (*sanguinarios superbos*) to whom went much of his bounty, but the king was also a judge, a patron

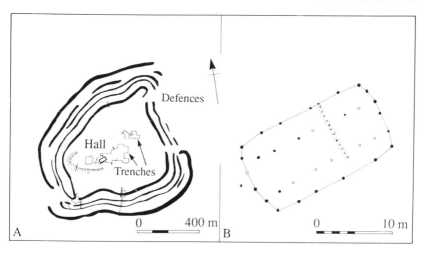

4.5 South Cadbury: the defences, the excavations and the fifth/sixth-century hall (after Alcock 1972, 1982).

of the Church, a giver of alms and of rights to land (Davies 1978b), a gaoler and a police officer. Within their own little worlds, such kings had taken over the rights and duties of the Roman Emperors, now reorientated each to his own household and warband.

There are important differences between the developments in these highland zone kingdoms and the western lowlands. That those in control of a more 'peasantized' proletariat were able to draw on the labour services of the local community is the obvious implication of South Cadbury II (Alcock 1982), where ramparts 4–5 m wide and *c.* 1200 m long were fronted by a dry masonry revetment and equipped with a timber framework and gate-house which would have required 20,000 m of planks and beams (**4.5**). Although close parallels for this work are not currently available nearer than the Pictish forts such as Burghead and Dundurn, there are sub-Roman parallels in the sense of other sites requiring labour far in excess of that which could have been provided by the inhabitants, as at fifth-century Wroxeter. In several counties bordering the Bristol Channel, the reuse of hillforts is an important phenomenon of the fifth century (and the Roman period), with occupation serving a variety of functions including defence, high-status settlement and religion (Burrow 1981). Local communities may have turned to such sites as tangible links with the past in their search for legitimate authority as well as security, and several had religious importance throughout the Roman period and beyond. However, these findings have not been replicated with any degree of precision elsewhere, and this may be just one of many local responses to the changing circumstances of the fifth century.

If they be counted as a product of Celtic lordship, the several dykes and 'hedges' of the south and south-west demonstrate the capacity of the

British élite to conscript labour. Such works were already being erected during the later Roman period when, for example, the Bokeley Dyke (Dorset) was constructed, use of which appears to have continued into the fifth century (Rahtz 1961). The Giant's Hedge in southern Cornwall is another substantial example but, although still not closely dated (Fox and Fox 1960), the Wansdyke arguably ranks as the largest single demonstration of the ability of Celtic rulers to mobilize labour for political purposes (**4.7**). It is reasonable to suppose that labour for the construction of the dykes was marshalled in much the same way as for the later fourth-century repairs to Hadrian's Wall: that is by conscription on the basis of tax assessments within those communities over whom the commissioning

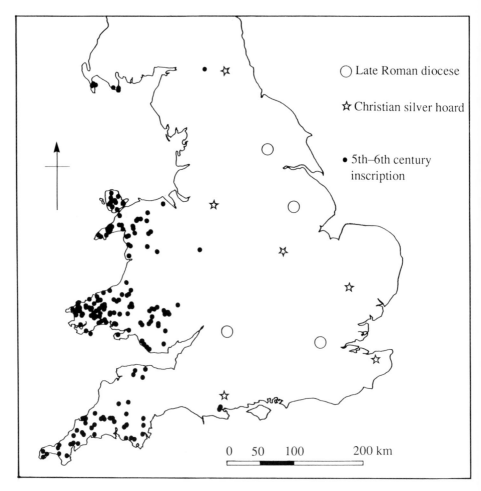

4.6 Late Roman and early medieval Christianity in southern Britain: the inscriptional and hoard evidence.

administrator had authority. For the Wall this involved work by men from several of the southern *civitates*. The Wansdyke was presumably constructed by labourers recruited from Wiltshire and Dorset. Whatever the date, the dyke clearly post-dates the Roman road on Morgan's Hill, yet is thought to predate the establishment of Wessex in the late sixth and seventh centuries. By the eighth century it was a well-documented estate boundary with no political or military purpose. The reasoning behind it may owe a debt to Roman frontier systems. It is difficult to conceive of a more fitting monument to the coercive powers and the Roman-style approach of the rulers of what had been the Durotriges, as that community responded to the pressures and tensions of life after Rome. It is tempting to think that his familiarity with such dykes, built like the Antonine Wall in earth or turves, may have encouraged Gildas to assign one of the great Roman walls across northern Britain to British construction. When he described the northern stone wall as being constructed 'in the normal way' (*solito structurae more*; *De Excidio* XVIII.2) he may have had in mind the use of conscript labour as much as some architectural notion of masonry construction, since the latter would not have been a familiar technique – except in surviving monuments or ruins – to his audience (Higham 1991b). Although current opinion is hostile to any attempt to localize Gildas (e.g. Sims-Williams 1983b), his familiarity with recent or even current British use of non-masonry constructional techniques would suggest that he was at least familiar with a type of engineering which was most widely used in the central south and south-west of England (Higham forthcoming b and c).

Once reintroduced to the social system of western Britain, warriors became highly mobile and might wander far in search of a generous patron. A man from Elmet (W. Yorkshire) was commemorated on stone in Wales, and Roman writers knew of British war-bands serving the Empire as auxiliaries in Gaul in the 460s or 470s, who may well have derived from the same areas. Those areas of Britain which evolved an indigenous military class in the fifth century were clearly capable of over-producing warriors, just as were the early English communities.

British migration to Armorica may have been spearheaded by under-resourced but ambitious warriors and priests from the west of Britain. The monks of St Gildas-de-Rhus long cherished the tradition that Gildas, the author of the *De Excidio* himself, was their founding father (**4.9**), and it is easy to believe that departure from Britain may have commended itself to him after his libellous foray into moralistic pamphleteering. Christian exiles travelled by ship across the sea from those parts of Britain under attack by the rebelling Saxon mercenaries and, although several destinations have been suggested, Armorica (or Brittany as it was to become in the sixth century) remains by far the most likely. The impact of Britons on the language (Jackson 1953) and on local Christianity (Fleuriot 1980; Chédeville, and Guillotel 1984; Davies 1988), indicate that the immigrants were

4.7 The Wansdyke on Horton Down, Wiltshire. This massive, north-facing ridge-top dyke defends or demarks southern Wiltshire and Dorset from the Thames valley. It is still undated but construction on the orders of British authorities against Saxon land seizure in the Thames valley as implicit in the *De Excidio* of Gildas is an attractive possibility (copyright the author).

extremely influential, although how this influence was achieved remains a matter of debate.

In Celtic society, aristocratic households stand out as the principal centres of consumption, of craft skills and of the distribution of imports and metalwork. It is only on sites of high social status that smithing has been identified, as at the multi-phase aristocratic stronghold of Dinas Powys, where bronze- and iron-working occurred beside the fashioning of wood and leather and the manufacture of cloth, within a period dated to the late fifth to seventh century on the basis of imported pottery and glass (Alcock 1963). In Somerset, small-scale metalworking was characteristic of hilltop sites, using pre-Roman techniques and favouring non-Roman forms, incorporating Roman glass fragments, scrap metal and gold (Rahtz 1982). Beads reached such sites from Ireland and pottery from Cornwall, although Roman pottery seems to have enjoyed a long period of use, some reaching Cadbury Congresbury after the Roman period as sherds (Burrow 1979) which may have been used as coinage or counters. Imported fine table wares and the contents of amphorae were presumably consumed on site, while wine may have found its way far up the coasts of the Irish Sea, if only in wooden casks.

By 500, upland British society had reorientated itself upon the aristocratic household, re-established its military capacity and forged a new society resilient enough to survive and even prosper in the immediate future.

Religion, burial and group identity

Britain entered the fifth century with a mixture of religious beliefs and practices which included episcopalian state Christianity as well as a multitude of local cults, many of which retained Romano-Celtic deities and served the traditional needs of local communities. The expansion of Christianity into the Gaulish countryside was under way only in the late fourth and early fifth centuries, a period during which Britain was intermittently, and eventually finally, detached from the Empire. This process of evangelism in Gaul is associated with the careers of St Germanus and St Martin.

In Britain, when direct Roman rule collapsed, Christianity was probably still largely confined to the declining urban communities and to the social and administrative hierarchy and their households, all of which were most strongly represented in the lowlands. It is unlikely to have had many committed recruits among the indigenes in the north and west.

Despite the generally non-missionary nature of the British Church, Christianity spread within the British Isles during the fifth century, expanding both within and without the provinces. The priesthood eventually gained the active patronage of the new leaders of western Britain, but this may have been delayed for a generation or more after 410, when the tribes of the upland zone were probably largely pagan.

A degree of evangelism may have been present before the middle of the century. Pope Celestine dispatched a bishop to Ireland in 431, although whether he was a missionary or not is a matter of speculation. Bede recorded the tradition local to Whithorn of a British cleric, St Ninian, and his mission to the southern Picts. The presence of an early British Christian community there is evidenced by several inscribed memorial stones, of which the earliest, the 'Latinus' stone, belongs to the second half of the fifth century. Excavations still under way on the small hill crowned by the medieval church of Withorn have revealed late fifth- or early sixth-century activity, at the start of a stratigraphy which extends through the Northumbrian and Viking Ages (Hill 1988). St Patrick's letter to Coroticus describes the Picts as apostate, implying that some missionary attempt had been made in their direction — supposing that his language should be taken literally. However, Bede's information may owe more to a competition for status between the eighth-century Northumbrian bishops at Whithorn and Abercorn, where the Northumbrian mission to the Picts was stationed, and should not be allowed much weight, particularly since it was framed in terms which imply that Bede reserved his own judgement, on its veracity. The very existence of St Ninian remains extremely doubtful.

Despite hostility from within the British Church, St Patrick, himself a Christian born and bred but now with faith kindled anew, followed Palladius to Ireland if that is the correct order of events, and his is the first certain, documented attempt to carry Christianity to the Barbarians outside the Empire, within the British Isles.

There is no evidence that Christianity made much impact on the provincial *pagani* before the death of Constantine III. The account of St Germanus baptizing his timerous British soldiers on the campaign which was supposed to have yielded the Hallelujah Victory (in 429) may not be strictly historical but it does suggest that Continental churchmen in the late fifth century expected the British to have been unbaptized pagans in the 420s. Patrick seems to have assumed Coroticus to have been at least nominally Christian, and to have been in contact with Christians although the questions of his place of residence and date bedevil attempts to draw conclusions from that fact. The fifth century would seem to have been the period when Christianity spread more widely, with the leadership of communities in the highland zone prominent among its new devotees.

As the Roman Imperial system failed as a system of government and defence, so its clerical wing assumed a growing importance. St Germanus was a papal agent, sent to ensure that Britain conformed to Roman views over the Pelagian heresy, but, if his visit to St Albans is any indication, his first mission at least appears to have been to the lowlands.

Beyond the stamping ground of Germanus, the tribal kingdoms which arose within the provinces did so by adopting in highly localized forms the social and political structure at the core of the Empire, centred on the Imperial household. A critical element in the Imperial system of government was its relationship with the Christian Church, which provided it with a hierarchically organized system capable of delivering ideological conformity and extensive opportunities for Imperial patronage. Christianity offered the nascent British dynasties an institutional dimension to their control over local society, the control of ecclesiastical patronage, an ideology which would recall their Romanity, and an entrée to more elevated notions of kingship consistent with Imperial status but alien to tribal society. By the third quarter of the fifth century, the petty Welsh princelings were at least nominally Christian, and the Irish were under instruction – a fact which Gildas totally overlooked. Each Welsh king exercised patronage over the Church within his own lordship.

The triumph of Celtic Christianity may have been delayed until the mid-century, by which time political leadership had stabilized and recognized the opportunities before it. In the meantime, the fortunes of some pagan shrines were in the ascendant. The temple at Pagans Hill was still roofed in the mid-seventh century and a skull cult survived in the fifth or sixth centuries at Cadbury Congresbury (Rahtz 1982). The Wroxeter cult site was more probably that of a pagan healing deity than Christian.

However, the victory of Christianity is evidenced archaeologically in the Celtic west, at least by the end of the century. At Uley (Glos.) the masonry temple was entirely dismantled in the fifth century and replaced by a new timber structure, which used the pagan altars as building material, set within an enclosing bank (Ellison 1980). The last phase of the temple at Nettleton Scrubb was probably Christian. At Lamyatt Beacon (Som.), the pagan temple may have been converted to Christian use before abandonment, and the site was reused for an orientated inhumation cemetery after the Roman period but up to two centuries after the shrine fell out of use (Leech 1986).The temple at Henley Wood was similarly cut across by a cemetery of west–east oriented inhumations devoid of grave-goods, which may have been Christian.

Some later churches may have developed from late Roman mausolea, as has been argued for St Albans, Stone-by-Faversham (4.8) and Wells Cathedral (Rodwell 1982), although such mausolea need not be Christian. At Poundbury, one interpretation of the extensive but poorly evidenced fifth- or sixth-century occupation of the late Roman cemetery was as a monastery, perhaps reflecting the burial place of an important local saint (Green 1982, 1988). Elsewhere, links between springs, pagan shrines and churches may imply the conversion of local religious sites successively from one deity to another throughout the Celtic world (e.g. Cole 1985; Scherr 1986). The high incidence of later churches built over or adjacent to Roman ruins (e.g. at Woodchester and Rivenhall) may imply a link across the vicissitudes of the period (Morris and Roxan 1980), although alternative explanations are available and often appear more plausible. Many Celtic church foundations survived to be incorporated into the later Anglo-Saxon minster system in Devon (Pearce 1982, 1985) and other areas of late sixth- and seventh-century conquest.

4.8   The Anglo-Saxon Church of Stone-by-Faversham, Kent, the core of which was a late Roman mausoleum (copyright the author).

To what extent did the Celtic Church emerge from the Christianity of Roman Britain? There are signs that it owed more to reintroduction and transformation in the fifth century, than to roots already deeply embedded. British Christianity had been episcopal, urban, high status and official. No known fourth-century church survived in use into the later fifth century and the urban congregation, the Christian villa owner and the provincial diocese were all pushed towards extinction by the passing of Roman Britain. However, although the Church of the lowlands was extinguished as an institution in consequence of the Anglo-Saxon conquests, it seems likely that the expansion of Christianity in the west and in Armorica owed much to the arrival of a trickle of well-educated and Christian refugees from the British lowlands. Having abandoned the wide estates that had supported them hitherto, and themselves with little expertise as soldiers, their natural recourse was to their religion and they were probably instrumental in injecting a high degree of literacy and of intellectual vigour into the western realms. Against their dependence on the patronage of local kings Gildas railed but in vain.

Inscribed stones are the most widespread evidence we have for late fifth- and sixth-century Christianity. About 150 survive in Wales, 50 in the south-west and a dozen or so in the north (**4.6**). Throughout Britain, the custom of making inscriptions on stone was declining rapidly in the fourth century; it had in any case been most commonly associated with the army rather than the general populace. Fifth-century examples post-date the adoption of semi-uncial characters, which occurred on the Continent early

4.9 The Church of St Gildas-de-Rhus, south-east Brittany. In the treasury are human bones contained in fifteenth-century reliquaries, which are claimed to be the arms and legs of St Gildas. An eleventh-century tombstone behind the high altar is also assigned to him and it is clear that this community already believed by that date that their founder was the author of the *De Excidio* (copyright the author).

in the century and may be present in the west of Britain in the decades following the mid-century. Several scholars have taken this to imply that the insular Celtic Church owed more in its inception to links with the Continent than to any putative British heritage (Nash-Williams 1950; Ralegh Radford 1971) but this may be an accident resulting from chronological and cultural factors. Certainly, contacts between the west and parts of Gaul and the Mediterranean were developing during the later fifth and sixth centuries, when cross-Channel links between Gaul and Christian communities in the British lowlands were failing. However, Britain could still be seen as a single entity when Gildas was writing and its Christian communities apparently maintained communication across political boundaries.

Whatever links there were between Celtic Christianity and the Continent, they were insufficiently influential to halt the drift of the insular Church into forms of organization which were inconsistent with Continental practices. It may be that Christianity in the upland zone and under the influence of its kings diverged as early as the late fifth century, even from what remained of the episcopal Church of lowland Britain. The Welsh Church ignored Continental reforms occurring after the mid-millennium, and the Christianity practised by British immigrants to Armorica was sufficiently different by 567 to attract the attention of the Continental clergy. In comparative isolation, the western British Church developed within a system of patronage and organization which mirrored the emerging kingdoms, and reflected the greater importance of the family and kin within society. Royal and aristocratic influence within it was clearly considerable when Gildas inveighed against those numerous clergy who found their careers enhanced by royal interest, or who purchased benefices. Such men found themselves of necessity making greater concessions to the violence and marital instabilities of a leadership which was attuned to the realities of power politics in a dangerous world, than to the pontifications of a European Christianity with which their contacts were incidental, and whose commands they could ignore with impunity.

Yet when the Roman and Celtic churches eventually began a new dialogue (*c.* 600), it was not intransigent Welsh kings whom Bede blamed for its failure but the advice of the abbot of a British monastery, implying that much authority over the British Church was by that stage external to its secular patrons and associated with 'families' of monks, after the Irish model.

The needs of its patrons seem to have enticed the Celtic Church into some major departures from normal Continental practice, where fifth-century Christian burial was characteristically unaccompanied inhumation in an orientated cemetery. Western Britain probably had very different traditions of mortuary disposal and local Christianity had to adapt to these as well as to the changing social needs of its patrons. A sixth-century inscribed gravestone formerly stood at the ancient route crossing at Pen-y-stryd, Ardudwy (Merioneth). Reconstruction of the inscription reads, in translation, 'Here lies Porius in a mound. He was a Christian Man.' (a chi−rho follows, Gresham 1985). Burial in a cairn was commemorated elsewhere: '*in hoc congeries lapidum...*' (Nash-Williams 1950, No. 101: 'in this heap of stones...').

In the churchyard at Tintagel, several mounds imply the presence of a group of tumuli. When the interior of one was exposed a lintel-grave was revealed. It is possible that these mounds hide aristocratic tombs of the fifth century (Thomas 1988), but it is premature to guess at the results of excavations now under way on the site by the Cornish Archaeological Unit. The young hero posthumously praised in poem A1 of the group of verses published under the title of the *Gododdin* was buried beneath a cairn (Jackson 1969).

In Clwyd, recent excavation of a group of square-ditched barrows suggests that they belong to this period[1], in which case they presumably represent earthen mausolea based, ultimately, on the square-ditched barrow of the Arras culture in late Iron Age Yorkshire. Similar mortuary practices were adopted during the Roman period in Pictish Fife and Angus, where they contrast with the more common adoption of long cist graves on a Roman model (Close-Brooks 1984), of which carbon-dated examples belong to the fifth and sixth centuries.

These several experiments in mortuary practices occur beside the more normal Christian cemetery, such as is represented at Cannington (Som.) and elsewhere. Many inscribed stones are to be found in medieval grave-yards. Although some have been removed from their original sites to the church, others commemorate burials in Christian cemeteries; one Welsh example records that this body lay 'with the multitude of its brethren'.

Burial in tumuli or cairns is of great antiquity in Britain; the rite was not dead in the Roman period and was to be revived in the Anglo-Saxon areas. To find it here in conjunction with the burial of high-ranking Christians is indicative of the experimental nature of sub-Roman culture, and the need to find expression in public ritual of the competitive and heroic ethos of the aristocracy as that overturned more Romanized ideo-logical perspectives. The burial of a prominent individual at the crossroads was not unusual and occurs at several sites in the south-west, where burial at or near the settlement is also a well-known phenomenon. These aspects of Celtic Christianity underline the transitional nature of society, adapting a Roman/British ideology which was in many ways now inappropriate by combining that with other forms of social and religious expression culled from the past, developed *ab initio* or borrowed from neighbours whose Christian and Roman credentials were entirely spurious.

Settlement archaeology

Palaces, halls and other sites of high status imply the presence of an extensive pattern of farming settlements in the fifth century. Yet, so far, the efforts of modern scholarship have failed to identify more than a handful of these sites, and the current tendency is for the sample to decline in numbers as more existing examples are rejected than are being added. Now that vessels of 'very coarse pottery' have been reinterpreted as salt containers of the Iron Age, sites consistent with farming occupation in the period have been reduced to a handful of often dubious and poorly dated examples.

At Gwithian (Cornwall), several small sites were occupied during this period, their occupants subsisting on mixed farming and food collecting, and exploiting local ores (Thomas 1958). In Wales, aceramic levels were identified at Cae'r Mynydd, which post-date fourth-century occupation (see Edwards and Lane 1988 for discussion). Carbon dates suggest occupation of Ty Mawr (Holyhead) in the fifth to the eighth century in unenclosed and mostly round huts; eight homesteads are visible but no more than one or two were ever in contemporary use (Smith 1987).

The inability of archaeologists to identify sub-Roman farm sites has deeply influenced interpretation of the Anglo-Saxon settlement (e.g. Myres 1986: 217). Yet the problem is a technical one and varies little across the interface between the Celtic and Anglo-Saxon regions of Britain. Much of the farming population had never been highly Romanized and alternatives to pottery were probably always in use. When Roman manufacturing collapsed, there is no reason to think that the peasantry did other than continue with their traditional economic activities as well as they were able, within the changing constraints of a social system in transition, and against a background of growing threats from outside. Archaeologists have been misled by the ease with which Roman levels can be identified and dated, into the belief that they ought to be able to identify occupation levels of the early medieval period. Yet, Anglo-Saxon finds apart, the material culture which confronts them is almost without diagnostic artefacts, at most levels of society. If rural settlements were henceforth unenclosed by ditches, it is understandable that they should be difficult to detect.

Buildings which could belong to the period are also poorly evidenced. This becomes explicable if we take account of the evidence for even high-status buildings, such as have been identified at Wroxeter, where Philip Barker abandoned established methods of site stripping to masonry levels, in favour of a more cautious process of removal of the overburden. Above the baths, which were abandoned early in the fourth century, he identified a large group of timber-framed buildings, some boasting timber façades modelled on Classical lines and some constructed far more modestly in a lean-to style, built of wattle and daub (**4.10**). The largest building was a vast 38.5 × 16 m, on a platform of selected rubble and constructed with cill beams. Construction of the complex had required the removal of 65 m of a Roman road (Barker 1975). The work of site preparation and construction leaves an impression of a large workforce, but one lacking masonry skills. The buildings belonged to 'a post-mortar generation', using crushed stone, plaster or brick and timber. The occupation was aceramic. The site is easiest intepreted as a high-status residence which may combine the function of a cult centre.

What is important in the present context is the evidence of fifth-century building techniques. By far the most prominent features uncovered were the floor surfaces made of recycled Roman debris. Evidence for the superstructure is extremely limited. A minority of buildings utilized sandstone padstones or post-holes, but many walls were constructed by methods which necessitated very little disturbance of the substrate. Without the floors, many of these phantom buildings would be extremely difficult to identify through excavation.

These findings are supported by evidence from other urban sites. The public baths at Canterbury fell out of use during the fourth century, but a series of timber buildings succeeded it on the south-west side, the last of which made hardly any impression in the silt from a blocked sewer on which it was erected. Fifth-century building was also evidenced in the baths portico, and outside a private bath suite on the Marlow car park site (Blockley 1980; Blockley and Day 1979 and forthcoming[2]). None produced structural evidence of this period which would have been likely to be visible through crop mark photography, and artefacts were almost entirely absent.

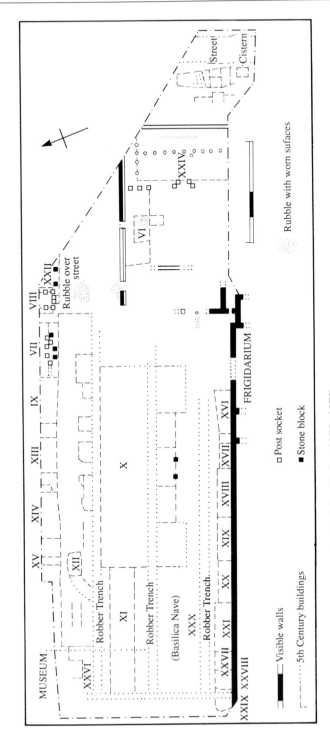

4.10 Wroxeter: the fifth-century levels (after Barker 1975, 1979).

Earth-fast posts do occur: the main structure at South Cadbury was a post-constructed hall 19 × 10 m, forming an approximately double square with slightly tapered ends, with parallels with the hall at Doon Hill, Lothian (Alcock 1982; **4.5**). Undated post-holes were identified cutting into the eastern corridor of the Roman make-up above the basilica at Silchester (Fulford 1985). Late fourth- and fifth-century buildings at Latimer were based on posts in trenches, with the possibility that cruck construction was also in use (Branigan 1968). Such buildings find any number of precursors in the Roman period and most belong to a consistent

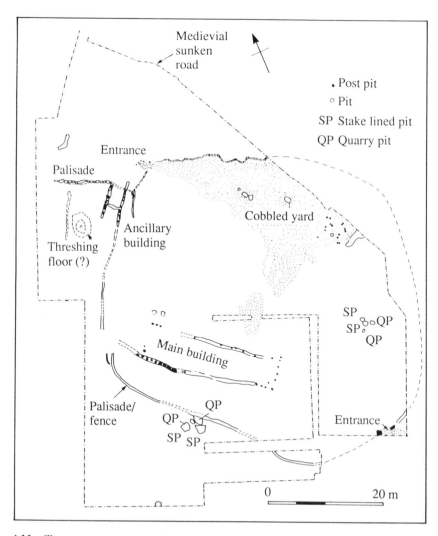

4.11 Tatton: an aceramic enclosed farmstead on the northern edge of the Midland plain.

tradition of building. However, such easily identifiable forms are uncommon and most buildings have not left sufficient evidence for reconstruction to take place, but were founded variously on posts erected on surface cill beams, on the subsoil or in slight trenches cut into it.

At Tatton (Chesh.), excavation of a deserted medieval settlement revealed a stratigraphically early structural episode, centred on a long building at least 24 × 5 m constructed with close-set timbers set into pits in trenches which were so shallow that most had been ploughed away, even though associated cobbled surfaces had survived. An ancillary structure was constructed in similar fashion and the buildings stood in a fenced and cobbled yard (**4.11**). A range of carbon dates suggests occupation towards the latter end of the period 190 BC to 445 AD, but the complete absence of diagnostic artefacts implies that occupation did not begin before the collapse of the Roman economic system (Higham forthcoming a). Coring at an adjacent mire revealed farming activity, dated from 430 to 670, which should probably be attributed to the occupants of this settlement.

Doubts must remain about the dating of this occupation, but if this is what a Dark Age Celtic farm site reveals to the archaeologist, it is hardly surprising that discoveries have been few and mostly derive from excavations intended to examine other periods. Without artefact scatters to alert the field walker or deep subsurface features visible from the air, such sites are virtually undetectable by current methods. There is clearly no direct correlation between the real number or distribution of such sites and the tiny handful so far identified, particularly given the palaeobotanical evidence referred to above which implies that the farming population of Britain remained comparatively numerous throughout the period.

Notes

1 My thanks to John Manley for providing me with interim reports on this excavation.
2 My thanks to Paul Bennett and his staff at the Canterbury Archaeological Trust for discussion of these sites and access to the final reports prior to publication.

CHAPTER FIVE

THE LOWLANDS IN TRANSITION: SETTLEMENT AND LANDSCAPE

In Chapter Four, we surveyed the palaeobotanical evidence for the fifth and sixth centuries across the ex-diocese and concluded that reforestation was neither ubiquitous nor massive in scale. Although some woodland regeneration occurred after the long plateau of extensive clearance of the Roman period, this was substantial only in marginal areas, occurring elsewhere alongside evidence of maintained or even extended clearance. We then examined those societies in the north and west which were successful in retaining their indigenous languages through the period of social transition which followed the Roman period.

Next we must examine the lowland zone, where Roman Britain was centred and where Anglo-Saxon England began. Because of the scale of the evidence and the breadth of the issues involved, discussion will be divided between two chapters. Chapter Five offers a survey of the pattern of rural settlement, land-use and enclosure systems, while Chapter Six discusses the cultural evidence of the English settlement.

Settlement in the landscape

The evidence for the landscape of much of the lowland zone differs little from that of the west and north. Identified settlement sites are few in many areas and the total known distribution is unlikely to reflect real population levels or distribution. Field systems unique to this period are practically unknown (e.g. Taylor 1975; Hinton 1990: 10).

To an extent, the problem has been one of misconception. Since the Anglo-Saxon settlement has traditionally been seen as a major watershed in the historical, linguistic and cultural development of Britain, we have anticipated identifying a distinctive Early English landscape. During the first half of this century, this expectation seemed largely fulfilled, since the Anglo-Saxons were believed to have arrived in Britain already equipped with open field villages. However, evidence of open field is non-existent before the somewhat equivocal reference in the laws of Ine (cap. 42) in the seventh century, and certain examples have so far been entirely elusive prior to the Viking age, with many more apparently coming into existence in the late Saxon and early post-Conquest periods in conjunction with the nucleation of rural settlement into villages. The earliest medieval village so far identified is that at Raunds (Northants.), coming into existence probably in the ninth century (Cadman 1983) at a time when similar settlement reorganization was commonplace throughout western and central Europe. Such a date is probably not atypical for those areas where nucleation of settlement and reorganization of land first occurred. Neither nucleated villages nor open fields — both so characteristic of some areas in the medieval period — currently seem directly relevant to the study of the fifth and sixth centuries, even though some medieval villages were sited on, or even developed from, settlements first founded in the Roman or Saxon periods, and other pre-existing landscape features, such as banks, lynchets and ditches, can be shown to have been incorporated into medieval field systems.

Our understanding of the settlement pattern in the fifth and sixth centuries depends heavily on aerial photography detecting subsurface features, and on the use and deposition of domestic pottery which can be identified by field walking. In parts of eastern England, the use of the latter technique has resulted in the identification of significant scatters of pottery (Foard 1978: RCHM(E) 1979, 1981, 1985; Hayfield 1987; Lane 1988; Newman 1988, and forthcoming). The results of these several surveys are not entirely comparable one with another. For example, small pottery scatters have been interpreted as settlements in Northamptonshire and East Anglia, while those conducting the Wharram survey were inclined to suggest some alternative interpretation where the number of sherds was very small. Results in all areas are faced by interpretational problems stemming from ceramic traditions which changed little over a period as long as four centuries.

In Great Doddington (Northants.) and neighbouring parts of Welling-borough, seven scatters of early to mid-Saxon pottery have been interpreted as probable or certain early Saxon occupation sites, of which two were on sites in use in the Roman period. Both the Wellingborough sites sat astride the parish boundary, a common phenomenon to which we will return (p. 135). In the same area, the ruins of several Roman villas had attracted Saxon burials, a common phenomenon also examined at a later stage (p. 116–7).

The distribution of early Saxon material in Northamptonshire and Suffolk has much in common with the late Roman period, but many Romano-British sites were abandoned in favour of fewer new ones, albeit that the same areas were occupied and the same avoided. Some sites which had been abandoned for several generations were reused. The Stanwick Villa, near Raunds, may be an example of this, since a small concentration of Saxon pottery was identified by field walking within the site, but excavation of this area revealed no trace of Saxon structures and the site is a poor candidate for continuity since occupation apparently ceased within the Roman period (5.1).

In the Fens, widespread flooding drove sections of the late Roman

5.1 'Stanwick', the Roman villa, Raunds, Northamptonshire. An overall view showing the enclosure wall around the 'home farm'. The rubble spread is infilling a late Iron-Age ditch forming a small oval-shaped defended enclosure. Although no structural evidence of fifth- or sixth-century occupation was identified a scatter of early to mid-Saxon pottery from the south side of the enclosure indicates that it was reused for some purpose within that period (courtesy of David Neal and the Central Excavation Unit, English Heritage).

community off the land but a degree of reoccupation occurred in the early to mid-Saxon period over parts only of those areas occupied in the Roman period, with numerous small pottery scatters in the area around Spalding (Hayes 1988; **5.2**). These scatters do not recur on old Roman sites, suggesting that abandonment of these was general. On the several islands, such as Thorney, Eye, March and Whittlesey (Hall 1987), early Saxon cemeteries and occasional sunken-featured huts (at Whittlesey) may indicate continuing use of the drier areas untouched by marine inundation, but again settlement seems to have shifted to new sites.

In contrast, the two villas within the parish of Wharram Percy (Yorkshire Wolds) and the three (of nine) farmsteads in the same parish where pre-Roman Iron Age occupation is most clearly demonstrated all produced ceramic evidence of settlement in the early to mid-Saxon period (Hayfield 1987). At present, it seems that patterns of settlement on the Wolds were less susceptible to relocation under the pressures which characterized the

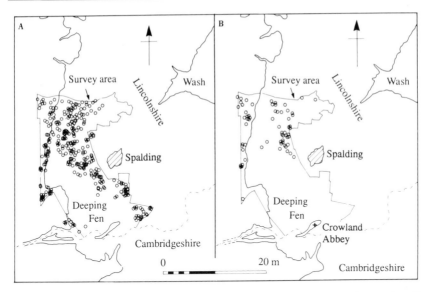

5.2 Roman and early medieval settlement in the Lincolnshire Fens: the results of systematic field survey (after Lane 1988): (A) Roman artefact scatters; (B) early to mid-Saxon artefact scatters.

fifth and sixth centuries than were settlement systems in East Anglia or the south-east Midlands.

Throughout East Anglia, sites with ceramic evidence of both Roman and Anglo-Saxon occupation occur but are nowhere typical. At Stonea, Cambridgeshire, Anglo-Saxon timber halls were constructed adjacent to a Roman villa-residence. At Gestingthorpe (Essex), Roman and Saxon material was found on the same site but no structural remains have been identified. At Grays, a second-century Roman cemetery was reused in the late Roman period, then in the sixth to seventh century, when an inhumation cemetery was associated with a small group of buildings (Wilkinson 1988). However, small-scale excavations are unlikely to provide the full picture of settlement and land-use. The addition of methodological problems to the real incidence of settlement removal makes it unsurprising that many sites of both periods betray no evidence of occupation in the other; even where occupation of both Roman and Saxon periods is identified there is rarely any certainty that settlement was continuous.

The field-walking survey associated with the Sutton Hoo project has identified numerous dispersed Romano-British farms with a density as high in some areas as one per km^2 (**5.3**). Datable artefacts were reaching a declining number of these sites during the second half of the fourth century. Sites yielding pottery or metalwork of the early Anglo-Saxon period are fewer, although numerous by contrast with the evidence from many parts of England. Newman (1988 and forthcoming) suggests that his

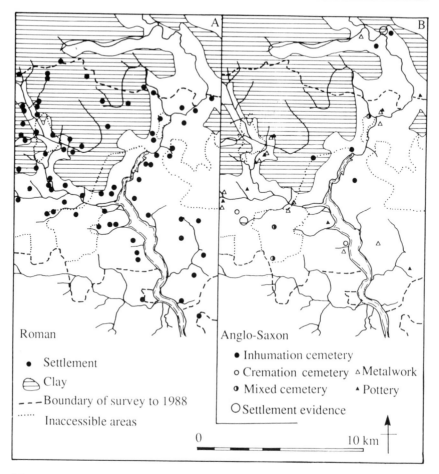

5.3 Roman (A) and early to mid Saxon (B) sites in south-east Suffolk: the results of the East Anglian kingdom survey (after Newman 1988, and forthcoming, whose assistance is gratefully acknowledged).

evidence demonstrates a dramatic drop in population levels between the late Roman and early Saxon periods, followed by a gradual increase in settlements thereafter. However, unless evidence is forthcoming redolent of large-scale woodland regeneration, a crash in the rural population remains problematic. Given the changes under way in the late Roman period, this phenomenon could be explained by reference to the decline of pottery distribution which coincided with the end of Roman Britain, which necessarily left low-status sites, in particular, without diagnostic artefacts. If there was a gap between the decline of Romano-British manufacture and the arrival of Germanic pottery on settlements of low status, then settlements were either aceramic, or dependent on their own, on-site production of poor grade vessels with poor qualities of survival. The small numbers of identifiable early Anglo-Saxon sites are as easily explained as an indication of high status or distinctive culture, as of total population.

In south-east Suffolk, identified settlements of both periods are situated on the lighter sands and gravels of the valleys of several rivers, and their inhabitants seem to have shared opinions concerning the factors which made a particular site attractive for settlement. Around them, the landscape probably changed comparatively little over the period.

Attempts to demonstrate continuity of occupation of specific sites have generated considerable controversy. It seems beyond reasonable doubt at Wharram Percy, where early Saxon material accumulated in the upper fills of ditches initially opened in the pre-Roman Iron Age, but none of the remaining sites within the parish has been adequately tested with the spade. A case for continuing use of late Roman buildings has been offered at Rivenhall villa (Rodwell and Rodwell 1986), but this interpretation has since been challenged (Millett 1987). The evidence from several villas is discussed below. Successive occupations of a specific site may be common. For example, at the Orsett 'Cock' enclosure (Essex), a Romano-British ditched enclosure in use at least until the early fourth century was succeeded by a group of sunken-featured structures and a possible post-hole building, in use after the ditches were filled but possibly when hedges still survived on the site (Toller 1980). Settlement associated with early Saxon pottery and graves at Meonstoke (Hants.) occurred close by a villa deserted not before the late fourth century (Hughes 1986) and the far better-known settlements and cemeteries at Mucking were located on land which had been enclosed, adjacent to a villa complex (Jones 1974). The West Stow settlement (West 1985) has yielded large amounts of Roman material which implies settlement or intensive land-use of that period on the same site, or one closely adjacent. Four Saxon settlements at Witton (Norfolk) were all identified in fields which yielded a medium density of Roman pottery (Lawson 1983), which probably indicates long-term cultivation from a farm close by.

These instances are anecdotal but several common themes emerge. Most identified fifth- and sixth-century settlements were sited on land which was well drained and already cleared, rather than freshly cleared from pre-existing woodland. The evidence of settlement continuity on any one site varies from region to region and the conditioning factors are unlikely to have been either ethnic or cultural. When combined with evidence of reoccupation of what may have been recognizable but deserted settlement sites, Roman–Saxon settlement continuity is far more impressive.

It seems probable that the area of intensive land-use shrank during the fifth century, under pressure from climatic, institutional, social and economic factors. The result was a changing pattern of land-use. Climatic change may have encouraged farmers who retained an interest in agriculture to shift towards and claim a share in the best drained soils available, abandoning much land which had been in arable use during the climatic optimum of the Roman period. Settlers at Mucking, West Stow and Chalton Down adopted sites which were the driest available. The valley edge settlement at Heslerton (N. Yorks.) implies an abandonment of the valley bottom farm sites which characterized the Roman period, in favour of reorganized settlement on a subsoil of broken chalk on the very edge of the valley, beneath the Wolds, where they were better placed to cultivate the higher of the fields in use during the Roman period (Powlesland *et al.*, 1986; 1990). Such relocation may have been necessitated by changes in the water table and the balance between rainfall and surface runoff.

Not all early Anglo-Saxon settlements were situated in the countryside. Some were situated in Roman towns, such as Heybridge (Drury and Wickenden 1982), where they may have performed a role within the fabric of urban life before that ceased during the mid-fifth century. Others settled, or were settled, inside military installations, as occurred at Portchester Castle (Cunliffe 1976), where their presence may imply an attempt by sub-Roman British authority to recruit barbarian warriors as soldiers. At Dorchester-on-Thames, sunken-featured buildings coincide with early warrior graves and early Saxon pottery, providing perhaps the best evidence outside Canterbury for intentional reuse of a Roman town by German warriors in the early fifth century (Kirk and Leeds 1952–3; Frere 1984). At Canterbury, local hand-made pottery and late Roman wares were still being deposited in the 420s, perhaps even later. Excavations in Stour Street revealed that a Roman courtyard sealed by black loam had been cut by a large pit containing a multiple burial, of an adult male, an adult female, two children and two small dogs associated with fifth-century Romano-British type ornaments (Bennett 1981; 5.4). Such a burial clearly post-dates the collapse of the civic administration of the town but life, albeit not urban life, may either have continued on the site, or been subject to an interruption as short as two decades (Brooks 1988). Sunken-featured buildings began to be constructed on the Marlow car park site in the second half of the fifth century, and may have been attached to a palace complex, the main structures of which remain as yet unlocated. In the light of these Anglo-Saxon settlements in urban contexts, it would be a mistake to assume that all early Saxon settlements were those of farmers.

In the countryside, the analysis of pottery scatters is clearly only as useful as the domestic use of ceramics permits. In other areas of known fifth-century Anglo-Saxon settlement, intensive field walking has failed to identify early Saxon period sites (or those of the Iron Age for that matter) as for example in the Cuckmere valley (Garwood 1984–5) and near Lewes (Biggar 1977–8), even where human settlement clearly existed in the fifth and sixth centuries. Pottery use appears to have declined to very low levels or ceased altogether across most of the lowland zone during the early and mid-Saxon periods, away from the North Sea coastal shires.

The evidence available is, therefore, unusually dependent on surveys carried out where the break between Romano-British and early medieval

5.4 Multiple burial in a large pit of the fifth century, Stour Street, Canterbury: two adults – one male and one female – two children and two small dogs were discovered above a thick deposit of waterlogged organic material, perhaps originally constituting a wooden structure. Late Romano-British personal jewellery contrasts with Anglo-Saxon beads (courtesy of Paul Bennett and the Canterbury Archaeological Trust: for further details, Bennett, 1980 and forthcoming).

ceramics was as small as possible – that is, in East Anglia and the south-east Midlands. However, even here, the pattern of settlement which can be reconstructed may be only partial.

The late fourth and fifth centuries witnessed a high rate of settlement mobility; numerous sites of all ranks were abandoned. As already noted, abandonment is one of the key characteristics of all parts of Britain during this period and is not specific to areas attacked or settled by Germanic immigrants. Indeed, it is a characteristic of most peripheral parts of the Roman Empire at this time, being as easily identified in the deserts of North Africa as in Britain, and any explanation must be capable of transfer from one part of the Empire to another. Within Britain, it is as clear-cut a phenomenon on the hills of north Wales and Cumbria as on the gravel terraces of the upper Thames valley or the River Deben. Yet, across Britain, land-use seems to have continued at an intensity not far short of that characteristic of later prehistory, so that, on its own, population collapse and replacement by immigration is an inadequate explanation. We seem instead to be witnessing a period with a high incidence of site abandonment. In some areas, this is most marked among those sites which had been the most recently established; elsewhere it may have been less discriminate, with evidence of unprecedented settlement abandonment in favour of new sites.

There may have been several reasons for this, dependent on the type of site involved. Several major groups of sites, including villas, forts, and towns, were inappropriate to the direction of social and economic change in the early post-Roman era. Farm sites are more likely to have adapted to changes in circumstances than to such deep-rooted functional change within society.

To take a single example, villas had been civilian homes and social centres in which the late Roman élite were segregated from their inferiors, and their high rank displayed by their exclusive use of a range of Romanized facilities. The number still occupied as such by 410 was probably comparatively small, many already having been abandoned during the fourth century. Many of the remaining examples ended with what has been described as 'squatter' occupation, which may merely indicate continuing occupation by the owners or their agents at a time when the social and economic system which had hitherto sustained them and the fabric of their homes had collapsed. Eventually abandonment followed, as the occupiers recognized the inadequacies of their homes in the changing social and economic conditions of the day and found themselves alternative niches within society. However, it seems possible that the focal importance of the villa or its proprietors may have survived, on the same site or another.

What replaced the villa in the course of the fifth century was the hall complex, in which the high status of the owner was advertised not by his segregation from his inferiors but by the number and status of his dependants in immediate attendance. The architecture required was fundamentally different, and better attuned to a generation which had lost the Roman masonry skills. If any villas had survived into the second quarter of the fifth century in those areas taken over by Germanic warriors, they were demolished, or pillaged of portables of any value and allowed to fall gradually into ruin – an epitaph for a life-style which was no more – to be used for sepulchral purposes, perhaps by the new élite. This process is visible at a handful of sites. Reference has already been made to the excavations at Stonea (Camb.). At Orton Hall Farm (Oxon.; 5.6) a villa was largely demolished after *c.* 400, and early Anglo-Saxon pottery reached those residing in an adjacent cottage. This in turn was abandoned and a timber-framed hall and associated sunken-featured structures were built in the sixth century on an adjacent site (Mackreth 1978), when several burials were inserted into the villa ruins. At Barton Court (5.5), the masonry villa was again demolished, perhaps for the sake of its building materials which can only have been used for Roman-style building in the area in the first half of the fifth century. Building 2 stood a little longer. Typical early English buildings were erected outside the villa precinct in the second quarter of the century, the earliest being constructed while the

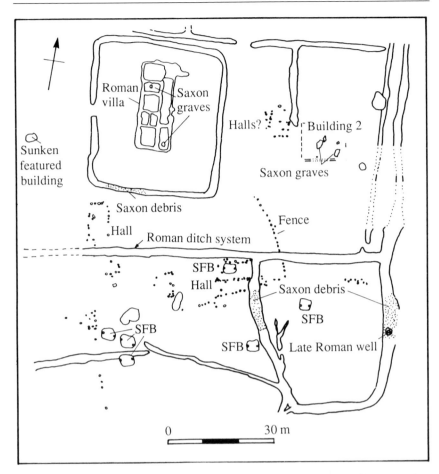

5.5 Barton Court Farm: A second example of the interface between Roman and Saxon settlement, with the latter initially utilizing late Roman ditches, which silted up before the construction of the last, sixth-century buildings on the site. Sixth-century Saxon burials were inserted in the ruins of the villa and building 2 (after Miles 1986).

late Roman paddock ditches were still open. Occupation continued into the sixth century, when, once again, burials occurred in the ruined Roman masonry buildings (Miles 1986).

The attraction of such villa sites for timber-framed halls and ancillary buildings of the early Anglo-Saxon period may imply that these foci of the late Roman estate system retained their importance during the next century or two as the recognized centres for the operation of the estate. If that were the case, the survival of an indigenous workforce seems probable. That the ruined buildings should attract burials in the sixth century suggests a continuing connection between the Roman villa site and a

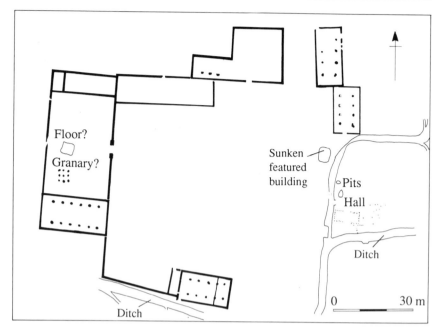

5.6 The Roman/Saxon interface in settlement archaeology: Orton Hall Farm, a small Roman villa, parts of which continued in use into the fifth century, and which was subsequently replaced by a timber-framed hall and associated sunken-featured building of characteristic Saxon type (after Mackreth 1978).

proprietorial interest in the estate, the burials perhaps being intended to defend the proprietorial interests of the descendants of those buried, in a fashion comparable with those burials which appear to have been intentionally sited on estate boundaries (p. 186).

Among the farming population, the apparent reduction in the number of settlements might be explained in several ways: one is a decreasing ability on the part of modern researchers to identify occupation sites on which a far less obvious material culture was in use; the second is the possibility that population declined; the third stems from the observation that the settlements which replaced the late Roman farms and villages often consisted of more than one hall with attendant buildings, which might represent more than one farm unit and family. Although nucleated rural settlements existed in Roman Britain, the commonest settlement form was the individual farmstead, probably inhabited by only a single family. The commonest settlement form of the early Saxon period was a group of farms, ranging in number from four or five to twenty or more.

For archaeologists, the most disturbing possibility is that, even where very early medieval pottery seems comparatively abundant, there may be contemporary sites without pottery, for reasons which could be social, economic or cultural. If that were the case, the apparent rise in the number of sites occupied, and therefore of population, in the middle Saxon period may be no more than the increasing dispersal of artefacts which are archaeologically identifiable, among an ever-growing proportion of the population. Demographic rise in the seventh and eighth centuries finds little support in evidence of any other kind and is at best unproven.

Population decline may go far to explaining the high rate of settlement mobility. On analogy with evidence from early medieval Ireland, the late Romano-British peasantry operated a system of land tenure within customary land units, in which the right to an equal share in land was transmitted by birth. If the population declined during the fourth, fifth and sixth centuries, whether as a result of climatic change, raiding, flight, disease or general dislocation, the number of working farms would have declined, but after a pattern entirely disassociated from the geography of exploitation. The resulting distribution of settlement is likely to have become progressively less well suited to the exploitation of the same fixed territory as the demographic shift occurred. At the same time, the demands for a surplus and the very agricultural characteristics of that territory may have been changing under governmental social and climatic pressures (5.7). We may anticipate an unusual concurrence of factors favouring settlement mobility during the period. Given changes of this order, it can be supposed that new social conditions and the economics of land-use would have made reorganization of settlement very desirable in many areas, and encouraged a shift towards less intensive forms of exploitation. The problem facing the archaeologist stems from the concurrence of so many factors at a time when the rural community had become aceramic or begun to experiment with the manufacture or use of new types of pottery and other artefacts introduced from outside the Roman world.

That this process should have encouraged the reuse of settlement sites which had been abandoned at some previous stage is not surprising, since many of the new social and economic conditions would have found parallels in the recent past. Most of the pre-conditions for the adoption of a particular site for settlement will not have changed (the availability of water, building materials and access, for example), and the establishment of a pattern of settlement based in part on sites previously occupied is likely to have had much to commend it. Where few locations were deemed well suited to settlement occupation, then reuse of abandoned sites or actual continuity from one period to the next on the same site would be more likely, as in the particular topographical circumstances of Wharram Percy, and elsewhere, where settlement was concentrated in hospitable niches within a landscape which was generally less attractive to occupation.

Settlement abandonment and mobility are, therefore, phenomena which are explicable without recourse to the theories of large-scale immigration and population replacement which have tended to be popular explanations of this evidence.

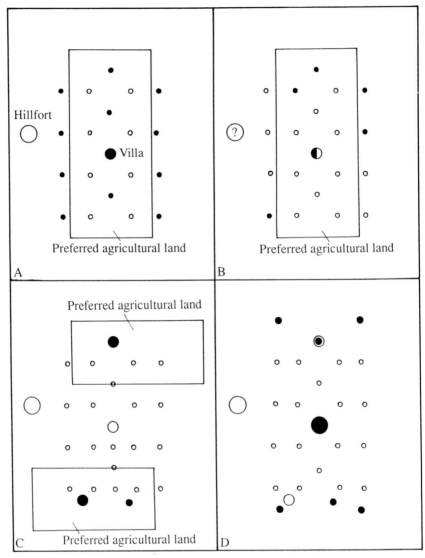

5.7 Models illustrative of settlement mobility in the fifth and sixth centuries: (A) the central Roman period: densely occupied territory with central villa, abandoned hillfort and a scatter of abandoned Iron Age and early Roman farms; (B) late Roman/early sub-Roman: activity at the villa site is in decline and population decline leaves many more settlements abandoned. The population takes occasional refuge inside the hillfort where a shrine may be in use; (C) fifth/sixth century: environmental changes alter the pattern of preferred agricultural land, while demographic and organizational changes enable population to regroup in small hamlets and individual farmsteads on well-drained soils; (D) mid/late Saxon: demographic growth and environmental improvement create the conditions which enable estate lords to nucleate settlement and systematize agricultural land, so as to exploit the opportunities offered by changing technology, at minimum cost, by converting a large part of the territory into open field. Individual farms survive only on the periphery.

The archaeology of settlement

Settlements which have been subjected to large-scale excavation are not numerous and examples which have been fully published are extremely few – principally Bishopstone (Bell 1977), Yeavering (Hope-Taylor 1977), Raunds (Cadman 1983), Cowdery's Down (Millett 1983) and West Stow (West 1985), of which Cowdery's Down and Yeavering are sixth-century and later, and the latter is exceptional in being a royal palace site. Publication of Mucking is now imminent. However, by far the most extensive excavation so far undertaken is still in progress at Heslerton (N. Yorks), under the direction of Dominic Powlesland.

Two types of building are characteristically found in association on sites of the period. The sunken-featured building (or *grubenhaüs*) was the first type of early Saxon structure to be identified in England (Leeds 1923). The principal feature is a large pit, around which are arranged two, four, six but rarely more post-holes to support the superstructure. Two post structures are by far the commonest (**5.8**). In some, the base of the pit has been interpreted as the floor of the structure, around which planks may have walled out the surrounding earth, as reconstructed at West Stow (**5.9**). At Canterbury, wickerwork had been used to stabilize the edges of the pit and a combination of trample, stakes and small posts implies that the pit bases were the floors of a small group of ancillary buildings which

5.8 Sunken-featured building under excavation at Meonstoke, Hampshire. This example is characteristic of the simplest and commonest type, with post-holes for two large uprights to support the ridge (courtesy of Mike Hughes, Hampshire County Council).

5.9 Reconstruction of a sunken-featured building at West Stow, Suffolk. In this example, the base of the pit is interpreted as the floor and dwarf walls of plank hold back the unstable earth around (copyright the author).

may have been attached to a high-status settlement, otherwise still unlocated, dating to the later fifth and sixth centuries (Blockley and Day, forthcoming).

The form and function of such buildings is still debated, arguments centring on the significance of worn floors on the base of the hollow and on the occasional presence of side walls. In some instances there is positive evidence for suspended timber floors but both sunken and suspended floors may have been commonplace and the former were probably the earlier. If Tacitus's description, in the *Germania* (XVI), of covered pits is relevant to the origins of these buildings, then they began as sealed stores for agricultural produce rather than residences or workshops (Higham, forthcoming d). Whether or not their form had changed before the *adventus Saxonum*, it seems likely that storage remained an important function on Anglo-Saxon settlements in Britain, particularly where households of high status found it necessary to store the renders, or rent in kind, by which they were supported from one harvest to another.

Adaptation of this primary role certainly did occur. Early medieval houses in Bohemia, for example, had sunken floors and were constructed in a style reminiscent of Germanic *grubenhaüsen*. However, residence was probably not a primary role in England (Ralegh Radford 1957), although sunken floors were occasionally used in houses where these were vulnerable to gales, as on the Downs in the Dunstable area (Matthews and Hawkes 1985).

On many settlements, sunken-featured buildings were segregated from the timber buildings, On others they seem to have been grouped around each hall. Within them finds of loom-weights are common and some may have served as workshops for a variety of industrial, craft or domestic functions but, in most instances, the fill of the pit derives from the ultimate phase of use as a midden and the finds from inside need not be related to the use of the earlier structure.

Sunken-featured buildings were barely present in Britain in the Roman period and they were introduced to Britain from the Germanic world in the fifth century. They were simple buildings, easily constructed and ideal for well-drained locations. The techniques of construction were not complex and could have been learnt without difficulty by the insular population, keen to fill the gap left in produce storage by the demise of stone-built barns. Other uses may have commended themselves and considerable variation seems likely, much of which probably developed in an insular context.

The characteristic ground-level structure of western Germany in the fifth century was an aisled longhouse in which both humans and animals were accommodated under a single roof in a building which often reached a prodigious size. Such aisled buildings were commonly present in groups substantial enough to be described as villages, in association with lesser timber-framed buildings and sunken-featured structures. Buildings of this kind are very rare in Britain (Dixon 1982) and have nowhere been found in the sort of orientated groups present at, for example, Tofting (Bantelmann 1955), and Feddersen Wierde (Haarnagel 1979), where they were regularly paired with square-built granaries, also absent in England.

The main residential structures of the fifth and sixth centuries in England were post-constructed, timber-framed buildings, which occur on every rural site where large-scale and careful excavation has taken place, occasionally being present without sunken-featured buildings. The earlier examples tend to be post pit rather than trench constructed but were clearly substantial buildings and probably well carpentered. They are comparatively uniform in their architecture across the whole of England over two or more centuries, although they range widely in size and sophistication. Many had internal partitions which probably segregated private and public spaces (see discussion in Rahtz 1976a).

Although the characteristic timber-framed hall in England can be matched with the lesser structures of a German village or with temporary structures on the coastal marshes of the Continent, there are significant discrepancies between the ranges of buildings present in each case. Anglo-Saxon settlements in England employed a limited suite of structures from which several elements typical of coastal Germany are missing. Crucially, the omissions include the largest, most characteristic and commonest types of German buildings. It has been plausibly suggested that the above-ground structures of the Anglo-Saxon settlements in England had an insular

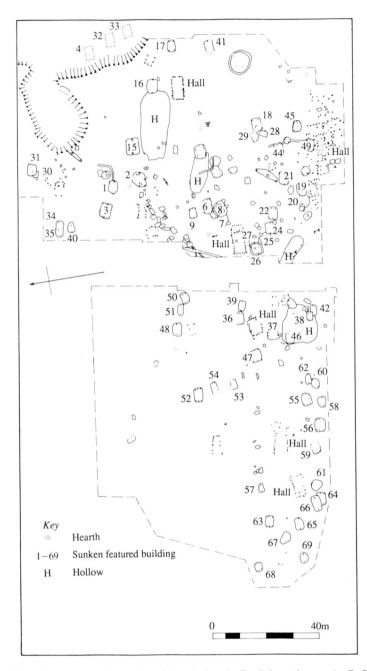

5.10 West Stow: a complex and multi-period early English settlement in Suffolk (after West 1985).

origin and were based on common prototypes found all over the provinces in the later Roman period (James *et al.* 1984; see also Green 1982).

The extent to which any of the English settlements constituted villages is a matter of debate. The group of buildings at West Stow has been interpreted as a small group of farms which were successively rebuilt on different sites, resulting in the appearance of a settlement larger than was ever present at any one time (**5.10**). A similar case was made at Catholme, where 66 buildings were interpreted as a slowly developing group of 5−7 farms, gradually evolving and shifting over a period of 400−500 years (Losco-Bradley 1977). Much depends on the expected lifespan of a timber-framed building and this has always been assumed to be relatively brief. However, such structures are not substantially different in their durability from the numerous timber-framed halls of the late medieval period which survive to the present day and, provided they were maintained, their life expectancy need not have been so short. At West Heslerton, more than 50 timber-framed buildings of the fifth and sixth centuries have been uncovered, associated with an inhumation cemetery with at least 125 graves, and a scatter of more than 60 sunken-featured buildings at a distance from the main structures (Powlesland *et al.* 1986; 1990 and personal communication; **5.11**). It is difficult to describe the large groups

5.11   Post-hole based timber-framed halls and sunken-featured structures of the Anglian period under excavation at West Heslerton, north Yorkshire (courtesy of Dominic Powlesland and the Heslerton Anglo-Saxon Settlement Project).

of buildings at Mucking or Heslerton without recourse to the notion of a nucleated settlement, but the status of such sites remains a matter of debate. The high incidence of deposition of artefacts, the large storage facilities and the association with cemeteries containing furnished burials all imply that the majority of the Anglo-Saxon settlements known to archaeology were the residences of people of considerable status, ceorls, thegns and kings rather than peasant farmers. As such, they were centres of patronage (hence evidence for craft activities) and consumption, but not primarily of agricultural production.

On this basis, aisled halls were scarce in Anglo-Saxon England because the Germanic immigrants were characteristically of a status to be supported by the labours of others and were not themselves farmers, so had no need of cattle stalls attached to their own houses. They inhabited halls. Where these occur in groups they may have resulted from the ubiquitous partition which characterized Anglo-Saxon inheritance customs.

The buildings themselves would have been raised by professionals, aided in all probability by the conscripted labour of the unfree. Such labour services were a normal part of obligations to both state and estate in later Roman Britain and recur in the late Saxon period. They may have existed in the period of transition between the two, so that it seems probable that most Anglo-Saxon buildings of the fifth and sixth centuries were largely the work of Britons.

Land-use and enclosure

It is difficult to distinguish between the agrarian economy practised by the peasants who supported a site such as Bishopstone, and nearby Iron Age and Romano-British settlements such as that on Slonk Hill, Shoreham Sussex; (Hartridge 1977–8). Both communities practised mixed agriculture in which sheep played an important part, the breeds in use over these centuries changing little. The balance of livestock being slaughtered indicates greater similarities between the site economy of a late Roman farm and that which followed, than with that which preceded it. The use of a more sophisticated plough capable of turning a furrow appears not to have survived the final decay of demesne farming in the late fourth century. There is no evidence of the use of comparable ploughs in early Saxon England and, like their Iron Age and Romano-British predecessors, the inhabitants of Bishopstone probably relied, for cultivation of this well-drained, light soil, on an ard or scratch plough of the type found at Sutton Hoo (**5.12**).

That is not to suggest that cultural, social and demographic changes during this period left no mark. There was certainly a retreat from the extensive agriculture of the Roman period, and numerous luxury foodstuffs and garden crops fell out of cultivation. At Barton Court Farm there was a decline from the Roman to the Saxon period in the intensity of land-use

5.12 Inhumation of individual in a hurdling pose in association with an ard or simple plough, excavated at Sutton Hoo in 1985 (courtesy of Nigel Macbeth: Sutton Hoo Research Trust).

(Robinson 1981). Roman deposits produced evidence of the cultivation of spelt wheat, barley and flax but later deposits yielded only barley and flax, crops better suited to wetter conditions. The various exotic garden species disappeared. Grazing levels declined and shrub pollen began to increase. The evidence points to the abandonment of plants which were peculiar to upper-class Roman eating habits and those which were most vulnerable to increased rainfall (such as wheat), as well as a shift to a lower density of livestock, commensurate with lower demands for food — evidence either of lower population or declining demands from the social hierarchy. As the drinking of grain-based alcohol replaced wine, so barley became a more important crop. At the same time, rye was more widely grown in the early medieval period than hitherto (Chambers 1989), reflecting either dietary preferences or the abandonment of clay lands in favour of sandy soils for their better drainage qualities.

A major problem is to know what manner of enclosure systems were used by early English farmers. Settlement sites at Church Down, Chalton and Cowdery's Down were subdivided by lines of posts, perhaps supporting wattles. At West Stow, ditches were introduced in the late sixth century but there is little evidence of internal divisions in the fifth. At Heslerton, the ditches and banks of the Roman landscape continued in use as field boundaries during the life of the Anglian settlement, which was the last of a long line of settlements to use an enclosure and management system first laid out in the late Bronze Age (Powlesland *et al.* 1986). The evidence from Wharram Percy is similar, and indicates that pre-existing enclosure boundaries survived in use during the early medieval period. New ditches were briefly introduced at Raunds after *c.* 550 but were abandoned by the seventh century, and large-scale enclosure did not occur until around 700.

Elsewhere, Saxon fences are unusual and there is little direct evidence of the fields which the inhabitants of these sites were using to grow their grain and pasture their flocks. In some instances, as at Bishopstone, the settlement was sited in pre-existing, lyncheted fields and the various cereals which were consumed there were probably grown on fields which had been laid out in the Roman period or before. If immigrants ever found themselves having to work such fields, they would have seemed very familiar since similar systems were commonplace in many parts of Germany and Holland during the Roman and migration periods.

That Anglo-Saxon settlements tend to be identified without associated field systems may owe much to the modern ploughing which has brought so many to light, but which has destroyed the hedged or banked boundaries with which they may have been associated, leaving traces too vestigial to be identified from the air.

As already noted (p. 21−3), large swatches of the British lowlands were extensively enclosed during the later prehistoric and Roman periods, resulting in grids of small fields, often laid out between long axial boundaries which exhibit a considerable degree of regularity over large areas. Examples are widespread, from Cumbria to Kent, and are not confined to either Celtic or English areas of England. They occur both as relics identifiable only from the air, and as field systems which were still in use into the twentieth century, identified at sites in Wales, as well as in England. Unfortunately many of the latter have been severely damaged by twentieth-century agriculture, particularly in eastern England.

The recognition and study of these fields have been pioneered by a group of scholars working in East Anglia (Rodwell 1978; Williamson 1984, 1986, 1987, 1988). The identification of specific types of landscape was not especially difficult, but dating fields which have been in use over a long period presents a range of problems and remains contentious. However, sample excavation at Asheldham Church demonstrated that one of the principal axes of the surviving road and field system on the Dengie peninsula on the Essex coast was open in the Roman period, but sealed by a medieval church and cemetery (Drury and Rodwell 1978), in a fashion that is repeated in other comparable systems, as at Shimpling Church (Suffolk).

Elsewhere, it can be shown beyond reasonable doubt that Roman roads cut across what must be pre-existing systems of tracks and field boundaries, ignoring the basic alignments of the landscape. If the roads have survived in use to the present day, it follows that the field systems are extremely unlikely to have been laid out over the road alignments. This phenomenon has been identified in its most uncontroversial form where the Pye Road cuts across extensive field systems around Yaxley in Suffolk and Tivetshall St Mary in southern Norfolk (Williamson and Bellamy 1987; **5.13**).

These ancient landscapes are typical of the better drained claylands of East Anglia. They are not noticeably associated with sites producing Anglo-Saxon pottery or with Anglo-Saxon cemeteries, which have generally been identified on the drier soils of the river valleys. Sherds of Anglo-Saxon pottery are far less often identified in scatters derived from manuring than either Roman or medieval sherds, so we might not expect pottery evidence of use during this period away from settlements.

Similar landscapes can be identified throughout the north and east of Kent, and in Sussex. The former, in particular, is a county which was

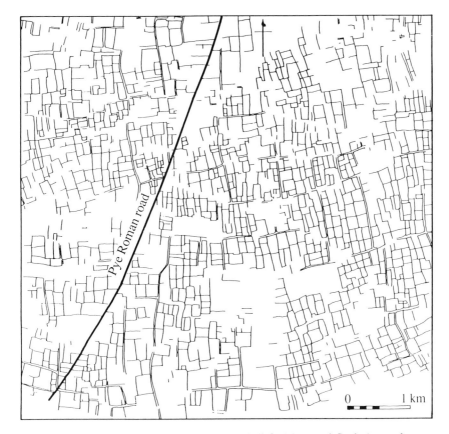

5.13 Pre-Roman field system between Tivetshall St Mary and Scole in southern Norfolk, which was cut by the Roman Pye Road but was maintained and remained intact, presumably in continuous use, into the modern period (after Williamson and Bellamy 1987).

barely affected by large-scale enclosure in the modern period (Tate 1978) and saw little open-field agriculture or settlement nucleation in the medieval period. The orientation of these south-eastern landscapes was more obviously dominated by geographical factors than those of East Anglia, because of the Downs, the coastal marshes and Wealden Forest. During the Roman period, the latter was exploited as an area of intensive iron working for the British fleet, and timber taken to provide charcoal (Cleere 1975). The degree of settlement within it is now a matter of debate, but its wooded character seems to have survived and it was probably already then used as seasonal pasturage by communities normally resident in the periphery (e.g. Tittensor 1977−8). Place-name evidence indicates that the Weald was extensively used in the mid to late Anglo-Saxon period (if not earlier) to pasture pigs and other livestock, and there is every reason to think that this usage was already old by this stage. It is, after all, more probable that the exploitation of distant pasture would be characteristic of periods when woodland was scarce, than when it was plaintiful, and Gildens arguably made reference to transhumance in his geographical introduction (III.3).

The trackways which connected settlements with their woodland rights were generally long-distance, running across the grain of the landscape. It has been suggested that those crossing the scarp of the North Downs in Kent are cut by the Pilgrim's Way (Everitt 1986). If the latter was a prehistoric track (as is generally assumed), then the basic pattern of these sinuous droveways also predates the Roman conquest (**5.14**). Detailed examination of a sample of these junctions suggests that the relationship between the Pilgrim's Way and the transverse trackways is more complex than has been allowed, but a proportion of the latter do seem to predate the pilgrim route, which dog-legs before re-establishing its scarp-base progress.

That relationship alone is a slender indicator of the antiquity of the Kentish landscape. More important, elements of the Roman road system which have continued in use as routes of varying status up to the present day cut across extensive boundary and trackway systems. This occurs in the vicinity of Chichester, where the modern A29 passes diagonally across a landscape which is orientated on a north/south alignment. More dramatically, the same phenomenon occurs in east Kent, where Roman roads connecting Canterbury, Lympne, Dover and Richborough post-date a system of sinuous trackways and regularly aligned field boundaries (**5.15**).

These systems are merely parts of a wider landscape, which extends over much of the two counties, sharing an alignment which is determined by the need to move livestock between the peripheral agricultural settlements, estuarine or coastal marshes and the Weald. That parts of this aligned landscape were cut across by the Roman roads implies that the basic fabric of this enclosure system was already in existence when the Roman roads were constructed. Both the track and enclosure systems and

5.14 A sunken cross-Downs routeway, crossing the Pilgrim's Way at the base of the wooded scarp slope of the Downs, photographed from close to the Coldrum Stones long mound, Trottiscliffe (courtesy of David Higham).

the roads and other routeways which provide their terminal date survived the Saxon period into the modern era.

These studies in East Anglia and Kent imply that many enclosure systems which were in use during the Roman period continued to be used and maintained during subsequent centuries. Most are now defined by hedges and, although it is difficult to be sure, they were probably hedged from the beginning. These hedges needed regular maintenance. A gap of only three or four decades is sufficient for a hedge to revert to standing trees. If neither grazing nor cultivation occurred during the same length of time within the fields, the result would be dense scrub, the first stage of recolonization by secondary woodland. Such may have occurred patchily among several of the field systems identified in East Anglia, where some of the medieval commons may represent localized reversion to woodland.

Although a ditch might remain visible even in woodland over a considerable period, most boundaries were probably without ditches, and it would require very special pleading to imagine that abandoned fields could be brought back into use after decades − even centuries − of disuse, within the same boundaries. That this did not happen is widely demonstrable in the north-east Midlands and southern Yorkshire. All this would

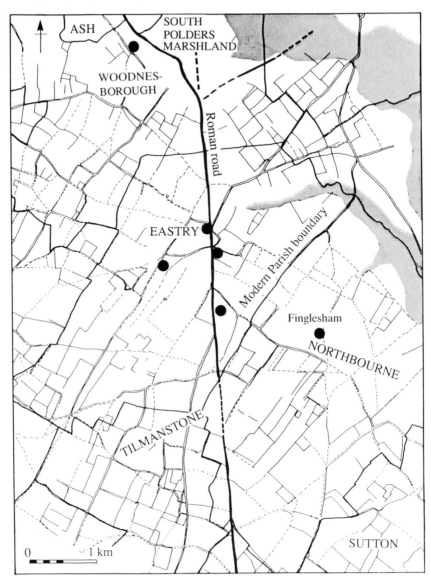

5.15 Eastry, Kent: fields, rights of way and township boundaries in the heart of the Kentish kingdom. The earliest element in the human landscape seems to be the basic field pattern which was already in existence before the construction of the Roman road between Richborough and Dover. The medieval/modern township boundaries seem to have been a later addition to the field system. Solid dots indicate Anglo Saxon Cemetaries. (based on OS 1:25,000, 1914).

seem to indicate that only continuous use and maintenance of these enclosures is compatible with the fact that they survived. Such survival is entirely inconsistent with substantial dislocation of the rural community in the migration period and the mass replacement of one peasant community by another. In other words, the large-scale survival of working landscapes from Roman Britain to Anglo-Saxon England is a strong indication that there was substantial continuity within the mass of the indigenous population at the base of society.

That this can be demonstrated in the areas of the earliest English settlements – in East Anglia, Kent and perhaps Sussex – is particularly important, since, if mass migration occurred, these areas were always the most likely candidates to have been affected. If a peasant settlement is absent here, it is intrinsically unlikely elsewhere.

However, such considerations do not explain the peculiarly well-preserved landscapes of these areas, as compared with other parts of England. Why did field complexes survive in East Anglia and Kent when they failed elsewhere? To an extent these discrepancies are a matter of differences in the research effort which has gone in. Examples are known from elsewhere. Around Gloucester, a strong case has been made for the survival of a gridded landscape from the Roman period over 500 km^2. (Wacher 1974a), and a Romano-British field system has similarly continued in use on the Wetlooge Levels beside the Bristol Channel (Allen and Fulford 1986). Other examples will probably come to light over the years ahead. Many parts of England, such as Cheshire and Lancashire, probably had much lower levels of population and were not extensively enclosed during the pre-Roman or Roman periods, so such research methods are fruitless. Elsewhere, our knowledge of Roman-period enclosure systems is insufficient to be able to judge the degree of continuity during the fifth and sixth centuries. Population density probably varied as much in Roman and Saxon times as at Domesday, and the more densely settled areas in 1086 are likely to have been areas with similarly high levels of settlement at an earlier date. These included East Anglia and parts of the south-east.

However, these instances do not explain the widespread abandonment of similar field systems on the Downs, in the Pennines, or in the east Midlands and south Yorkshire, where decayed field systems closely resemble those which survived further south and east. It seems likely that a series of other factors played their part: population decline, changing demands on arable land, lower densities of grazing, climatic change, all or any of which could have been significant. The maintenance of extensive field systems was a time- and labour-consuming activity which would have been abandoned as soon as they were no longer necessary, or the labour available was insufficient.

If the fifth and sixth centuries did become markedly wetter, the effects would have been very different in different areas. Parts of England which had regularly suffered from summer droughts during the Roman period may have found productivity rising. Such conditions were particularly pertinent to East Anglia and eastern Kent, although many other east coast districts were also affected as far north as the East Riding (Higham

1987b). In contrast, other parts of the Midlands and the west of England where such conditions did not apply could have experienced a decline in yields.

Near-optimal climatic conditions probably provided the backdrop to the very obvious wealth of East Anglia in the sixth century, the basis of which was agriculture. In addition, it will be suggested (p. 166) that immigrant war-bands based in these areas were taking captives from other parts of the British lowlands and concentrating them within their own areas of control, principally in East Anglia. By such means those areas may have been artificially protected against population decline at the expense of their neighbours.

Whatever else, the retention or abandonment of enclosed landscapes do not seem to have been matters which were decided on the basis of ethnicity or migration. The survival of British culture and language was no guarantee of the survival of settlement or land-use patterns. It was those landscapes where English dominance was first achieved that enjoyed the least traumatic transition from Roman Britain to medieval England.

There is a further possible explanation. A weakness of much of this discussion lies in our ignorance of the date of the abandonment of many field systems and in the appraisal of what followed. The dating of a field system is determined by documents, or by its relationship with datable artefacts or other landscape features. The presence of Roman pottery in secure deposits in ditches is enough to demonstrate that such fields were in use during the Roman period. However, given the low levels of dispersal typical of fifth- and sixth-century artefacts, the absence of later material from trial trenches does not demonstrate that the system went out of use soon after the collapse of the Roman pottery industries. In practice, that abandonment could have occurred far later than the fifth century. After all, when describing the local landscape in his own day, Gildas pointed to the existence of widespread cultivation on the plains and 'stretched' hills (Higham forthcoming c.).

In the east Midlands and in south Yorkshire, some systems were replaced by medieval open field systems which probably began within the period 800 to 1200, with the majority coming into existence in the second half of that period. Many north-east Midland communities were still widely dispersed in 1066. Parts of this landscape could easily have survived throughout the Dark Ages only to be entirely lost when a thoroughgoing reorganization brought about settlement nucleation and agricultural systematization into open fields. If this was, in part, a response to the widespread adoption of the heavy plough, there is some sense in the view that the first stage in this reorganization was the abandonment of settlements on sandy or chalky soils in favour of nucleated settlement central to heavier loams and clays which could be cultivated with the better equipment and under the more hospitable climatic conditions of the late Saxon period. Such changes may help to explain the high incidence of deserted Roman—British and early

Saxon sites on free-draining soils and their common occurrence on or close to medieval boundaries, in areas peripheral to medieval villages. Where such boundaries had become routeways, settlements may have been attracted to them, as seems to have occurred at Wharram Percy, where routeways were probably one of the strongest factors in determining the location of new settlement in the pre-medieval periods (Hayfield 1987).

It has been remarked that township and parish boundaries in relevant parts of the east Midlands frequently cut early field systems as plotted from the air (Unwin 1983). If these boundaries are early, then the fields were clearly abandoned early, and Unwin has argued that township boundaries in this area were a product of an influx of Anglian peasant cultivators in the fifth and sixth centuries. However, there is little reason to place the township and parish boundaries of the Danelaw as early as this, nor to ascribe them to immigrant peasants. Many probably represent major reorganization in the late Saxon period – during the Scandinavian conquest and subsequent 'reconquest' by English kings, or even in the Norman period. In East Anglia and east Kent, township and parish boundaries clearly post-date many ancient field systems and weave their way across them (Williamson 1986; **5.15**). In parts of the east Midlands there are indications that early parishes were far larger than those present

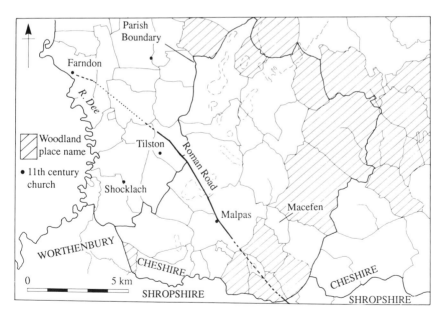

5.16 Malpas/Depenbech: a pre-English land unit or estate mirrored in the parochial and secular structure of land tenure in the later Middle Ages (based on OS one inch tithe apportionment).

by Domesday and these are more likely to represent the early estate boundaries of the area (Stafford 1985). The high incidence of early Saxon settlements on or close to township and parish boundaries may indicate a preference for such a location, rather than imply any particular chronological pattern. The incidence of rural settlement on township boundaries is similarly commonplace in many areas in the early modern period.

Land units and estates

From the third quarter of the seventh century there are charters extant that reveal the existence of estate boundaries which were recognizable features in the landscape, well and long known, defining blocks of land which contained all the basic resources of the rural economy, such as arable land, pasture, woodland and meadow. While it seems likely that some of these units were later than the earliest Anglo-Saxon settlements, others were comparatively ancient.

The aristocracy of late Roman Britain exercised sufficient rights over large areas of land for these to be defined as estates. If Roman law was in use by this aristocracy (see p. 27), then those estates were liable to division or augmentation by purchase, inheritance or gift, and the aristocracy probably enjoyed a highly developed sense of property. The likely result was the build-up in the lowlands of the type of great estates which are well documented on the Continent, consisting of numerous separate blocks of land, some of them very large, and dispersed across one or more provinces. This estate system may have been far more complex than that which prevailed in England in 1066 or in 1086, but with similar combinations of large and small holdings. If it differed markedly in kind, it was probably in favour of large blocks of land under the control of fewer individuals.

Whatever the scale of its various parts, the estate was the crucial point of contact at the end of the Roman period between the primary producers of goods and services and the hierarchy of state and aristocracy to whom they paid over a large part of their production, in rent, in taxation in kind, in services, and in cash where that was available to them. In that sense, they were already to a degree seigneurial estates.

Large and widely dispersed estates delivering a surplus to a distant high-status site were vulnerable to political change, a decline in the monetary economy and weakening security. By the early fifth century, the aristocracy had lost the capacity to sell large surpluses for cash and had, therefore, probably abandoned demesne agriculture. What remained to them was the exercise of patronage. The greater aristocracy may have used their influence in the local law courts to enlarge their own estates at the expense of lesser neighbours but, by the date Gildas was writing, Roman law was under considerable pressure. A minority of influential men had usurped Imperial authority and, as judges, were making their own decisions without regard to the 'rules of right judgement' (*De Excidio*

XXVII). The law courts were an obvious theatre for such kings to exercise patronage and, in their own household warriors, they had the power to enforce whatever judgements they handed out. The Roman civil law had, hitherto, protected the civilian aristocracy. It was now in retreat, if not entirely routed, and the leaders of the Britons had taken the first tentative steps from Romans subject to Roman law to medieval lords presiding over courts within which their word was sovereign.

The lands most vulnerable to confiscation or appropriation were those at a distance from the household of the owner and these probably had to be sacrificed in favour of blocks of territory nearer home. State revenues in kind, and labour, may still have been demanded by the king and used to support soldiers attendant upon his person and under his personal control. Gildas's complaint concerning the plundering of the innocent by kings (XXVII) may imply that, in succession to legitimate Roman authority, late fifth-century kings were attempting to tax or appropriate the estates of the landholding aristocracy.

These developments may have been made more complex by Christianity in its various guises. Pelagian teaching was hostile to the inheritance or accumulation of massive wealth and both Pelagianism and more orthodox Catholicism were sympathetic to monasticism and the ideals of chastity and personal poverty. Both Patrick and Gildas shared these enthusiasms and their writings provide important evidence of the role of the Church as an institution in fifth-century Britain. That Patrick's father and grandfather were in holy orders suggests that church office offered significant advantages: fourth-century precedents imply that these may have included tax exemption. Gildas was probably a deacon, perhaps for similar reasons. His complaints concerning the clergy imply that the Church was a wealthy institution, to gain entry to which there was savage competition. His world included monks and at least one monastery ruled by an abbot, and his putative authorship of a monastic rule may imply that Gildas himself later converted his own household and estates to a monastic institution. Such may have been the ultimate fate of a significant number of late Roman villas in the West Country in the second half of the fifth century.

Although the evidential basis of this review is small, it does imply that estate structure and the relationship between peasant and landowner, on the one hand, and landowner and king, on the other, were undergoing change during the fifth century, with or without a shift of ownership to immigrant barbarians.

In the much-raided eastern lowlands, a comparatively Romanized British aristocracy had recourse to the normal Roman device of hiring barbarians and treating them as Roman soldiers, supported by taxation in kind. Unwilling to release taxpayers to become soldiers, they were eventually supplanted by their own Saxon employees, who brought to the role of landowner a military competence which contrasted with the judicial and administrative skills of the Romanized British élite. The new men were immigrants, keen to pass from the role of mercenary and pirate to that of landowner or retainer, and so to regularize their own entrée to the agricultural surplus.

In the western lowlands, where the Saxon rebellion was contained, Gildas's strictures underline the tensions between the British government of his own community and the civil aristocracy and churchmen within it with whom he identified. In such circumstances, British efforts to harness resources to military ends were inhibited and British kings disadvantaged *vis-à-vis* their Saxon neighbours.

In the upland zone, Romanized aristocracies and churchmen were far less firmly entrenched and tribalism and local war leadership were able to emerge without a bruising contest for control of the agricultural surplus. Despite their comparative poverty and low population levels, the tribal kingdoms of the less Romanized areas proved comparatively robust and competed successfully with English kings until the rise of universal English 'over-kingship' in the seventh century.

Beneath or within the hypothetical estate systems, peasant farmers operated a mixed farming regime adapted to the natural ecosystem and sensitive to the opportunities offered by the environment, but subject to various and changing demographic and seigneurial pressures. Their farms were dispersed across much of the landscape. Most farms controlled the land immediately adjacent to their own yards but shared the use of other resources with their neighbours. Such systems operated within specific land units, within which property rights were assigned on the basis of equal division between all free householders. Partible inheritance and heredity were probably the crucial mechanisms, as in early medieval Ireland and Wales. Land units should be seen as units of exploitation and common interest on the part of farmers. Estates were proprietorial and defined access to that part of the agricultural surplus which was paid over as a render in goods and/or services. Estates and land units were two very different things, even though the boundaries of the one might often coincide with those of the other.

In the fifth century, these peasant communities were adapting to the changing economic and social circumstances. The principal form of adaptation – with an obvious appeal for them – was the sloughing off of peasant status (as imposed by the Roman state system) and a shift towards tribalism with all that that entailed. In other words, there may have been pressure from within the indigenous community to reverse the processes of Romanization and 'peasantization' (see p. 25–6).

The land units within which they exercised their hereditary interests are likely to have been relatively stable over a long period, if only because their integrity was fundamental to the functioning of the social system within them. They provided the optimal framework for the exploitation of land from settlements which were predominantly dispersed but which varied in number, size and location as the population rose and fell. With the demise of the Roman estate system, it seems likely that relationships between the farming population and the élite still tended to be expressed through these units, some of which may have become fossilized as long-established estates or areas with extensive formal linkages, and so lasted into the Middle Ages.

In no instance is there any certainty that a particular medieval estate can be traced back to the Roman period, but there is considerable evidence that such land units passed from Celtic Britain to England during the expansion of the latter in the seventh and eighth centuries. The evidence can derive from late Saxon charters, or from the post-Conquest parochial structure. Let one example speak for many. Malpas, in the south-west corner of Cheshire, was a minster parish comprising numerous townships in the Middle Ages. At its core was an estate held by the earls of Mercia in 1066, all of which had passed by 1086 to Robert fitz Hugh, and he or his descendants built the castle on which their barony was focused beside the parish church. In 1086 the manor was still known by the Celtic name, Depenbech, a topographical name which appears to describe the deep valley of the Wych Brook on the southern edge of the parish, but not the township. On the eastern periphery is the township of Macefen, another Celtic place-name, meaning 'boundary' (Dodgson 1967). The Roman road from Whitchurch to Chester bisects the parish, the boundaries of which could, but need not, predate the road. At the core are a group of English topographical and settlement place-names. On the periphery to the south, east and north, place-names are typically derived from woodland terms (5.16), reflecting a well-wooded belt separating this area from its neighbours. There is no way of knowing how old this land unit is, but it clearly predates the advent of English place-names. It may be far older.

Similar units are scattered across the same county, and can be recognized in the minster parishes of Runcorn (with emendations), Prestbury, Aston and Great Budworth, to name but a few. Across the Mersey, comparable examples seem to have been in existence until major reorganization occurred in the tenth century, when blocks of land such as Makerfield lost their integrity in favour of a new hundredal system put in place, probably, by Edward the Elder (Higham 1989). The pattern of place-names incorporating the element *eccles* both here and in the West Riding implies that these 'shires' predate the English take-over in the seventh century.

Closely comparable examples of land units have been identified in all areas of England by specialists who have reached their conclusions from several different directions. Hooke (1981) argued for a boundary system with pre-Roman origins in the central Avon valley, the Vale of Evesham and across the Cotswolds, parts of which accommodated transhumance links between relatively open land and wooded pastures such as Arden (another Celtic name). Gelling (1976b) remarked on the probability that many Saxon estates in Berkshire originated before the English settlement. Bassett (1989) has suggested that the parish boundary system around

Great Chesterford (Essex) contains substantial relics of a Roman or early post-Roman land unit. Barker (1984) has made similar suggestions for Sixpenny Hundred (Dorset), Dunley Hundred (Wilts.), Cirencester and Malmesbury, and Pearce (1982) has made comparable observations in the same region. The territorial shires of Northumbria have repeatedly been viewed in this light and fieldwork around Wharram Percy has tended to support rather than negate such views. The royal estates and lathes of Kent offer similar possibilities. Suffolk examples have been discussed in some detail (Warner 1988). Although many may derive from late in the Roman period or even from the fifth century, that numerous land units passed from Celtic to English lordship intact seems plausible, and their populations presumably passed with them.

Concentrations of Bronze Age and pagan Saxon burials on or close to medieval boundaries have been taken as evidence that the boundaries themselves date back to prehistory (e.g. Bonney 1976). Such concentrations occur in Wiltshire and along the South Downs in Sussex, as well as in parts of the Pennines and the Yorkshire Wolds. Many barrows are strung along major watersheds and the notion that these reflect ancient boundaries is an attractive one. The view that burial on the boundary was a method of influencing succession finds support in early Irish law (Charles-Edwards 1976). Dispersed barrow burial, often of affluent individuals, continued through the Roman period in parts of Britain later taken over by the Anglo-Saxons, and these, too, may have been boundary burials. Many of the dispersed inscribed memorial stones of western Britain which are sited at crossroads, for example, may derive from a similar practice, and it is at least possible that parallel thinking encouraged Anglo-Saxon burials under isolated mounds in prominent but peripheral locations, such as characterize the late Anglian or Anglo-Saxon burials of the White Peak or Westmorland. It may be that it was the aristocracy as the proprietors of estates who were most likely to be buried on the periphery of them. Later English society was familiar with the burial of political leaders on the borders of their people's territory, in order to defend it. Such notions are prominent in *Beowulf*, and similar ideas may explain the siting of the Sutton Hoo cemetery on the periphery of East Anglia. By the early ninth century, comparable ideas were current in Wales, where the author of the *Historia Brittonum* claimed that the fifth-century British leader Vortimer had wished to be buried on the coasts on a site chosen so as best to protect Britain from Saxon invasion. There may also be a link with the reuse of ruined Roman villas for small numbers of Anglo-Saxon burials in the sixth century.

Such notions were surely pre-Christian in origin. They were either common to both Celtic and Anglo-Saxon communities prior to their respective conversions (as the Irish evidence might suggest) or transferred from one to another at a later date. If the latter occurred, then this custom necessarily came from the British community to the Anglo-Saxons.

If there was a tendency to bury a few persons of high status on the periphery, the majority of pagan English cemeteries were probably closely adjacent to settlements. Although these two distributions might appear contrary, in practice there need be no tension between them. Few settlements with cemeteries have been identified with any certainty on major boundaries, but this too remains a significant possibility where boundaries were also routeways which attracted settlements − taking us back once again to the memorial stones sited on crossroads in Wales.

Computerized analysis of Saxon boundaries and burials initially suggested that a correlation existed between them only from the sixth and seventh centuries onwards, implying that most such boundaries were Saxon in inception (Goodier 1984). However, the methodology used in this study has since been severely criticized (Reilly 1988), and it is probably premature to offer any generalizations concerning the value of boundary burials as indicators of the antiquity of the boundaries with which they are spatially associated. We are left with the fact that both Celtic and Anglo-Saxon communities believed that boundary burial offered certain advantages in the defence of land, and that many burials and putative barrows are associated with boundaries, even though these by no means constitute a majority of known burials.

Although many land units can realistically be seen as British in origin, there is still no certainty that any specific estate boundary in use in the mid to late Saxon period originated in or before the Roman period, unless it lay along the coast or some similar barrier. It has already been suggested that estate organization came under considerable pressures for change during the late Roman and early post-Roman periods, and to these must be added the pressures deriving from the processes of the English land seizure and reallocation. While economic systems and land units may have changed little, proprietorial estates may have been far more volatile, and early English royal patronage probably tended to carve off slices from kin-based systems of land-use for the support of individual warriors. The reintroduction of Christianity brought further pressures for change within the landscape and within the structure of landownership, with the granting of both entire, and small portions of, estates (once granted, estate boundaries tended to ossify in church custody). Thereafter, there was substantial landscape reorganization in those areas where open fields were introduced.

Do these various pressures for change render meaningless the discussion of early land units? Not necessarily, but they do encourage extreme caution, and render many of the most optimistic claims which have been made open to the criticism of the cynical.

However, it is the continuum that we should seek to explore, not the ossification of an Iron Age or Roman estate system in a rigid form. There is plentiful evidence for land units of pre-English origin, adopted with boundaries little changed in the early Christian era, and incorporated in that form into the settlement and landholding hierarchies of Wessex,

Mercia and Northumbria. Malpas (Depenbach) is of this kind. These are Celtic land units, but not necessarily Roman estates. The best chance of identifying Roman land units or estates must lie in those areas first occupied by Anglo-Saxon immigrants, in the southern and eastern lowlands and particularly in East Anglia and Kent. There numerous large and compact estates or parishes evidenced in the later Saxon or medieval periods have invited the suggestion that they are early English in origin or even predate the English settlement. The 'Roding' group of parishes in Essex has recently been used as an example of an early English kingdom in the making (Bassett 1989). Like Malpas, this territory has a geographical cohesion. Unlike Malpas, the major boundaries within this territory have been claimed to predate the Roman road system (Rodwell 1978; **5.17**). Although at present still unproven, there is a possibility that such units predate the English settlement and were examples of Celtic land units – even Roman estates – associated with specific communities which were renamed and incorporated wholesale into early England (see p. 206).

Lordship, land and society

The estate was the critical interface between the creators of wealth and the social élite who were supported by their labours. This was as true of early Anglo-Saxon kings and *gesiths* (military retainers), with their food rents, as it had been of the Roman state, sub-Roman kings and the landholding aristocracy. It was also the point of collection of payments to both the late Roman emperors and Anglo-Saxon kings. The yield from the estate to the élite *c.* 400 included both tax and rent, and was forthcoming in goods and services.

Early barbarian settlements in Gaul were probably exempt from taxes (Sivan 1987) and the early English may have enjoyed similar privileges (p. 160), in contrast to the indigenes whose taxes in kind were used by Vortigern to supply his Germanic mercenaries. Other kings presumably used the same system to support whatever British soldiers they employed. By the lifetime of Gildas himself kings seem to have been collecting labour through the same system for the construction of massive dykes (Higham forthcoming, 6). The successful rebellion of Saxon mercenaries established territories which were autonomous *vis-à-vis* the British state system, under English kings who supplemented the surplus of the estates which they controlled by raiding and collecting tribute from those which they did not. Like Visigothic kings in seventh-century Spain (Collins 1983), they may have continued to collect revenues – as is suggested in the *De Exidio* 1.5 – but they themselves paid taxes to no one.

The major pressure for territorial expansion of these primary lordships probably came from the warrior companions of a Saxon chieftain. The lack of documentary evidence cripples any attempt to write a social history of the fifth and sixth centuries but it is possible to make some extremely

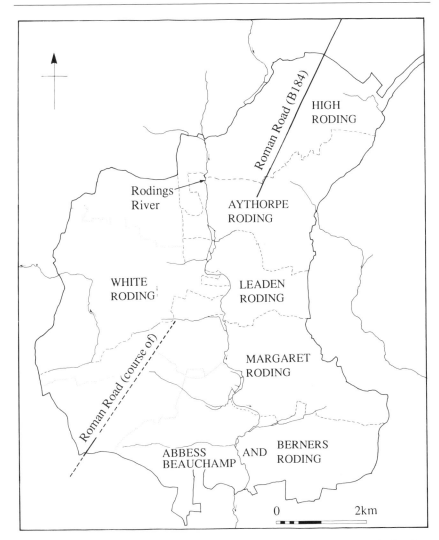

5.17 The Rodings, Essex: a putative early land unit and kinship group in the Rodings valley, where it has been claimed that significant landscape features predate the Roman road system (based on OS 1 : 25,000, 1914, with additional information after Rodwell 1978 and Bassett 1989).

hesitant deductions concerning the likely structure of this élite system by establishing common ground between Classical sources (particularly the *Germania*) and legal evidence and other forms of written material from the seventh century. In a system with close parallels to Celtic war-bands, Germanic warriors took service with well-established leaders in the expectation of reward, within their own community or without. Ultimately, the reward which was most eagerly sought by warriors was land, tenure of which would enable a warrior to establish his own household, marry and raise a family. In the law code of King Ine (cap. 51: Attenborough 1922), those *gesiths* who had obtained land were distinguished from the landless *gesiths* who were still household members attached to the person of their lord. In his letter to Egbert shortly before his own death, Bede stressed the importance of this system to the military strength of the Northumbrian state.

The more successful the early chieftain, the greater the land at his disposal and the greater his capacity to endow his warriors with estates from which previous landowners had been evicted. Aggression was in the immediate best interests of the landless warrior, provided it was successful.

What was sought by the military retainer was not land to farm but land which was already worked, or that could be worked by newly acquired slave labour. The warrior was a prospective estate holder, not a prospective farmer. As English tenure expanded through seizure on behalf of the chieftain and subsequent gifts to his supporters, the value of the annual render from a land unit became a matter of critical concern to both chieftain and warrior.

By the seventh century, this render was being expressed in hides, a term which served as a unit of audit for both rent in kind from within an estate and the tribute paid by one king to another, as documented in the Tribal Hidage (Higham forthcoming, e). In the former context it was translated in anonymous Latin charters as *manens* or *mansa* ('a household landholding or income') and by Bede as the 'land of a family'. Since renders from land dominated the income available to support a 'gentry' family, the terms were synonymous. The word is Anglo-Saxon (*hid*, often Latinized as *hida/ hyda*) and derives from 'the household' or 'marriage'. The association with a unit of render or tribute probably stems from the Germanic customs recorded by Tacitus (*Germania XXV*). He noted the custom of voluntary payments or gifts by households of lower status to the nobility and by the leaders of one tribe to another, as well as the involuntary payments in kind made by unfree peasants to their masters. A household of high status could only be established, by marriage, when sufficient renders were available to it, hence the use of the term. Note the landless bachelor thegns of Bede's writings. It was the involuntary form of payment which was paramount in the seventh-century instances, so, within the estate, the word probably means 'the minimum peasant renders sufficient to support a household of free status'.

The status of this notional household was clearly not that of an 'earl', gesith or thegn, who would normally be granted royal land and its renders in blocks of several hides. Ten-hide estates were common in Northumbria and were probably the norm for a life grant to reward the military service of a single warrior (Bede *H.E.* III, 24; *Letter to Egbert*; Yorke 1990 for discussion). The household pertinent to a hide was almost certainly that of the ceorl, the lowest rank of freeman in this highly stratified society, beneath whom were numerous peasants, servants and slaves. It is clear from the laws of King Æthelberht (*c.* 600) that ceorls were not peasants (*contra* Stenton 1971: 277–80). They were weapon-owning freemen and the heads of substantial households.

If the ten-hide estate of the seventh century was expected to yield renders sufficient to maintain a household of thegnly rank, it seems unlikely that the ceorl households in which it was measured were actually present, since they would have been direct competitors for those same renders. This is borne out by the static nature of hidation over very long periods. The number of households would be expected to change over time but the hidation did not change in parallel. The hide of the earliest charters was, therefore, a unit of account, of demand and of tribute, based on a notion of the renders required to support a ceorl household of 'gentry' status and expressed by the best means available in a coinless society.

The laws of King Ine of Wessex make it clear that many of the 'gentry' subject to him were recognizably Welsh, accorded a lower wergild and legal status than an English ceorl on lands and renders of similar size. This inequality raises a number of significant issues concerning the hide and its origins in Britain.

Similarities between the tenure systems of early medieval England, Ireland, Brittany and Wales are too numerous to be accidental (Charles-Edwards 1972). In both Ireland and England, Charles-Edwards argued that the origin of the unit of account (in England, the hide) was the territorial expression of a particular form of kindred allied to a particular status system. In England one must be prepared to differentiate between the hide as a unit of account and the hide as the household of a ceorl. The latter notion was imported and gave rise to the term used for the former. However, as a unit of render, hidation approximates in its functions to the system of obligation which we can deduce as underlying the collection of goods and services in fifth- and sixth-century Britain. Instead of being imported wholesale and *de novo* from Germany, it is as likely that the system of obligation within the English estate resulted from the application of a word common to several Germanic languages to pre-existing and comparable systems of render by which British élites customarily drew resources from the Celtic system of kinship and land tenure.

This interpretation was mooted, but discounted, by Charles-Edwards in favour of parallel developments in different parts of the Indo-European community. In 1972, to make a case for early Anglo-Saxon society owing a large debt to Celtic systems of land tenure across England would have been out of step with the perceptions of Anglo-Saxon society then current.

In Kent, the hide never became established. Few early charters give hidage (although those which do use the term *manentes*, which is directly equivalent) and the basis of later valuation is the *sulung* (ploughland), subdivided into four 'yokes'. The nomenclature of the larger unit is

Anglo-Saxon and the smaller Latin (*iugum*). In origin, the *sulung* appears to replicate the hide. The relationship between *sulung* and *iugum* mirrors the eight-ox plough and cannot predate its widespread use. The earlier term might be the *iugum*, the terminology of which is identical with the basic unit of tax assessment in the late Roman Empire, in which case this system might have been in continuous use in Kent from the Roman period onwards. Given the comparatively early date of the English settlement there and the degree of landscape continuity which is apparent, this is an attractive possibility, but it is equally possible that the *iugum* was reintroduced from Frankia at a later date.

In Sussex, early charters document estates measured in *tributarii* ('taxpayers'), directly equivalent to hides and implying the measure of renders valued in 'ceorl' household units.

Ceorls either received their land during the English settlement by royal gift, or they descended direct from the existing British population. The references to free Welshmen in Ine's laws were not repeated in those of Alfred, by which time their descendants had become fully fledged Anglo-Saxons. This process of acculturation may have been normal outside areas of primary settlement, particularly since *gesiths* or thegns, rather than ceorls, were the normal recipients of royal patronage in the seventh century. British freemen may then have passed *en masse* into the lower ranks of Anglo-Saxon society. Such a suggestion is compatible with the low wergild of the English ceorl when compared to other Germanic societies, with the poverty of Anglo-Saxon terms expressive of kinship beyond the nuclear family and the exceptional differentiation between ceorl and thegn in Anglo-Saxon England.

If many ceorls derived from insular stock, so surely did the peasants and slaves at the base of society. Æthelberht's laws divided Kentish society into three groups of three, of whom only the highest, of king, earls and ceorls were free. The middle group, of *læts*, were apparently peasant farmers, and the lowest were household slaves. If the lower two orders supported those of free status, they were necessarily far more numerous, and were, therefore, far more likely to be of British stock even in areas of the densest English settlement.

The tax system of the late Empire rested on a unit of yield, the *iugum*, through which the demands of the state for money, goods and labour were apportioned. This was a highly complex and tightly documented system which necessitated regular updating. By *c.* 400, the demands of the Emperor for gold coin had broken direct contact between peasant and government. For the future, British taxation, like the royal renders of Anglo-Saxon England, was estate-based, delivered without recourse to coin and collected by the owner.

This system survived in some form into the mid to late fifth century and was familiar to Gildas. As government fell into the hands of kings, so tax collection probably ceased to be properly documented and the obligations owed by a specific estate or land unit became customary, excepting only exceptional labour corvées of the kind necessary for dyke construction. If land tenure was a matter of equal division between households, then the assimilation of the unit of assessment to the household was equitable and offered the easiest solution to the problem of establishing a consistent unit capable of audit by local administrations in the process of abandoning bookkeeping (for Gallic parallels, Percival 1985).

Did Roman and British taxation survive the Anglo-Saxon settlement? Labour services were a normal part of obligations to the late Roman state, apportioned by the *civitas* on the *iugum*. Gildas's comments on the northern walls (*De Excidio* XV. 3; XVIII. 2) imply his familiarity with the building of non-masonry barriers (Higham forthcoming, b). The stone wall was constructed 'in the normal way' by using 'miserable British' labour. Implicit in his account is the assumption that his audience understood how earthwork barriers were constructed. Gildas's contempt for the turf wall is best understood as a veiled reference to comparable engineering work in his own day and in his own vicinity. Gildas probably represents the voice of the estate holders, that is the church and aristocracy, faced with the demands for goods and labour placed upon them by a local tyrant. The obvious way to gather such a workforce would have been by conscription, using obligation to the state as the necessary constraint and dispersing it among the estates on the basis of the *iugum* or whatever comparable unit had replaced it as a customary measure of the obligations of the land unit and estate. Within, the equality of landholding meant that such demands could be equitably divided among the householders.

Although the Wansdyke is undated it was presumably built by labour drafted from the countryside. Similar banks protected the east borders of Elmet and can only have been constructed under British authority at some date before *c.* 626, when the kingdom lost any semblance of independence. Other dykes could equally have been constructed on this principle before the Saxon conquest.

If such labour services could be demanded in exceptional circumstances, it seems probable that the rural population habitually and regularly did labour services as part of their obligation to the state. Such may have included the carriage of renders, building services and the repair of fences on sites of high status. They may also have included road and bridge maintenance. The battle sites of seventh-century England from Chester onwards (where identifiable) imply that English armies regularly used Roman roads. Bede noted King Edwin's frequent journeys along them and his organization of refreshments at wells. If they were unmaintained, the provision of a network of facilities seems a trifle excessive. Bede also recounted a miracle putatively performed by John of Beverley which centred on a horse-race conducted along what was almost certainly a well-maintained section of Roman road (*Eccles. Hist.* II.16; V.6). In many areas, Roman roads were to be important estate and parish boundaries in the mid to late Saxon periods. There is at least the possibility that the obligation to maintain them persisted during the sub-Roman period, into the early English period, with labour extracted as a continuing part of their obligations to the state from local communities, assessed on a unit of taxation descended ultimately from Roman Britain.

Similarly, food rents provided the normal system of support for both British and English kings and must have been assessed on some notional unit of yield throughout the period, be it the *iugum*, the *uncia* or the hide.

Tangible evidence for the early English capacity to assess and collect resources from the countryside comes in two forms. One is evidence of the levying of tribute − hence Bede's interest in the hidation of Anglesey, Man, Iona and other Celtic territories, − and the document known as the 'Tribal Hidage'; the second is the continuing capacity to construct linear boundary systems, in the eighth century and earlier, of which the several crossing the Icknield Way near Cambridge provide an early sample.

The 'Tribal Hidage' (Dumville 1989) is a list of thirty-five named peoples (under thirty-four kings), each with a number of hides alongside. It is generally interpreted as a rough and ready tribute list, the figures of which are expressed nowhere more precisely than hundreds. Although it has been traditionally assigned to a Mercian king, Mercia actually heads the list and there is a strong case for interpreting it as a Northumbrian document of the seventh century, since Bernicia and Deira are the main omissions (Brooks 1989b). It was presumably a document written to act as an *aide-mémoire* according to which demands could be dispatched and against which incoming tribute could be checked. This two-part list is a prime example of the use of hides as a unit of account and carries no implications concerning the number of households in each community. In a coinless era, payment by one king to another in recognition of his superiority would have been in precious metals and objects of high value and exceptional workmanship, not foodstuffs (for parallels see *Beowulf*). The value of these payments was expressed in the only medium available, the hide, based on the value of annual renders capable of supporting the ceorl's household.

Since Elmet appears on the list, the Tribal Hidage must predate the usurpation of that kingship by Edwin of Deira, but it can only have been produced at the court of a king in a position of superiority over all southern Britain, who had one or more clerks capable of writing it. Edwin himself is the obvious candidate. His position as a northern 'overking' under Rædwald of East Anglia (*c.* 616−24) underpins the bulk of the first list of peoples or kings. With Rædwald's death, Edwin was threatened by the rise of Cwichelm of the West Saxons and allied himself by marriage with Eadbald of Kent, accepting into his court at this stage Bishop Paulinus and apparently extending his protection over Eadbald's allies, including the beleaguered king of Wight. Cwichelm attempted to assassinate

Edwin at Easter 626 (*H.E.* II, 9) and Edwin responded by a wholly successful campaign against Wessex later that summer. It was this campaign which catapulted him to a general 'overkingship' of all southern England and led to the second tier of names being added to the Tribal Hidage (Higham forthcoming, e).

Among the kings of peoples listed in the Tribal Hidage are several who may at this stage have been Celtic, including the 'Wrekin-dwellers', the *Hwicce, Westerne* (apparently the Celtic kings of the Irish Sea region) and Elmet. Several others (e.g. *Hendrice*) are also candidates. The 'overking-ship' was, in other words, operative in a political world which spanned the Anglo-Celtic divide. Edwin was the fourth 'overking' known to Bede, the sequence beginning with Ælle whose superiority cannot have much post-dated the middle of the fifth century. The campaign by an insular Anglian king against the Continental Varni recorded by Procopius in the 550s was probably undertaken by someone of similar status, if not Ælle himself. An 'overkingship' can, therefore, be pushed back into the mid-sixth century, only a half century or so after Gildas's description in the *De Excidio* of the system of obligation then operative. Indeed, in describing Maglocunus, the most powerful king in Wales, as only 'almost' the most powerful *dux* in Britain, Gildas implies the existence of one more powerful who was most probably English and a tribute-taking 'overking'. The use of the hide to enumerate tribute payments to 'overkings' is further removed from the origin of the term than that of the estate renders to a king; it thus pushes back the latter into the early sixth century at latest, when it was necessarily contemporary with the last written evidence available to us of taxation in kind. A degree of continuous development from one to the other seems probable, in which case the origins of the hide lay in a compromise between the Anglo-Saxon language, Celtic systems of tenure and the demands of sub-Roman British authority.

The Devil's Dyke at Newmarket provides evidence of a very different type (**5.18**). Although only 11.5 km long, this is the most substantial bank and ditch of the British Dark Ages, running from what is generally assumed to have been wooded land at Wooditton to the Swaffham Fens at Reach, blocking the wide natural routeway carrying the Icknield Way at a point where it runs along a narrow ridge. Excavation in the 1970s demonstrated that the dyke had been dug and built by gang labour but that the ditch had never been cleaned out. This was an example of crisis management at its most urgent. The dyke is undated, except that it is post-Roman and pre-903 but it fits most easily into the context of the late sixth or seventh centuries, when East Anglian kings were in contention for the dominance of all England. It is only one of four dykes across the Icknield Way (**5.19**), of which the Fleam Dyke may be the latest, given that the Bronze Age barrow at Mutlow Hill, on which it was orientated, was the corner of three parishes and the meeting place of the Domesday Hundred of *Flamendic*.

5.18   The Devil's Dyke at Newmarket, Cambridgeshire: the most substantial profile of any Dark Age dyke, this example was apparently designed to defend East Anglia by impeding approach up the Icknield Way. Although generally undated, a context around 600 seems most likely (copyright the author).

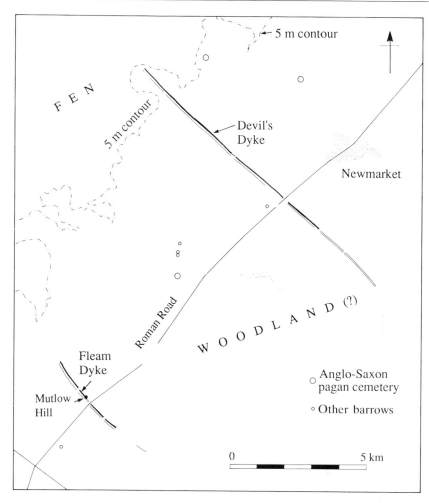

5.19 Dykes on the Icknield Way between Cambridge and Newmarket. These massive earthworks are no earlier than late Roman in date, and may belong to the early Saxon period. They were clearly constructed against enemies from the south-west.

Unlike the Devil's Dyke, this was maintained over a long period and it is difficult to imagine a more cogent assertion of the responsibility of the local community for this work than meeting on its apex.

The obvious means of building these and other dykes of the period was to call upon the labour services of the rural community through the hide system. Parallels with late Roman and sub-Roman Britain are obvious and there is a good case for the one being a direct continuation of the other.

While it is not possible to demonstrate beyond any doubt that the basic structure of late fourth-century taxation still continued in the seventh century, it is at least possible to establish that the two systems were extremely close in several important respects. A need for a system of assessing value and extracting goods and services continued throughout the fifth and sixth centuries, when several major earthworks were probably constructed by means of labour conscripted on this basis.

Conclusions

In conclusion, settlement abandonment and mobility in the lowland zone seem to contrast with other evidence of landscape and land-use continuity, and may be explicable by a variety of internal mechanisms, without relying on large-scale migration. It is possible to argue for the material survival of large and complex enclosure systems, the origins of which lie in the expanding agrarian societies of later prehistory and the Roman period. A form of assessment on households and on yield seems to have passed with them, assessed on a farming population whose origins lay in the British past, but whose future lay in Anglo-Saxon England. This discussion has ignored the major stumbling blocks of changes in material culture and language. It is to these that we must turn next.

CHAPTER SIX

THE ENGLISH SETTLEMENT: HISTORY AND ARCHAEOLOGY

Historical sources

In his *Historia Ecclesiastica*, completed in 731, the Venerable Bede implied that England had been peopled by a mass migration from Germany. He claimed that it was the 'three most formidable races of Germany, the Saxons, Angles and Jutes' who had settled in Britain (*H.E.* I.15) and described the various English peoples of his own age as being descended severally from them. His further list of German tribes that remained unconverted in the late seventh century (*H.E.* V.9) appears to imply that he thought these tribes, too, were those from whom settlers came to Britain (Campbell 1982), but the text is ambiguous and it was probably not Bede's intention that it should carry this meaning.

The Anglo-Saxons were well aware that they did not originate in Britain. If Gildas preserved an early foundation myth from Saxon sources (XXIII.3; Sims-Williams 1983b), then the basis of Bede's account was 'English'. Like their neighbours, the eighth-century English were keen to secure a clear idea of their own origins. 'Nennius' recorded foundation myths for the Britons based on the *Aeneid* and for the Irish based on the Bible (*Hist. Brit.* 10–15). Both derive ultimately from Roman or Christian traditions which had been borrowed and converted to their own needs, producing entirely artificial but simple and acceptable perspectives on the past. If Gildas believed that the Picts resided outside Britain in the early fifth century (Wright 1984), then we have a valuable illustration of changing beliefs concerning the origins of another of the peoples of Britain who were clearly recognized in the fourth century as being indigenous. In the *Historia Ecclesiastica*, Bede provided the English with answers to the more basic questions concerning their origins, making their ancestors immigrants, placing their arrival in the joint reign of Martian and Valentinian (post-449), establishing Hengest and Horsa as their leaders and noting a stone monument recording the death of Horsa in east Kent. The when, who and where of the *adventus* were thereby established, and later chroniclers were emboldened to take other English foundation myths, assign them dates and surround them with the aura of history.

However, Bede knew very little about these events. He offered no historical information at all between Gildas's Ambrosius Aurelianus and the coming of St Augustine, though the gap is to an extent plugged by a discussion of St Germanus whose exploits he inserts at this point. His information concerning the Hengest episode was less reliable than he and his contemporaries supposed. There is no evidence whatever that he was aware of the information which has reached us from southern Gaulish sources, nor any evidence that he was referring to two separate events in dealing with the employment of mercenaries under Hengest and discussing what he explained as a mass migration. The latter was a necessary construction given Bede's belief in large-scale migration but his comments are unhistorical since they suffer from a major problem of transmission (for a different view see Thompson 1984).

Horsa's death is unlikely to have been commemorated in stone in the third quarter of the fifth century by his illiterate following. If such an inscription did exist, then it was probably Roman, perhaps containing the word *(CO)HORS* and deriving from the activities of the garrison of Reculver. Alternatively, a monument might conceivably have been erected by the Kentish kings, early in the seventh century, to give substance to current attempts on their part to associate themselves with the Hengest stories and so justify their 'overkingship' of southern England. The appearance of Hengest in the royal Kentish genealogies smacks of a retrospective insertion. The Kentish dynasty were the *Oiscingas*, deriving from the eponymous Oisc (possibly a god), not Hengest (Dumville 1976; Brooks 1989a). In legends recorded in early English and Celtic literature, Hengest originated in Jutland, and Bede recorded that the peoples of Kent and of Wight were Jutes. While strong contact between the two should not be doubted, it would be wrong to give any undue credence to the Jutish connection between these three. The Hengest/Horsa doublet may have arisen from an explanatory gloss added to a regnal list, to explain that 'Hengest' meant 'horse', in much the same way that geographical elements were incorporated into regnal lists elsewhere in Anglo-Saxon England. Having said all that, the name of Hengest's British employer, Vortigern, finds some implicit support in the *De Excidio* and is an early form, so the British 'tyrant' who invited the first Germans into Britain may be historical.

Bede's dating depends entirely on Gildas's juxtaposition of the appeal to Aëtius (in or after 446) and the invitation to the Saxons, a subject to which we must return. The names Hengest and Horsa derive from oral sources which we cannot substantiate, but the historicity of which we must doubt. They recur in the *Historia Brittonum* (Chapters 31, 44, 45) and the several versions of the *Anglo-Saxon Chronicle* (449–73), but are not on that account any the more historical. Bede's record of the several tribes and the descent of the several peoples from them has all the hallmarks of retrospective analysis and, unsupported, should be treated with maximum caution. Alongside the Hengest legends there were recorded in the ninth century a further series of localized foundation myths, attached to several of the historic kingdoms, opening with Ælle in 477 and Cerdic in the mid-

490s. The associations established between personal and place-names in several of these accounts are clearly spurious examples of folk etymology (Sims-Williams 1983a). Port, for example, was associated with Portsmouth and Wightgar with Wight (Roman *Vectis*). Despite the recording of several events which were not obviously fabrication, history cannot be wrought from the Chronicles until, at earliest, the late sixth century. Bedevilled by their reliance on a chronological framework based retrospectively on Easter tables and by what must be later attempts to render oral traditions and tales into sequential form, these Chronicles entries are essentially myths, and no more than that.

The geography, chronology and characterization of Bede's account must, therefore, be placed to one side. His account of the fifth century depended heavily on two works, the *De Excidio* of Gildas and a version of Constantius's *Life of St Germanus*. The first is one of the most contentious texts of the early medieval period, while the second is a piece of hagiography, the details of which were set down at a considerable distance in both space and time, for purposes which should not be confused with the writing of history. To these we can add only very few independent historical sources. Under the year 441, laconic entries in the 452 Gallic Chronicle recorded that 'The provinces of Britain, which up to that time had been harassed by various disasters and accidents, are brought under the control of the Saxons' (trans. Jones and Casey 1988). The Chronicle of 551 noted that 'The British provinces, lost by the Romans, fell under the sway of the Saxons' (trans. Thompson 1984). This information probably reached Gallia Narbonensis (where the chronicles were probably being written) with refugees from Britain, such as were carving out new homes for themselves in Brittany and northern Spain. If it has any credibility at all, the initial conquest of parts of Britain – almost certainly parts adjacent to the Channel coast – by what were then conventionally known as Saxons must have occurred by this date, so that Bede's dates (derived ultimately from his reading of Gildas) are too late. It is possible to compute dates for the arrival of the Saxons from the *Historia Brittonum*, resulting in a date in the late 420s or *c.* 430, but these remain no more than vague guesses, the factual bases of which are unknown. Otherwise, it is to Gildas that we (like Bede) must turn for anything even approaching a contemporary account of the *adventus Saxonum*.

The *De Excidio* is undated, except by reference to the siege of 'Badon Hill' 43 years and one month before, in turn an event which is insecurely dated, the only annalistic reference to it being one in the *Annales Cambriae* under the year 516, an entry and a date which probably owe much to Gildas and which attribute the battle to the pseudo-historical Arthur. On several counts, modern scholarship has tended to place authorship in the second quarter of the sixth century, or very soon thereafter (e.g. Dumville 1984b), although a date as early as 500 has much to commend it and is perfectly feasible (Sims-Williams 1983a). That Gildas had himself received a traditional Roman education (Lapidge 1984) might incline us to place his youth as early as possible after the end of Roman government in Britain, and so pull the date of composition towards the earlier end of the feasible range, *c.* 490–510. However, it is quite clear from his own account that Gildas was not a contemporary of the *adventus*, although his childhood necessarily coincided with the tail-end of the struggle against the Saxons, after *Mons Badonicus* which was almost the final encounter, not the last one.

To Gildas, the arrival of the Saxon 'wolves' was the last of a series of self-inflicted wounds. The sins of the Britons had brought down upon them the punishment of God, executed through a series of disasters. The juxtaposition of moral failings and their penalty is the key to the ordering of book I, the *Historia*: Chapter XXI details the crimes, XXII and XXIII intimations of divine vengeance, peppered by biblical analogy, and XXIV the punishment. Gildas's view of an active, vengeful and omnipotent God mirrors that of Orosius (writing 418):

> Whenever man sins, the world also becomes subject to censure,... this earth on which we live is punished by having its animal life die out and its crops fail.
>
> *(Seven Books against the Pagans* II.1)

Gilda's sequential account of the appeal to 'Agitius' and the Saxon *adventus* is however, the only one available (De Excidio, XX-XXVI). No dates were given and there is no indication that the author knew any, but the sequence was set within a chronological framework and with some indication of the time lapses between events. By the eighth century it had become possible to establish a fixed point within Gildas's account, when 'Agitius' (Aetius) was thrice consular (446–54). Aware that the *adventus* needed to be as soon after 446 as possible, Bede adopted a mid-century date.

The result is inconsistent with the Gallic Chronicle entries for 441, and the archaeological evidence for English settlement in the first half of the century. The resulting dilemma has led to various attempts to distance Gildas from southern Britain, so liberating him from this chronology (e.g. Thompson 1979), yet every such explanation requires special pleading and is inconsistent with evidence internal to the De Excidio. The often-offered alternative, that Gildas was seriously mistaken regarding his sequence, is no more palatable.

This dilemma can be resolved. The appeal is only tied to the years after 446 if it were a document to which Gildas had direct access. If the 'quotation' from it is no more than Gildas's own reconstruction, then it could have been despatched at any date from *c.* 425 onwards. The garbled 'Augitius' and the implausible wording of the address both suggest an oral source. If Gildas had no more information than the fact of an appeal, the name of the recipient, (which he spelt phonetically) and the single biographical detail that this 'Agitius' had held a third consulship, then his reconstruction of the text used all the meagre information available to him without denoting the date at which it was sent. His choice of direct speech for this passage reflects his careful escalation of tension from one appeal to the next, (XV, I; XVII, I; XX, 1) and one threat to the next, all for rhetorical purposes. The idea may have come from the *Aeneid* in which such usage abounds. That Gildas abandoned his normal style in favour of a more classical one implies that he intended his audience to accept his 'quotation' as genuine. There is no value in the argument that the well-read Gildas was incapable of sustaining this style for such a short passage.

If this be accepted, the appeal to Aetius need not post-date 446. Had it been sent in the mid to late 420's then the invitation to the Saxons occurred *c.*430 and their rebellion, in or very shortly before 441. On this time-scale, Gildas's sequence is entirely consistent with all other evidence for the *adventus* and with appeals of other sorts, such as that which brought St. Germanus to Britain in 429 and again probably in the 430's. The subsequent revolt led to the Saxons overthrowing regional British governments and themselves securing control of provincial revenues. Hence the reference to 'the Britains' and 'rule' or 'jurisdiction' in the Gallic Chronicle of 452, and to 'tribute' in the *De Excidio* (I, 6).

Does Gildas's account deserve any credence? This must depend on his purpose. His 'historical' account was merely a preface in which he established the inevitability of divine intervention. Within it the arrival of the Saxons was the climax of a compelling juxtaposition of crime and retribution, by which Gildas was attempting to give local relevance and precedents to his warnings on the consequences of the sinful conduct of his contemporaries, in books II and III. Gildas was uninterested in history for its own sake but he used his own expurgated and partial account of the recent past to underline the sinfulness of the Britons and the plenitude of God's power, so as to reinforce and make terrible his strictures concerning the present.

If his preface was intended to reinforce his message, it was crucial that his account of recent events be believed. Had it been obvious fabrication then his historical preface would have fatally weakened his censures, rather than rendering them more credible, as intended. It is not entirely clear at whom the work was aimed. If it had been entirely personal and secret its survival would have been unlikely. It was, ostensibly, addressed to the kings and priests up-country against whom Gildas railed and the small coterie of clergy of whom he approved, but his sophisticated and cultured prose presupposes that, for full effect, his audience should have shared his Roman education and his knowledge of Vergil, quotations from whom he variously adapted to his own purposes. While he credited King Maglocunus with a superior education, there are reasons for thinking that may have been obtained in exile but not that his peer group in the far West need not have shared an education in rhetoric. Gildas was, therefore, more probably writing for a lowland, élite, Romanized and Christian audience, perhaps largely monkish or clerical by this stage: that is, the group with whom he so strongly identifies himself throughout the work. Such men might have been expected to be relatively well informed on the recent cardinal events occurring in areas of Britain hitherto closely linked with and adjacent to their own. While there was little general knowledge on which Gildas could draw for events earlier than the *adventus*, that event was probably 'recent' in terms of the narrative and could be remembered by a few of the elderly. He had far less room for extravagant departure from the general consensus when dealing with major events within the lifetimes of his parents and grandparents. His description must, therefore, be consistent with contemporary views of the recent past, if only back to the generation which experienced the Saxon *adventus* and rebellion.

In certain respects we can identify both a simplification of, and an intrusion of bias into, his account of even the recent past in the *De Excidio*. For example, the Saxons can have done no more than administer the *coup de grâce* to the dying towns of Roman Britain, if that. In his account of their sack Gildas appears to be indulging in highly charged interpretation on the basis of the physical fabric still very much visible in his own day, by making the Saxons scapegoats for what had, in fact, if unbeknown to him, been a long-term and deep-seated decline. His interpretation is couched in biblical language, reflecting a hiatus in the terminology concerning towns within Roman Britain. This interpretation is essentially archae-ological, and Gildas had few skills as an archaeologist. Yet it is surely something that he recognized the need to offer some explanation of the demise of the still recognizable towns of Roman Britain. The result mirrors his approach to the Roman walls, although the results are less far-fetched in modern eyes. In other respects, he clearly knew something about the Saxons and their customs, hence his knowledge of the Saxon word for a ship, of the Germanic practice of augury and of what is probably a Saxon view of their initial crossing to Britain to take up employment as mercenaries. Gildas either personally knew Saxons or was able to discuss such matters with those who did. Although his account makes only a meagre contribution to the geography (**6.1**), chronology and personalities of the participants, it does offer a structured and internally consistent account of the *adventus* which is both more detailed and certainly more credible than any other event in his *Historia* previous to his own lifetime.

Gildas described a political system in a part of Britain which he did not specify, headed by a 'proud tyrant', whose name he knew and on which he was savagely punning (Jackson 1982), making decisions with the aid of councillors. With their support, Vortigern responded to the threat or rumour of renewed raiding and attempts at settlement (by the old enemy, Picts and Scots) by recruiting Saxon warriors from outside the island, apparently from the Saxon homeland. These came in three ships, fortified

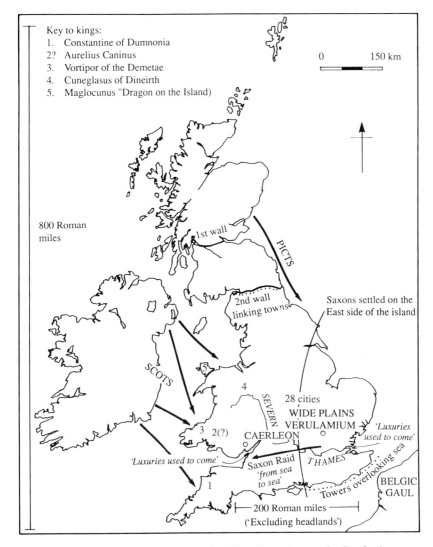

Key to kings:
1. Constantine of Dumnonia
2? Aurelius Caninus
3. Vortipor of the Demetae
4. Cuneglasus of Dineirth
5. Maglocunus "Dragon on the Island)

0   150 km

800 Roman
miles

1st wall

PICTS

2nd wall
linking towns

Saxons settled on the
East side of the island

SCOTS

5

4

28 cities

SEVERN

WIDE PLAINS
VERULAMIUM

'Luxuries
used to come'

3   2(?)   CAERLEON

THAMES

'Luxuries used to come'

Saxon Raid
'from sea
to sea'

Towers overlooking sea

BELGIC
GAUL

1

200 Roman miles
('Excluding headlands')

6.1   The geography of Gildas's *De Excidio*. The dimensions and other basic
information in the introduction derive ultimately from the *Natural History* of Pliny the
Elder, but Gildas followed Orosius in giving a breadth of 200 miles in error for Pliny's
300 miles.

by favourable omens obtained by divination, and were settled in the east of
the island. The numbers are probably apocryphal but the geography less
certainly so.

Aware of their success, a second and larger contingent joined them after
a delay of unspecified length, uninvited but accepted by the British
authorities as soldiers. At this stage (if not before) the mercenaries were

accommodated by means of a *foedus* (treaty) by which they were granted a regular issue of grain (*annona*), and promised to keep the peace. They were quiescent for a long period. Combined, the two periods mentioned by Gildas could amount to a decade or two, but the chronology is unknowable and it seems very unlikely that he himself knew how long either period lasted.

The Saxons then complained that their supplies were insufficient and were enraged by individual incidents (between Britons and Germans?), demanded increased payment and immediately set about widespread raiding, 'from sea to sea'. The damage they caused was sensationalized by Gildas, but he recorded that some Britons were killed or enslaved, or fled abroad, before the Saxons retreated *domum* ('home'), presumably to the area in the east of Britain in which they had been settled. There then began the series of wars in which Ambrosius Aurelianus, the last of the Romans in Britain, whose parents had 'worn the purple', led the Christian (and presumably lowland) Britons against the immigrants. The implication of the *De Excidio* is that these wars were eventually concluded by a treaty between British authorities and the barbarians, which was still in force at the time of writing and which recognized the rights of each in adjacent territories.

Gildas was careful throughout his work to distinguish between those he thought of as Romans and the native British community, whose successive rebellions against the Romans was a favourite theme. He seems to envisage Ambrosius as a member of the Continental Roman aristocracy, perhaps one of the great landed magnates of the western Empire who had taken refuge on his British estates from the mauling such landowners were experiencing at the hands of the Goths and Franks in Gaul. That such aristocrats were occasionally capable of military activity is borne out by the efforts of Ecdidius in the letters of Sidonius Apollinarius, and of the private armies raised (unsuccessfully) by Honorius's relatives in Spain against Constantine III. Gildas contrasted the behaviour of Ambrosius with that of his grandchildren (and by implication the kings with their household warriors in the West) who were contemporaries of Gildas, beside whom Ambrosius was in some respect deemed superior – less prone to the faults he labours in XXVI.2–4 and XXVII, perhaps.

Whoever this 'Roman' was, he was presumably a man of considerable power and authority, resident in the lowlands of Britain, who organized an effective British defence in the aftermath of the great raid. His achievements may have been extremely limited, since he was unsuccessful in evicting the Saxons from Britain; indeed there is no evidence he ever tried. We do not know where he was based. Peace was established soon after Gildas's own birth in the year of *Mons Badonicus* and this necessarily implies British recognition of at least one independent Saxon territory within Britain, presumably in the east of the island where they had first been established. *Mons Badonicus* is the sole conflict named by Gildas after Aquileia but he may have mentioned it not so much because of the scale of the victory achieved as for the coincidence of his own birth-date. Although the whereabouts of the site was probably common knowledge when Gildas was writing, it is now contentious, as is so much concerning the geography of the *De Excidio*. His own adult life was lived under a *foedus* which partitioned some part of Britain with the Saxons and was unaffected by any renewal of Germanic aggression. However, the *De Excidio* (X.2) implies that he and his audience were unable to reach either St Albans or Cærleon (or, perhaps, Chester) without running risks from Saxons now in acknowledged control of intervening territory. What Gildas especially feared was captivity in the hands of barbarians, a fate which he, like St Patrick, considered to be worse than death (*De Excidio* XIX.2). Given the geography of the earliest tier of archaeological evidence (**6.2, 6.3**), it is impossible to reconcile this statement with his being domiciled in the Midlands or the north. The presence of early Saxon burials in the middle Thames valley may represent the intruders by whom he felt threatened, in which case Gildas was writing in central, southern England, east of the Severn and south of the Thames, in the region of Wiltshire or Dorset (Higham forthcoming, c). The *De Excidio* is charged with the expectation of renewed onslaughts from the barbarians and we might envisage Gildas within territory defended from the Saxons of the Thames basin by the Wansdyke, the non-masonry construction of which may have influenced his assumption that the turf wall in the north (the Antonine Wall) had been constructed by Britons rather than Romans and encouraged his condemnation of it (XV.3).

Despite his exaggerations concerning the fate of the towns, and problems over dating, Gildas's account is generally plausible and internally consistent, becoming generally more consistent and more plausible as it moves towards his own lifetime. Gildas stood at the crossroads of later Roman Britain. Himself the author of a distinctly 'Roman' piece of writing, yet a distinctly 'provincial' one as well, Gildas had been educated in a late Roman style, after a fashion which implies that courts of Roman style were still operative in the community of his youth. His comments on Maglocunus suggest that this prince had enjoyed a similar education. From the ranks of such young men, recruits were joining Christian communities with most of the attributes of monasteries (*De Excidio* I.XXXVI.1), or rejecting the path of righteousness to follow a bloodier road to worldly power. Maglocunus, the nephew, not the son, and murderer of the previous king, toyed with the former then rejected it in favour of the latter. His career had similarities with that of St Guthlac, but in reverse.

To an extent, the contrast is between the emergent war-leadership of the comparatively un-Romanized upland zone and the survival of a comparatively unwarlike, Romanized élite in the lowlands, where both Ambrosius and Gildas himself should be placed. The leadership of the upland zone pragmatically restructured to meet the new circumstances. Something similar may have been happening in the lowlands, if we take

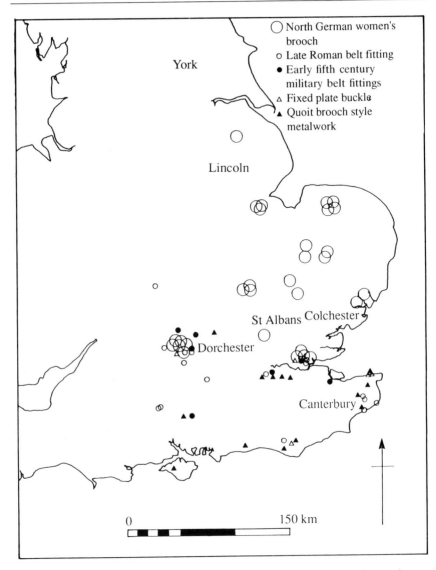

6.2 The *Adventus*: the distribution of north Germanic women's brooches and Romano-British/Saxon metalwork in the first half of the fifth century in Britain (based on Böhme 1986 and Hawkes 1989).

Gildas's comments seriously (XXI.3,4) but it had progressed less far and the employment of Saxon mercenaries proved a fatal weakness. An in-fluential contingent of the lowland gentry clung to a Roman and Christian ideology hostile to the social changes necessary to face the barbarian threat. The revolt of the Germanic mercenaries whose employment they had themselves recommended destroyed the very fabric of their lives and,

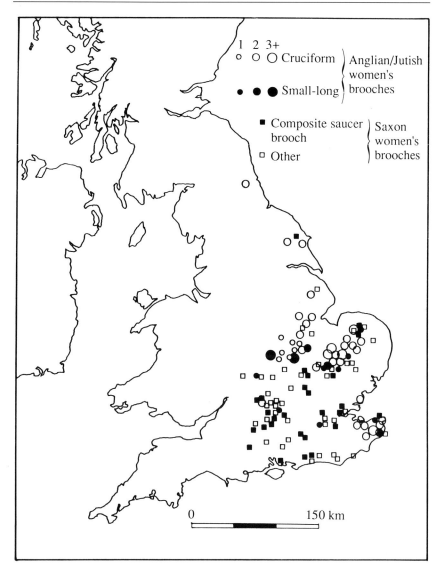

6.3 Anglian/Jutish and Saxon women's brooches of the second half of the fifth century in Britain (after Hawkes 1989).

by so doing, encouraged the élites of neighbouring British communities to cling ever more tightly to the rigging as their ship went down. Gildas and his audience remained essentially civilian. When threatened by outsiders their response was typical of late Roman authorities: to call in barbarian mercenaries − or Aëtius − to solve their security problems. Their continuing control of a large slice of the estate system rendered the kings, whose demands they resented, incapable of long-term defence of the community against determined and self-confident barbarians.

Their political system had remained Roman in form. Otherwise, how could Gildas portray the northern walls as being constructed with conscripted labour (XVIII.2)? The regular payments of the *annona* with which the Saxon soldiers were supported read suspiciously like late Roman taxation in kind, administered with a degree of regularity which implies continuing social control over the producer-classes (Stevens 1941). The experience of fifth-century Gaul provided precedents for the *foedus* with a barbarian leader (e.g. Sivan 1987), and the billeting of soldiers on civilians was a normal part of late Roman administration.

That Gildas could expect his audience to understand such terms in his own day says much about the survival of the Roman system in Britain. More important, he makes it clear that those who stood to lose in the event of barbarian raids on the east coasts were not confident of their capacity to defend it with the military resources internal to lowland British society. While these may have been adequate to see off minor raids (as in 429) or for disagreements between British leaders, the more Romanized parts of Britain had not yet evolved a professional warrior-class within the indigenous social system. Properly trained and equipped soldiers were probably at a premium and few in number. Great landowners may have been attended by gangs of strong-arm men, adept at extracting rent and taxes, or brawling with similar gangs from neighbouring territories, but such forces needed to be grouped around full-time soldiers to oppose barbarian raiders. For this role Vortigern and his council recruited other barbarians. These were then treated as if they were Roman soldiers and made a charge upon the tax-take, making it impossible for a British soldiery to emerge under his authority.

The Saxons were ideal troops to defend Britain against raiders. They came with their own arms and already trained in their use. As the Emperor Julian discovered in Gaul (Zosimus III.7), regular soldiers were far less effective at dealing with rural raiding parties than barbarian auxiliaries of the same kind. The Saxons had a formidable reputation:

> The Saxons, a tribe living on the shores of the Ocean in inaccessible swamps and dreaded for their bravery and rapidity of movement, undertook a dangerous raid in full force against the Roman possessions, but they were crushed by Valentinian in the land of the Franks.
>
> (Orosius, *Seven Books Against the Pagans* VII.32)

The revolt of such troops was always a probability. As mercenary soldiers they were in competition with the local aristocracy and the Church for a share of the agricultural surplus, yet their share was determined by their competitors. They consequently took advantage of the weakness of alternative forces to supplant their civilian employers as the controllers of land and tax revenues. Widely dispersed estate systems were peculiarly vulnerable to such appropriations. Again, Continental parallels are well known. At about this time, Sidonius Apollinaris was unable to secure two-thirds of an inheritance from his mother-in-law because a Visigoth had occupied it (Stevens 1933). The eventual establishment of Saxon control of estates in eastern England necessarily entailed the loss of those estates and their tax revenues to the lowland British aristocracy. Given the dispersed nature of Roman landholding, such may well have included estates of Ambrosius or Gildas's proud tyrant himself, whom subsequent chroniclers named as Vortigern and married off to Hengest's daughter. The history of the Visigoths demonstrates that such marriages did occur, even if Vortigern's remains a matter of speculation.

The Saxons of Gildas's account were few in number. The initial recruits numbered between 100 and 200, depending on the size of the ships, if his statement that there were three be accepted at face value. If not, they were still unlikely to have been much more numerous, if only because no British ruler is likely to have wanted vast numbers of Saxons within his territory. The reinforcements were more numerous but not so many that their hosts were unable to at least attempt to feed them. The great raid across Britain was undertaken by a force of hundreds or perhaps even a thousand or so, but not several thousand. The settlers detailed by Gildas were, therefore, comparatively few and characterized by their qualities as warriors. Whether their families accompanied them he does not say, but archaeological evidence suggests that they did from the beginning.

In respect of their numbers his account is at one with the several foundation tales recalled in the various versions of the *Anglo-Saxon Chronicle*. Ælle and his three sons were credited with three ships, Cerdic and Cynric had five ships, Port and his two sons had two ships and the West Saxons, in 514, had three ships. The actual numbers of ships probably owe more to the fabric of heroic verse than to historical reality and may indicate no more than a tendency for Saxon foundation myths to be clones of one another. However, all instances concur with the view that the Saxon settlement was undertaken by very small numbers of warriors. There is no literary evidence of any historicity that argues for or is even consistent with a mass migration.

In the west of Germany, whence they came, recent interpretation of archaeological evidence at sites such as Federssen Wierde (Haarnagel 1979) supports the view that German society became increasingly hier-archical during the Roman period. The warriors who entered Britain were likely to have been already men of free status within their own communities, ranking above the large 'thrall' population. They were presumably led by men who originated from rich, influential families, to whom they were connected by the bonds of companionship as *comitatenses*. It was in groups linked by blood ties and commendation that German warriors normally went to war, and a German army consisted of an agglomeration of such groups, each fighting in their 'wedges', around and on behalf of its own leader as, for example, at the Battle of Strasbourg. The statistics of the several invasion myths recorded in English and British sources seem to imply that later commentators expected a retinue or war-band of the migration period to approximate to a single ship-crew.

The companions of a powerful leader would normally be unmarried men with little or no land of their own, dependent on their patron for maintenance and reward, as documented by Tacitus in the *Germania* (cap. 14). This system directly parallels the war-bands of Gildas's British tyrants, and emerges very clearly in seventh-century Wessex through the role of the *gesith* in the laws of King Ine (Attenborough 1922; discussed in Abels 1988). Kings sought control of lands on which they could support themselves by the labour of the less privileged, and from which they could confer slices on their leading warriors, and raid for portable wealth to be distributed to their unlanded followers. The notion that barbarian *foederati* secured not land so much as tax revenues from the Roman authorities is an attractive one (Goffart 1980) but control of estates would suffice at least as well. Indeed, it is difficult to distinguish between the two.

The great raid detailed by Gildas fits neatly into this picture. In order to satisfy the demands of his following, a German leader needed booty such as fine horses, precious metal and raiment. Peace and employment within a provincial society devoid of coin and niggardly with luxury goods was incosistent with his status and the demands made upon him by his companions, just as it was for the war-bands of the British tyrants, whom Gildas characterized as criminals.

The booty which the Saxons secured included slaves some of whom, Gildas assumed, had given themselves into slavery as an alternative to starvation. Slave-raiding was commonplace on the Rhine frontier and throughout the western provinces in the fourth and fifth centuries. St Patrick was familiar with the Gallic practice of ransoming captives from the Franks, and the Saxons may have intended to follow their example. However, many slaves were not ransomed. Hydatius described the Suebi carrying off captives as they passed across Gaul into Spain in the first decade of the fifth century; these were probably either sold or used as agricultural labourers, as was Patrick in Ireland. Ammianus recorded the retention of prisoners as standard among the German tribes along the Rhine. The slaves of the Sarmatians outnumbered their masters and rebelled successfully against them in the mid-fourth century, forcing them into distant exile, and forming themselves into a new tribe called the Limigantes (Ammianus XVII.13). The soldiers of Coroticus took slaves in Ireland who were destined for Pictish markets. The documentary evidence for slavery among the northern barbarians is overwhelming, and it was arguably increasing in the fifth century.

It is, therefore, surprising that most modern scholars have made little of Gildas's reference to enslavement of the Britons by the Saxons and his own obvious terror of enslavement. One example will suffice. Writing of the rate of survival of the Britons, Thompson wrote:

... isolated individual place-names have survived because isolated enclaves of Britons managed to escape annihilation.... In general the names disappeared along with the people who used them. Nor were the people enslaved, except no doubt for some of the women and children. Germanic society at this date had little place for slave labour even in the relatively highly developed communities just beyond the Roman frontier,...

(Thompson 1982b: 214)

German warriors in Britain did kill Britons. It was a disgrace for a German warrior to survive the destruction of his war-band and this viewpoint discouraged the giving of quarter on the field of battle. At Pevensey (*Andredesceaster*), the *Anglo-Saxon Chronicle* credited Ælle with killing every one of his British opponents (annal for 495) and, true or not, this was at least consistent with what later generations thought might have happened. Gildas recorded the shock of the British when some of those who surrendered themselves to the Saxons as slaves were killed at once. It was not the custom of British, Irish or Pictish raiders to kill their captives. An explanation is offered by Sidonius Apollinaris (*Epistolae* VIII.6.15), who noted of Saxon raiders in Aquitaine that they habitually sacrificed a tithe of their captives before sailing home. Tacitus also recorded human sacrifice by the Germans – significantly, to Mercury (probably Woden). Yet, however macabre, even this left nine in every ten alive and enslaved, and slavery was to be an important facet of Anglo-Saxon society for centuries to come (Pelteret 1981).

Gildas describes a Saxon settlement on lands in the east of England. If sections of the indigenes fled, their new masters would have needed to replenish the workforce on their lands. They achieved this by the standard method of the day, by slave raiding, establishing most of their captives as thralls to work their new estates, but perhaps sacrificing a small minority to their native deities.

Gildas provides us with a single example of Saxon settlement, albeit necessarily the first one, within a geographical context which poses as many problems as it solves. The immigrants were warriors, of free status, in search of fame and fortune. Their leaders contracted to serve a British authority, then found this insufficiently rewarding and set about independent activities on their own behalf. The remainder were tied to the chieftains by reciprocal promises of service in return for protection. However, the military resources of each leader were relatively small and the ties between chieftain and warrior were personal rather than dynastic.

Among the Goths or Burgundians, a permanent form of dynastic kingship had already begun to emerge as the settlement on Roman soil occurred. Many of the Continental migrations involved relatively large numbers, forming an entire people in transit. There is no documentary evidence that either was characteristic of the Germanic settlements in Britain. In contrast, the sense of group identity was extremely localized in early England, much on a par with what we know of early Welsh lordship. Kingship was initially overwhelmingly military (and perhaps sacral), only certainly accumulating other social functions during the sixth and seventh centuries, when the patently artificial kingdoms of the so-called heptarchy came into being.

On the basis of the literary evidence, there is no reason to believe that the English settlement was on the same scale as that of the Franks or the Vandals. Nor does it reveal the same degree of social organization. Incoming kings had no need of literate bureaucrats, since their territories were sufficiently small for face-to-face contact to suffice for the management of their affairs. No niche remained for a Christian British gentry and clergy.

This is not to imply that the Germanic settlement of Britain occurred in isolation from the Continent. That it did not is graphically evidenced by a curious story told by Procopius, concerning a war between the Varni (on the Continent) and the Angili in *Brittia* (Britain), sparked off by a broken engagement of marriage (*History of the Wars* VIII.XX.1–41). Internal evidence strongly suggests that this tale came from a German source and it probably reached Byzantium with a Frankish embassy. It offers a telling insight into the tortuous patterns of personal alliance, insult and vengeance which must have characterized the barbarian society now dominant on both sides of the North Sea.

When Gildas wrote, Britain was divided between a Christian and British west and an eastern area in parts of which pagan Germans were recognized as being in control. While his and other parts of the lowland zone remained at this date outside direct Saxon control, these were only the remnants and were soon to fall to the immigrants. In his eyes and those of later British commentators, the English *adventus* was catastrophic in its impact. It swept away the last autonomous Romanized community in the West, and created in its place the largest pool of pagans to be found anywhere within the old Empire in the sixth century.

To what extent was this the result of a mass migration? Such a thesis finds no support in the writing of Gildas, who was aware of Britons entering Saxon society in a servile capacity, probably in numbers sufficient to fill the ranks of the lower classes and outnumbering the warrior class many times over. It was, however, the popular perception on both sides of the language divide by the age of Bede. To proceed further, it is necessary to test hypotheses culled from literary sources against the archaeological and linguistic evidence. Both provide data of very different types and both have consistently been interpreted as diagnostic of a mass migration.

Of graves and men: the archaeology of the Adventus

The practice of inhumation was only introduced to Germany during the later Roman period. Germans serving in the Roman army before *c.* 350 who died within the Empire seem to have been buried according to Roman rites and are barely distinguishable from other Roman soldiers.

This practice continued into the later Empire. Ammianus noted that the Gothic chief Athanaric of the Greuthungi died at Constantinople and was buried with splendid rites in the Roman manner, at some stage after 369. Whether his burial was furnished or not, he was clearly inhumed. Inhumation was probably exported back to Germany by soldiers returning from mercenary service to a position of high status within Germanic society, but it was uncommon in free Germany before the end of the fourth century.

Furnished inhumations are widespread in northern Gaul in the late Roman period (Böhme 1974), where they have been described variously as 'warrior' or 'Germanic' graves. The rites used are a hybrid of late Roman and barbarian practices (for discussion see e.g. Hills 1979). They are characteristically orientated in a manner which would not be out of place in a purely Roman cemetery. The principal feature which distinguishes these graves from 'Roman' ones is the high incidence of grave-goods, which include pottery, glass and jewellery as well as weapons. Objects from Roman and from a variety of Germanic traditions lie side by side.

The drinking sets and other apparently expensive grave-goods imply a comparatively wealthy group within frontier society which differed from Romano-Judaism either in its social use of the ritual of burial or in its view of the afterlife. These depositions occurred when many provincials were still pagan, and Frankish influence within the Rhine army may have been hostile to Christianity. The presence of graves of this kind outside certain of the Rhineland forts implies that some at least of their occupants were soldiers. Although the ethnic origins of any individual grave must remain in doubt (Whittaker 1989), the majority of those buried were presumably Germans in origin, probably predominantly Frankish, the vanguard of the Frankish settlement in Gaul north of the Loire. What we are witnessing in north Gaul is the emergence of a mortuary rite which combined elements drawn from three traditions, Christian, Roman pagan and Germanic, and adapted to suit the social and ritual needs of the warrior élite of this particular community.

Comparable inhumations accompanied by fixed-plate buckles, military belt-fittings and metalwork in the quoit-brooch style occurred in small numbers in southern England in the first half of the fifth century (**6.2**). Graves of this kind have been identified at two sites close to Dorchester-on-Thames, in the cemeteries at Mucking (Essex) and on the south side of the lower Thames at sites such as Milton Regis (Hawkes 1989). Both sexes are represented, the women accoutred with a mixture of Roman and Germanic ornaments.

These burials probably reflect the presence of soldiers showing characteristics of – even recruited from – north Gaul or the Rhineland at the very end of the fourth and early in the fifth century. On the basis of his examination of the metalwork which accompanied them, Böhme suggested that they included Franks, Alamans, East Germans, Saxons and Angles,

6.4 Cremation and inhumation cemeteries in Anglo-Saxon England: a representative sample (after Hawkes 1989).

all of whom could have been recruited from the northern frontiers of the western Empire, for military service in Britain (Böhme 1986). In practice, their individual ethnic origin need not have been identical with that of the diagnostic pieces of metalwork among their belongings − individual objects clearly travelled widely as gifts or plunder − but it does seem clear that the warrior graves of the Rhineland frontier spilled over into nearby parts of Britain, perhaps in the late fourth and certainly in the early fifth century, present at least by *c.* 420.

6.5 Male inhumation surrounded by a ring-ditch at Snape. Two small plaques of tin from a decorated belt survive at waist level (courtesy of William Filmer-Sankey, Snape Historical Trust).

That these were Frankish graves was suggested a quarter-century ago (Evison 1965) and the idea has more to commend it than was then appreciated. However, there is no literary tradition of Frankish settlement in Britain and it is probably best to think of these incomers as merely Germanic, rather than of any specific tribal group, bringing with them ideas on mortuary practice recently developed in the Rhineland. The quoit brooch was derived ultimately from late Roman motifs, but via northern German annular brooch styles (Ager 1985), and the presence of metalwork of this type may imply the presence of Germans from further north, but with experience of Roman employment at first or second hand.

The presence of these graves scattered in very small numbers implies that the British aristocracy were recruiting what were in their own eyes Roman soldiers, from the only pool of equipped and trained men available to them, that of northern Gaul. Recruitment may have been continuous: there is little evidence of a break between the *comitatenses* in Britain in the years before Constantine III, and the 420s. The excavators of Mucking have argued consistently that the location of that site on elevated sandy heathland reflects the strategic needs of British rulers rather than the choice of the inhabitants. In grave 117 of cemetery I a military belt was found set in early quoit-brooch style, and a second cemetery with comparable material was founded within the next few decades (Evison 1977; Böhme 1986). If this small group of well-accoutred warriors were 'watchmen' guarding access to the middle Thames, we must assume them to have had ships and to have been capable of deployment as marines.

Such communities represent an influx to Britain of a new material culture combined with some adaptation in mortuary rites. These changes reached Britain along the same conduit as had the Roman Conquest and Romanization. They may, at the time, have been viewed in Britain as no more than a minor adaptation of existing practices, in line with current policies elsewhere in the western prefecture of the Empire where employment of barbarian soldiers was a routine fact of life.

Below the Thames, these warrior communities were dispersed in much the same areas as the forces of the Saxon Shore and they may have been intended to perform a similar function, protecting the exposed coasts from raiders. Only one group does not fit this interpretation. A cluster around Dorchester-on-Thames is entirely land-locked and it may be significant that while groups using Germanic equipment seem to have stayed on and prospered at Croydon and Mucking, there is no evidence of continuous warrior settlement at Dorchester, although several later fifth-century cemeteries were established near by. Even so, the high rate of deposition of late Roman coins within the town implies a special function in the last years of the Empire, when it may have been an important border town between the two southern provinces of the British diocese. As such it may have still required a share of the small number of available soldiers in the early fifth century. If the *civitates* remained significant in the early fifth century, then this looks like a frontier of some importance, close to which were the several borders of the Atrebates, the Catuvellauni and the Dobunni. Alternatively, if these *civitates* had been amalgamated into a single unit, this may have been the site from which they were administered.

The evidence is, therefore, consistent with the view that these graves reflect a late diocesan and early post-diocesan deployment of small numbers of soldiers equipped and recruited on the Continent, under Roman or Romano-British control.

The appearance of comparative normality breaks down north of the Thames. Within the first half of the fifth century, early cruciform brooches, equal-arm brooches, composite saucer brooches and supporting-arm brooches began to reach Britain, most being found in an area centred on East Anglia but overlapping with warrior inhumations in southern Essex and in the vicinity of Dorchester (Böhme 1986; **6.2**). This material culture and the cremations which accompanied it were characteristic of the areas of southern Denmark and north-west Germany with which the Angles and Saxons have traditionally been associated, and reached Britain unaffected by Romanizing influences.

Cremation had been the standard method of disposal in the Roman world in the early Empire, but was gradually abandoned in the second and third centuries. Quite independently, the rite remained in common use further north, throughout Germany, where its origins can be traced to the Bronze Age (possibly to the Neolithic), when comparable rites were present throughout Britain. Vast urnfields of the pre-Roman and Roman Iron Ages demonstrate the ubiquity of this rite, particularly in northern and western Germany where it persisted far into the post-Roman period. The ritual was integral to Germanic society and developed little; of the developments that did occur, several failed to reach Britain. Although some cemeteries of the Roman period in Germany, for example, display distinctive features such as sexual segregation, these traits are not found in England.

The arrival of urned cremation and personal jewellery characteristic of north-west *Germania* represents the earliest clear archaeological evidence of cultural contact between Britain and a part of Germany not already much affected by cultural contacts with Rome. Germanic immigration remains the single most likely mechanism for the arrival of this material in eastern Britain.

That this material is first encountered at the northern end of the old Saxon Shore may imply that immigrants followed the familiar European coastline to the northern reaches of the Channel, crossed from the mouth of the Rhine and made landfall on the north side of the Thames, in Essex or Suffolk. Thence it spread northwards up the North Sea coast of Britain, as well as inland to the middle Thames. The range of grave-goods implies that the immigrants were of both sexes.

Although further discussion should be expected, their burials have been dated relatively closely (Böhme 1986), without recourse to the literary sources. No objects of certain fourth-century date have been identified other than occasional antiques in later graves, but several cemeteries were in use well before the mid-fifth century. The total lack of Roman goods in the great cremation cemeteries of eastern England may imply that their settlement belongs to the decades after the breakdown of the Roman economic system, *c*. 420, and does nothing to support the notion that they could have been those of mercenary forces or treaty troops of the late fourth century (*contra* e.g. Myres 1969, 1986; followed by Morris 1973). The contrast between the early inhumations of southern England and the cremations of the east is clearly marked.

As Myres noted in 1969, the vast majority of all urns found in Britain have come from just ten cremation cemeteries. The numerical dominance of a small group of large cemeteries has, if anything, increased since then, with the total excavation of Spong Hill (Hills 1977; Hills and Penn 1981; Hills *et al.* 1984, 1987) yielding well in excess of the 2000 burials found at Loveden Hill. Whether these large cemeteries were used by single settlements or by dispersed communities is unclear. Recent excavations by the Norfolk Archaeological Unit have identified extensive early Saxon settlement adjacent to the Spong Hill cemetery which might be responsible for some, at least, of the burials there, and juxtaposed settlements and cemeteries are now commonly encountered elsewhere, but it remains quite possible that these massive and long-lived cemeteries accommodated many individuals from a distance.

What was the role of these eastern settlers? Böhme interpreted them as free Germans. One recent suggestion has been that they may have been the raiders of 409 or 410, who had emigrated from the seaboard of western Germany under pressure from marine incursions and political conflict (Hawkes 1989), and there is nothing intrinsically unlikely in this. It has long been recognized that a string of settlements on the *terpen* and *wurten* (mounds raised to provide dry sites for settlement) of the marshes of the Continental littoral were abandoned during the first half of the fifth century by groups whose material culture reflects that of the early cemeteries in England. Many of these communities had already proved themselves adaptable to changing sea levels (Brandt *et al.* 1984–5). However, around some sites agricultural pollen was not to reappear in significant amounts until the seventh century (Schmid 1977), suggesting that the environmental catastrophe which has been identified in the Dutch Rhineland *c.* 300 (Groenman-van Waateringe 1983) spread northwards over the following century and a half, and communities may have fled from this disaster.

However, this may be to make rather too much of the available evidence. Only comparatively small numbers of objects have been identified which indicate settlement in Britain before the middle of the fifth century, and, although many come from cemeteries where deposition continued into the sixth or seventh centuries, they are dispersed across a wide area, defined by the North Sea, the Thames below Dorchester and the Wash (**6.2**). Scholars are hard put to it to turn these early incomers into a tidal wave of immigrants, whether they were economic refugees or not.

Since they used cremation, they did not deposit weapons with their dead, a practice which had died out in Germany during the second and third centuries. However, these were families from free Germany, among whom a normal attribute of non-servile status was the use and possession of arms. We should, then, assume that warriors were numbered among them who may have seemed a formidable force to their immediate neighbours, the unarmed civilian gentry and peasants of the late Roman world. They settled in an area where there is no evidence of soldiers, once the northern end of the Saxon Shore system had been abandoned and the putative late garrison at Caistor withdrawn or dispersed. The local provincial community had no means of resisting them.

Their cemeteries are far from evenly distributed across the landscape. To an extent, this may be a matter of discrepancies in the discovery of sites. Cemeteries in this region have been found predominantly on the sands and gravels where quarries abound and aerial reconnaissance offers the best results, yet here too numbers have been augmented by recent field walking. It is possible that early arrivals may have enjoyed only a limited choice of settlement sites, and may have been excluded − or excluded themselves − from specific territories. Alternatively, they may have chosen to avoid specific areas and to scatter widely. Much depends on the view adopted of the social function of the immigrants. There appear to be marked discrepancies between different areas, sometimes reflected in the later Saxon hundreds. Whereas Blything Hundred (Suffolk) was characterized by the absence of pagan burials and by early Christianity (the first East Anglian see was at Dunwich), neighbouring Wicklaw Hundred had numerous pagan cemeteries which included Sutton Hoo, evidence of dislocation provided by six late Roman hoards, and a very different pattern of hundredal organization (Warner 1988). It is possible that such discrepancies mirror real differences in the pattern of early settlement, in which case successive British and Saxon rulers presumably exercised a degree of control over the geography of settlement.

Elsewhere, several Germanic cemeteries continue to use Roman extramural cemeteries (as at Ancaster), and site reuse later is common (as at Godmanchester; Green 1975). Others cluster around late Roman towns, such as Caistor or Cambridge. Myres (1969, 1986) offered the view that these burials reflected the fourth-century employment of north German troops as mercenaries to guard the northern Saxon Shore, but fourth-century finds do not occur within the towns themselves. More plausible is the suggestion that early settlers may have been attracted by or directed to important centres from which British *civitates* were still attempting to administer the collection of taxes in kind. If they were to be supplied from this source, the establishment of barbarian soldiers in the vicinity of the capital of the Iceni minimized the problems of supply and offered the tribal council advantages in their efforts to raise taxes from the peasantry around. Barbarian settlers in Britain were probably at least as independent in their attitudes towards local authority as those who were settling in Gaul, and freedom from taxation was probably fundamental to agreements between British rulers and Saxon incomers.

The distribution of these cemeteries suggests that, in the early decades of the settlement, the cremating Germanic population was comparatively small and scattered. It occupied territory which on the Thames overlapped with that of inhuming warriors, and the thin density of their early cemeteries implies that elsewhere they were scattered among the dwellings and farms of the less archaeologically visible indigenes. It is difficult to believe that such an immigrant community was initially completely independent of British society, whatever the nature of the relationship between the two.

It is possible that this evidence of Germanic immigration reflects the settlement which Gildas described, of barbarian forces employed by British élites ostensibly to guard against sea-borne barbarian raids. Attempts to interpret any particular body of archaeological evidence by linking it with Gildas's comments can be no more than speculative. However, the best fit at present would be the view that British leaders in the vicinity of the Saxon Shore to the north of the Thames recruited Saxon soldiers to bolster insular defences against sea-borne raiders of various nationalities now active in the ill-defended and vulnerable northern end of the Narrow Seas. Since troops recruited in Gaul and the Rhineland seem to have been monopolized by those in control of the short crossings of the Channel, whose interests lay within the southern half of Maxima Caesariensis, British leaders in East Anglia and the south-east Midlands had little option but to invite barbarian warriors from further north, that is, from the German homeland. These recruits then sucked in more of their own kind and later rebelled, taking control of a hotchpotch of territories in the east of England, from the North Sea to the middle Thames valley. If their example was followed by the inhuming soldiery of southern Britain, then the lower Thames valley was likewise separated from British control during this period.

There is one serious problem with this interpretation: the dating. To associate the earliest cremation cemeteries with the Gildas episode requires that we pull the conventional dating of his *adventus* back from the mid-century to the 420s or, at latest, 430s. There is, however, nothing intrinsically unlikely in this, since the internal dating of this section of the *De Excidio* depends entirely on the relationship between the *adventus* and the appeal to Aëtius, an event which Gildas is unlikely to have been able to date, and a document which he originally had to reconstruct. (see p. 156–7). The chronology of his *Historia* is in all other respects floating and the allocation of dates to separate parts of the story is a matter of conjecture (Dumville 1984a,b). It has already been suggested that Gildas is likely to have been writing in about 500, that is, several decades earlier than traditional dating would have us believe, and this would close the gap without difficulty. The rebellion of the Germanic mercenaries must have occurred before 441, if the Gallic Chronicles are to be reconciled with the *De Excidio*, and a build-up of Germanic mercenaries in the 420s and 430s is otherwise entirely consistent with the description of Gildas.

Archaeological evidence is very different in kind from that of literature and it will probably never be possible to offer anything more than suggestions concerning the links between them during the fifth century. However, both techniques have as their object the study of the past and links must exist and should be kept in mind. As things stand, there are major objections to the view that Gildas was referring to the recruitment of German mercenaries in the Rhineland by southern British leaders under the threat or even the reality of settlement in East Anglia of German 'backwoodsmen'. One is his insistence that the earliest English settlement was in the east of the island, a description which matches East Anglia to perfection but which correlates less well with the distribution of early inhumation cemeteries. Another is his apparent belief that the incomers came from the 'Saxon' homeland, rather than from the Roman Rhineland.

Another suggestion is that the Hengest episode should be identified in Kent, where distinctive Jutish pottery, bracteates and small numbers of early cremating urns have survived from the second half of the fifth century (Hawkes 1982). However, the *De Excidio* would have lost much of its impact if its audience had known the episode described was other than the first occasion when free Germans settled in Britain. We should be loath to assume either that Gildas took such a chance or that his audience was that ignorant. However, in the last resort any of these views are tenable and all have obvious advantages over recent attempts to place Gildas's Saxons in north-east England: archaeological traces of their presence are conspicuous by their absence beyond Yorkshire until the sixth century.

The revolt of their mercenary soldiers left British leaders powerless to intervene in the south and east of Britain, and the earliest Germanic cemeteries rapidly increased in number and spread to new areas. In the mid-fifth century, a series of cemeteries, largely of accompanied inhumations, was established in eastern Sussex (Welch 1976, 1983). That at Bishopstone at least was directly adjacent to a settlement and probably contained the dead from that community. Crop marks at Alfriston may imply a similar situation there, where burials were generally richly accoutred, with finds including beads of amber, rock-crystal, glass and porcelain. At Highdown, cremations occurred alongside inhumations, within and over a prehistoric defensive enclosure on a steep elevation above the coastal plain.

It has long been postulated that this group of burials resulted from a *foedus* with the British authorities at Chichester, since intrusive material of this period was long lacking from the richer, villa-dominated western plain of the *civitas*, occurring predominantly east of the Ouse and west of the Cuckmere (Morris 1965; Welch 1971). However, the discovery and excavation of a fifth − seventh century cemetery at Apple Down north of Chichester during the 1980s require that this view be abandoned. The suggestion that Highdown represents a settlement of strategic significance is also contentious. The site is one which may already have had considerable religious significance and the presence of a Roman villa on the slopes of the hill implies that it was the established focus of a local estate. The positioning of their burial ground at this focal point suggests that the Anglo-Saxons were conforming to existing patterns of settlement hierarchy in the area, establishing themselves precisely where their apparent wealth would seem to place them, at the apex of local society, displacing the pre-existing aristocratic household. Finds from the cemetery imply links with the Rhineland but weapons are not numerous, although the cemetery remained in use well into the sixth century.

During the second half of the fifth century, women's brooches typical of manufacture in north-west Germany spread throughout the upper Thames valley and the southern Midlands, Surrey, Sussex and Hampshire, with isolated examples elsewhere (**6.3**). Comparable pieces characteristic of Anglian or Jutish manufacture and associated with cremation spread in a deep belt around the Wash and in eastern Kent, with outliers in Yorkshire, and reached the Tyne by about 500 (Böhme 1986; Hawkes 1989). Along the Thames, inhumations accoutred with comparatively rich Frankish grave-goods suggest that links between the Rhineland and southern England continued, but north Germanic material was now numerically dominant, albeit largely in association with inhumation rather than cremation.

During the same period, numerous new cemeteries were established. Rites of cremation retained a dominant role in mortuary practice in eastern England above the Thames, and inhumation remained the standard rite below the Thames. Between the two, numerous cemeteries were eventually to contain both rites, either successively or in parallel (**6.4**), and several areas with early signs of mixed rites retained both practices over the next century. Regionalism and conservatism in this respect are both traits long recognized and well marked, which suggest that habits established locally within the fifth century, and often within the early to mid-fifth century, were often decisive in determining the rites used in the majority of graves within a cemetery throughout the pagan era. Although it has been suggested that in Kent, for example, inhumation replaced or drove out cremation of an early stage, the new rite was firmly entrenched within the fifth century. The rapid ossification of ritual makes it unlikely that fresh Germanic immigration occurred on a scale sufficiently massive to entirely alter the pattern of deposition in any of the early areas of settlement in the sixth century, in which case new recruitment to the Germanic colonies in Britain was via such channels of contact between Germany and England as were already established.

Status, population and ethnicity

The dispersal of Anglo-Saxon mortuary rites and material culture continued until the seventh century and mirrored the social, cultural and linguistic dominance which the communities using them rapidly came to exercise over the British lowlands.

The spread of Germanic equipment has generally been interpreted as indicative of the arrival and dispersal of incomers from communities scattered across north-west Europe, from the Rhineland to southern Scandinavia, and no one would argue against a degree of new immigration throughout the late fifth century, perhaps on into the early sixth. However, there are major problems of interpretation remaining when we turn to the scale of such postulated migrations. The central issue must be the confusion in the archaeological record between two separate but linked processes: those of immigration and of acculturation. Both are represented archaeologically by intrusive material in groups which can be comparatively consistent. How can we distinguish between migration and other forms of cultural contact?

Within a Germanic context, this problem has already been highlighted by the discussion of the Scandinavian input to the Anglian areas of eastern England (Hines 1984). An examination of material culture has identified a series of diagnostic artefacts (square-headed brooches, bracteates and sleeve clasps, for example) common to Anglian England (particularly Norfolk and Humberside), south-west Norway, Denmark and the Swedish Upland. Parallel developments in grave construction and ritual have also been identified. From this evidence, Hine has argued plausibly for continuing and complex forms of contact, including material exchange, two-way migration and ideological links across the North Sea. The mechanisms he postulates are not very dissimilar from those by which the material and ideological culture of Roman Britain was tied to that of the Empire. However, trade probably played a more significant role in the latter and gift exchange in the former, as young men sought patrons or brides in distant lands, in some of which they inherited a tradition of family contacts from earlier kinsmen.

However, the grave-goods used to imply contact between Scandinavia and East Anglia in the sixth and seventh centuries are no less, in context or in quantity, than those used to substantiate migration from north Germany to eastern England in the fifth century (Carver 1989). What has changed is not so much the material evidence as the standpoint of the investigator, who has chosen to challenge the established view that almost any imported grave-good represents an immigrant, in favour of a more complex view of cultural contact and exchange.

It is occasionally possible to demonstrate that an import was unlikely to have come with an immigrant. For example, the Frankish jewellery found widely in Kentish graves (Huggett 1988) was on occasion associated with Anglo-Saxon styles of dress and not always worn in the Frankish style (Owen-Crocker 1986), so perhaps not by a Frank. Such observations place discussion of immigration and ethnic origin in context. Elsewhere, the mixture of Anglian, Saxon, Celtic and even antique Roman grave-goods is such that the finds give no real clue to the ethnic identity of the occupant, outside the broad adoption of what we have learned to describe as an Anglo-Saxon culture.

The debt owed by Germanic inhumation rites to Roman ritual was immense. Although orientation alone cannot be sufficient to judge the religious opinions or ethnicity of an individual, the vast majority of Anglo-Saxon inhumations are orientated in a manner which would not be out of place in a Christian churchyard (Faull 1977). Nor was barrow burial necessarily an import. It was employed in Britain in the Roman period and was still in use in Wales in the sixth century. Many ancient barrows formed the foci of Anglo-Saxon cemeteries, just as they did Germanic cemeteries on the Continent, and as such presumably performed an important role in determining where a cemetery, and therefore perhaps a settlement, would be sited. Conversely, square-ditched graves at St Peter's, Broadstairs (Hogarth 1973) might recall late Romano-Christian practice, contemporary use of square-ditched barrows in Scotland and Wales, or mausolea in Christian Gaul.

Links between British and English burial practices are not uncommon. While inhumation appears to have come with troops from the Rhineland into fifth-century Britain, the rites used were so little different from those practised within the late Roman community in Britain that a shift by Britons from one to the other is entirely plausible. It is difficult to imagine how we might identify the burial of a Briton who had adopted Anglo-Saxon styles of dress and ornamentation.

This problem of acculturation is not one which will be easily solved, but it should not be ignored. We are confronted by two cultural and ideological traditions, one of which was spreading and comparatively profligate in its deposition of long-lasting artefacts. The other was geographically in retreat, had suffered a collapse in artefact production, and had inherited ideologies which discouraged furnished burial. The identification of British graves is fraught with difficulties, whether they are sought in the Celtic west or the English east of Britain. We are in no position to make statements about the probable incidence of British survival on this basis.

It is easier to speculate about population levels than ethnicity, although the two subjects are obviously linked. The rate of deposition in Anglo-Saxon cemeteries rose from modest beginnings in the early to mid-fifth century to a climax in the late sixth and seventh, when entire new cemeteries of accompanied inhumations came into use at the dawn of the new Christian era (e.g. Winnall II, Meaney and Hawkes 1970). At Buckland, deposition seems to have occurred only about once every four years in the late fifth century, compared with every two or three years, *c.* 700 (Evison 1987), a significant rate of increase.

The traditional explanation of this phenomenon is to postulate an increase in the immigrant population, either through fresh immigration or through an internal excess of births over deaths. However, migration is unlikely to have been significant by the mid-sixth century, and it was certainly not the force behind increases in the seventh century. Furthermore, it is unlikely to have augmented the population of individual small settlements of the kind presumed to be associated with the Buckland cemetery at Dover.

If fresh immigration was not responsible for the exponential rise in the numbers of burials in the sixth century, was it the result of population increase within Anglo-Saxon society? The possibility has been discussed *ad absurdum* (Arnold 1984) but palaeobotanical evidence is as hostile to a general and massive population increase in lowland Britain during the fifth and sixth centuries as it is to a massive collapse in the fifth century. Such suggestions are in limbo until better evidence is forthcoming.

There remains the possibility that this increase was a result of acculturation, by which local Britons were gradually integrated into the Anglo-Saxon social and cultural system through a process of recruitment internal to the local community.

The number of Anglo-Saxon cemeteries exceeds 1500 and burials must be numbered in several tens of thousands. However, these must be spread over at least 10 generations and possibly as many as 15, giving a population so far identified as averaging only 2000−3000 per generation. One recent estimate suggests that we have identified the graves of only 0.2−1 per cent of the population of lowland Britain (Campbell 1982), and there are vast gaps, particularly in the fifth century, when numerous areas (like the Chilterns) appear, on this evidence, as almost totally unpopulated. Yet the land was kept comparatively clear of woodland. Obviously, it is necessary to assess how representative these cemeteries are of the total population.

It is well established that the indigenous élite of lowland Britain had shown itself susceptible to incoming funerary practices throughout the first half of the first millennium AD. In the fifth century, a series of social, linguistic and ideological barriers may have stood between parts of this élite and the adoption of Germanic culture. Committed Christian civilians took to flight and sought social contexts which demanded of them less flexibility. However, the more far-sighted, along with some of their social inferiors, may not have been so severely inhibited: the latter were already disadvantaged within the highly exploitative Roman system, with low legal and economic status, yet undefended except by the use of mercenaries by their landlords; they were less likely to be committed to Christianity, and Germanic and Celtic paganism were closer in many respects than either was to Christianity. Links between the latter and the repressive state of the later Roman period are unlikely to have made it overwhelmingly attractive to the British peasantry. There may have been, among the peasantry of fifth-century Britain, many who welcomed the arrival of Germanic chieftains and the comparative security which they could offer (as implied White, 1988). Many may have taken advantage of the changing pattern of social control to shed the peasant status to which high population levels and powerful social hierarchies had reduced them during the Roman period. Their obvious route towards a greater freedom was to adopt the material, ideological and linguistic culture of the Anglo-Saxons. We should, therefore, expect Britons who had been freed from the late Roman system of social control and exposed to contact with Anglo-Saxon immigrants to be hammering on the doors of Anglo-Saxon cemeteries by the later fifth century.

There have been attempts to identify a British element within Anglo-

Saxon cemeteries, on the basis of accompanying objects and of orientation (Faull 1977) and it may be possible to argue on this basis that specific individuals were British and retained British beliefs into the Anglo-Saxon world. Some categories of British goods were deposited in Anglo-Saxon cemeteries, and may betray the cultural sympathies of those buried (e.g. Longley 1975).

However, the roll-call is neither long nor convincing. Despite local peculiarities, such as the crouched burials of the north-east which are likely to be indigenous (Eagles 1979), Anglo-Saxon burials do not generally hold individuals dressed or buried in styles which are specifically Roman or British, and coins are used for purposes quite divorced from traditional Roman rites (White 1988). It would be incautious to argue on this basis that many Britons were buried in Anglo-Saxon cemeteries (Rahtz 1978). The balance of immigrant to native cannot be established by this sort of reasoning. Among cremations, it is difficult to detect indigenous influence of any kind. However, this apparent diffidence on the part of putative Britons may be explicable.

The ritual of deposition was a public event, as is graphically illustrated in *Beowulf*. We should not be surprised if those responsible for any one burial took the opportunity to make a statement appropriate to the status, gender, age and religious beliefs of the individual. Computer analysis of the characteristics and associations of a large group of urns (Richards 1987) has suggested that urn design was not solely decorative but related to other facets of the individual that the relicts wished to stress, such as age, sex and status. This plausible suggestion will obviously create difficulties in reconstructing chronological typologies for funerary pottery which are in any way meaningful, and contemporary scholarship will not find it an easy matter to break the codes underlying burial ritual, with or without the help of a computer.

There are clear indications of exceptional status in many cemeteries. Of the 365 inhumations and 9 cremations excavated at Morning Thorpe, perhaps 4 burials were surrounded by a ditch and probably covered by some sort of barrow (Greene *et al.* 1987). Most of the 57 inhumations at Spong Hill were coffined but very few were in chambered tombs (or mausolea), and covered by barrows. One (Grave 40) was accompanied by an antique sword and influenced the orientation of other inhumations. The two most obvious barrows contained graves which were exceptionally well accoutred and accompanied by objects that were unique within the cemetery (Hills *et al.* 1984). At Snape, a cemetery which is famous for its ship burial also contained several further barrows of very varying size, beneath some, at least, of which were richly accompanied inhumations (Filmer-Sankey 1984; **6.5**).

High-status burial may occur in a cemetery where individuals of lower status were normally interred. Certain accessories are exclusive to such burials, such as gold braids and glass claw-beakers. Across the country, a small number of sixth- and seventh-century burials are exceptional for the complexity of the rites used and the number, value and wide associations of the objects deposited within the grave. Such include the ship burials at Snape and the specialist and high-status cemetery at Sutton Hoo (Bruce-Mitford 1975–83; Carver 1989; **6.6**), and other princely burials such as those at Taplow (Crowfoot and Hawkes 1967), Coombe (Ellis Davidson and Webster 1967) and Eastry (Hawkes 1979). The last of these can be hesitantly fitted into the social and territorial organization of the kingdom of Kent, where Eastry was a lathe focus, associated spatially with Wood-nesborough – a place-name which might indicate a pagan shrine.

These instances are few and late. Most graves are less clearly distinguishable by status. Early attempts to apply a crude system of numerical analysis to determine the status of the occupant have been refined by more detailed work, as on 234 inhumations at Sleaford Lincs., (Brenan 1984–5). It seems clear that no simple interpretation of status will be applicable across the length and breadth of Anglo-Saxon England; graves in areas such as Yorkshire are far less well accoutred than are those of Kent or Sussex, for example. There may be a link between the economic well-being of the community and the readiness of relicts to bury valuable possessions with the dead. Furthermore, the absence of grave-goods in some instances may be due to factors other than status, such as religious beliefs, or specific social roles, in the case of priests for example. Unaccompanied burials need not necessarily be of the poor. The ritual of deposition probably reflected the attitudes and aspirations of those responsible, rather than merely the social attributes of the dead person. In addition, the problem has a chronological facet, since many unaccompanied burials arguably belong to the Christian era.

Many of these cemeteries were still in use in the generation which produced the first written Anglo-Saxon law code, that of Æthelberht in Kent (Attenborough 1922), which contained much which would have been familiar to a German contemporary of Tacitus. This document demonstrates the presence in Kentish society *c.* 600 of numerous classes below the rank of the ceorl: we hear of female grinding-slaves of several different sorts attached to the royal household and to those of eorls and ceorls; ceorls regularly had a variety of dependants. The 'læts' who were immediately dependent upon these free classes, with a wergild which was dependent on the status not of themselves but of their masters or landlords, were apparently peasant farmers.

The picture that emerges from the laws is of a highly hierarchical society, within which the legal status of an individual was determined by his or her place in a complex class system. Many classes, probably containing the majority of the population, were of a status lower than that of the lowest rank of the 'law-worthy' and it has often been inferred that the lower classes were predominantly British, although læts also occur in Continental law codes and the term alone was not an indicator of ethnicity.

The seventh-century laws of Ine of Wessex discriminate in legal worth between the Saxons and the Britons alongside them, even when the latter were of free status. Later confusion in the Anglo-Saxon language between a Briton and a slave implies that most Britons within Anglo-Saxon society were of low class, descendants of those sectors of the local Romano-British peasantry who had so far failed to rise into the lower ranks of free tribal society, or had been recruited from neighbouring British communities by enslavement (see p. 193).

Anglo-Saxon burial rites seem to have been capable of conveying numerous messages, some perhaps of considerable subtlety. Indeed, the principal purpose of the relatively complex group of rites adopted may have been to advertise the social position of the deceased and his heirs. Such overt display for social purposes may have been necessitated by the considerable stresses which society was undergoing during the phase of transition in which England began. However, to broadcast the ethnic origins of a Briton in a society dominated by Anglo-Saxons invited the social and legal demotion of his heirs. Where they gained admittance to Anglo-Saxon cemeteries, British burials were probably as orthodox as possible. Where we can distinguish Britons it seems likely that local knowledge of Anglo-Saxon rites was flawed, and the entire social hierarchy was predominantly British, imperfectly acculturated to Anglo-Saxon ways. Such surely applies among the crouched inhumation cemeteries of Yorkshire.

Were agricultural workers and slaves generally, buried interspersed with their social superiors, or even in the same cemeteries? Among early interpretations of cemetery material, the question was irrelevant because Anglo-Saxon society was perceived as comparatively unhierarchical. Writing of great square-headed brooches, Leeds saw them as 'the ornaments of peasant agriculturalists among whom, too, grades of status and wealth must have existed' (Leeds 1949: 121). Such a view was conditioned by the historical tradition then current that the Anglo-Saxons were an egalitarian folk, but the historical assumptions on which this view was based can no longer be accepted. The extent of cultural contacts across the English and Continental cemeteries is remarkable, and implies that close links were maintained over two centuries or more across England and parts of the Continent. Peasant communities are unlikely to have achieved this network of wide and repeating connections, which are far more plausible within the upper tiers of a social hierarchy within which numerous young men borne to high status but without substantial lands opted for armed service as an alternative to farming, by entry to the household of a powerful man as a *gesith*, an armed retainer (Wormald 1978).

Weapons, even including spears, are not compatible with low status, let alone slavery, and the ornaments which were the normal grave-goods of women of comparable status should probably be viewed in a similar light. Such objects were all of comparatively high value, and were probably the exclusive preserve of the kings, eorls and, less certainly, the wealthier ceorls, and their households.

If this society had a wealth and status gradient comparable to that of Roman Britain or medieval England, then the rural workforce should have outnumbered the gentry and aristocracy by about 10:1. Such is not a common wealth profile within an Anglo-Saxon cemetery. In some, such as Eastry, it has been suggested that all social classes were present, but this example was probably the cemetery attached to a royal palace, and so is exceptional. At Buckland, the lower classes seem almost entirely absent. It follows that the agricultural workforce of the fifth and sixth centuries is unlikely to have been any better represented in the cemeteries of the day than were their forebears under a Romanized and urbanized aristocracy. They were to remain poorly represented until the Christian Church expanded its network of graveyards and funerary charges into every local community in the tenth and eleventh centuries.

One group of low-status graves can be identified in Anglo-Saxon cemeteries, where they occur in direct dependence on a small scatter of affluent burials. There are a few instances of double interments, where an individual of low status seems to have been buried with one of high status, perhaps even buried alive or killed for the purpose. A series of unusual graves at Sutton Hoo contained corpses in extravagant postures, and nine of the ten graves excavated around the high-status burial within 'mound' 5 (6.6) have been interpreted as sacrificial victims (Carver 1989). One of these burials was equipped with a plough (5.12). Another was a double inhumation (6.7). All probably contain demesne farm and household servants or slaves rather than the local farming population, dispatched to the next world in attendance on their patron or owner, an individual of the highest rank.

It seems probable that many Anglo-Saxon cemeteries, like Finglesham (Hawkes 1958), contain the remains of the households of the social élite, distinguished by their freedom at law and possession of a free wergild. Such included the kings and aristocracy and the warrior class, and perhaps their dependants and household staff, even down to the level of slaves. There is no reason to believe that the rural communities outside these focal households were normally buried beside their social superiors. An escalation of Anglo-Saxon type burial in the sixth century need denote no more than the gradual integration of surviving Britons into the Anglo-Saxon legal and social system and the culture that was its hallmark. In late anglicized Bernicia, the presence of only small numbers of high-status burials may imply that an Anglo-Saxon aristocracy was still culturally and socially distinct from the remainder of society until the conversion to Christianity in the seventh century.

The continuation of this process carried Anglo-Saxon burial rites into ever new areas, such as the Derbyshire Peak, where the rite seems to have been adopted only by a small élite, who emphasized their high status not

6.6   General view from the air of intervention 41, showing mounds 2 and 5, Sutton Hoo. The several secondary inhumations were associated with mound 5, to the right of the picture (courtesy of Nigel Macbeth, Sutton Hoo Research Trust).

only by the deposition of elaborate grave-goods with far-flung and complex parallels but also by the reuse of many of the ancient burial cairns that were a feature of their landscape (Ozanne 1962–3; Collis 1983). Such may have been boundary burials, the impetus for which could have come as easily from Celtic as from English customs. It is impossible to determine whether these graves contain the bodies of ethnic Anglo-Saxons or the anglicized aristocracy of a British community, who had 'become English' under the influence of the Mercian political and military hegemony. In such a context, the use of the term 'Anglo-Saxon' is acceptable as an indicator of a cultural tradition, but not of ethnicity.

The recent revival in the study of cemetery material by physical anthro-pologists is unlikely to solve the knotty problem of ethnicity, even when samples are drawn from the very latest Romano-British cemeteries and the very earliest Germanic inhumations (e.g. Stuckert 1980, quoted by Arnold 1984; see discussion in Renfrew 1987). It is impossible to be certain what proportion of the genetic material in a Roman cemetery in Britain is British rather than deriving from the pool of the Empire, if only because late Roman cemeteries of any size are exclusively outside towns

6.7 Double inhumation, with some bone surviving, on the buried soil peripheral to and east of mound 5, Sutton Hoo (courtesy of Nigel Macbeth, Sutton Hoo Research Trust).

wherein were concentrated the genes of immigrants from the rest of the Roman world. What is needed is a cemetery used exclusively by the rural community of late Roman Britain. Without this as a starting-point, it is difficult to imagine any value in comparisons between the skeletal remains in late Roman and early Saxon cemeteries, or from different groups within an Anglo-Saxon cemetery. By the sixth century, it is entirely possible that some cemeteries that can be diagnosed as Anglo-Saxon on cultural criteria were dominated by British stock; others could be entirely immigrant. We have not in England the distinctive skeletal deformities which have enabled scholars in Hungary to positively identify fifth-century Pannonians (Salamon and Lengyel 1980–1). We will not have the yardstick by which to assess the remains until scientists are able to use genetic fingerprinting on a vast scale, and early essays in that direction have not so far provided the critical information (e.g. Mitchell and Sunderland 1978). At this stage, the extent of gene penetration from Germany into England during the fifth and sixth centuries remains imponderable, but historians and archaeologists alike have tended to overemphasize the process, rather than the reverse.

The study of fifth- and sixth-century English cemeteries provides numerous insights into the societies that used them and the dispersal of the culture which they represent. It does not provide answers to the problems of ethnic continuity or discontinuity across the same period, and cultural unity may be an illusion created by the dominant role played by high-status sections of the community within many cemeteries. Significant sections of the community may be seriously under-represented. The search for these takes us back to the landscape, the systems by which it was managed and the settlements from which it was husbanded throughout the period.

CHAPTER SEVEN

LANGUAGE, PLACE-NAMES AND ETHNICITY

The preceding chapters have offered a re-examination of late Roman, sub-Roman and early Saxon society through the techniques of archaeology and history, with a view to establishing the degree of ethnic continuity from late Roman Britain to the early medieval period. The evidence so far examined points to an interpretation of the Anglo-Saxon *adventus* primarily as a warrior and high-status take-over of lowland Britain, rather than as a mass migration. On this assessment, the bulk of the Anglo-Saxon community could have been recruited internally from Britons, some of whom were able to take advantage of the transitional period to slough off the role of unfree peasant, while others continued to occupy the lower and less privileged strata in the social hierarchy, despite profound changes in the social system consequent on the collapse of Roman Britain.

However, it is English that we speak, not Welsh or a romance derivative of vulgar Latin. Place-name scholars have traditionally opposed all élitist views of the English settlement on precisely this point. The Germanist or folk interpretation of the English settlement depends heavily upon the opinion that:

> The smallness in number of words of British origin relating to agriculture or to domestic economy, to general household goods and services, is strong evidence against a substantial survival of British peasants and women-folk in Anglo-Saxon England.
>
> (Loyn 1962: 6)

The most complete trawl for British words in Anglo-Saxon has so far failed to bring the number as high as twenty (Jackson 1953).

A comparison has been made between the English input to place-name formation and that of the Romans, the Scandinavians and the Normans. The principal bench-mark has been the last of these, since it is by far the best documented. The Norman settlement was élitist and numerically small. Since the Normans had very little impact on place-name formation in England, it has been argued that an influx to Britain of small and élite groups *per se* would have the same limited effect. This view underlies most attempts to write history from the evidence of place-names but has rarely been expressed as succinctly as here:

Attempts to represent the Anglo-Saxons as a small aristocracy break down in the face of the place-name evidence... To bring about a change of language in most of the place-names, the number of the newcomers must be relatively high and the social status of the majority of them relatively low.

(Gelling 1976: 201–3)

If this is true, then there must be something fundamentally wrong with the arguments already laid out concerning settlement, society and the landscape. Not surprisingly, archaeologists and some historians have shrunk from such a conclusion and several scholarly works have recently appeared which virtually ignore place-name scholarship (e.g. Taylor 1983) or have all but denied its value (e.g. Myres 1986) – a stance which has understandably attracted an adverse response from place-name specialists (e.g. Gelling 1988b). We are in danger of confrontation between the practitioners of different research methods when we should be seeking ways of reconciling one method with another, and one set of conclusions with another.

As a generalization, the one quoted above suffers from two significant shortcomings: it uses a logical *non sequitur* and it confuses two phenomena best kept separate. The Norman invasion was certainly achieved by small numbers of persons who were predominantly of high status and it is agreed that it had little impact on place-names. It is not agreed that that association is sufficient of itself to suggest that the reverse is *necessarily* true, that is, that a profound impact on place-naming can only result from the influx of large numbers of immigrants, predominantly of low status. Such an argument entirely ignores the possibility that other factors might be involved and pre-empts what ought to be a valid and fruitful area of discussion among place-name specialists. The second problem is that this stance fails to distinguish between the replacement of one language by another and of one set of place-names by another. The former is an occasional phenomenon, but the latter is **ongoing**, occurring in all societies with a rapidity dependent in part on changes in the structure of settlement. The process of place-name change will only involve replacement with names derived from a different language when language change has occurred. However, the incidence of replacement need not be dependent on the adoption of a new language. Confusion between these two phenomena has stemmed from a confusion between language and ethnicity which begs the questions which are here being examined.

Language change

The Norman Conquest of England is an example of an aristocratic take-over which had little impact on place-name formation. However, there are other instances of élite dominance with a very different outcome.

An obvious contrast is with the Roman take-over of Gaul and Spain, where an indigenous population which numbered millions abandoned its own languages in favour of the Latin spoken by the few tens of thousands of soldiers and merchants who entered the country from Italy, whom very few of the indigenes ever met. By the end of the fourth century, the survival of Gaulish is improbable, yet the number of Celtic loan-words in Latin was small (about 150), common to vulgar Latin throughout the West but specific to certain subjects (including wheeled vehicles and clothes). That many pre-Roman place-names survived is due to the comparative immobility of settlement thereafter. New names were Latin-based.

Other parallels exist within Britain and Brittany. A recent survey estimated the population of one of the several tribes of Roman Brittany, the *civitas Coriosolites*, at 250,000 in the second century (Langouet and Daire 1989), and even in the fifth century we must allow a figure higher than this for the whole peninsula. Given that the linguistic evidence strongly favours formative contacts between Brittany and the never densely populated south-west of England, there are major problems in the way of interpreting the settlement of Brittany as a mass migration of Britons which swamped the local population by force of numbers (note the difficulties experienced by Jackson 1953: 16−27). Contemporary French scholarship is tending towards a theory of élite dominance, with successive and continuing linguistic and cultural influences from south-west Britain over a long period affecting a society vulnerable to cultural and linguistic influence and easily pushed into transition (e.g. Fleuriot 1980; Galliou 1986). The reintroduction of a Celtic language into Brittany highlights the social and cultural differences between Romano-German Gaul (and lowland Britain) and Atlantic Britain and Gaul in the fifth and sixth centuries (Wild 1976−7).

The introduction of Gaelic (Q-Celtic) to Scotland is another important instance. This appears to have been the result of the migration of a single, small Irish tribe to a new homeland on the west coast of Scotland around Argyll, where the kingdom of Dalriada took over territory, and possibly also populations, previously speaking Pictish and/or British. The Picts remained the largest of the northern language groups, in possession of the richest agricultural lands of Fife and Angus, and their kings frequently exercised a degree of overkingship over the Scots. However, in the mid-ninth century, Kenneth mac Álpin took advantage of a temporary weakness of Pictish leadership to move his own people to the east coast and establish the kingdom of Scone, a kingdom which was necessarily composed of a majority of low-status Picts but dominated by a secular and ecclesiastical élite who were Scottish. The language of the latter rapidly droveout the now lost language of the Picts. *Pit-* place-names, meaning 'a piece of land', are commonly combined with a Gaelic suffix and were probably the product of a bilingual period in the late ninth and tenth centuries (Nicolaisen 1976). The Scottish take-over of British-speaking Stratchlyde in the eleventh century also arguably left the local population in occupation, but they abandoned their language, probably within a few generations. In contrast, the seizure of the Lothians with their English-speaking population did not result in the conversion of that area to the Gaelic language; the English language was probably reprieved by major political and cultural developments associated with Queen Margaret and her children after the Norman Conquest of England.

Cornish died out as a spoken language in favour of English, without any known mass migration into the area by English speakers during the twelfth and thirteenth centuries. Similarly, Gaelic and Welsh have suffered severe decline, abandoned in favour of English even by communities which are ethnically largely untouched by immigration.

From all these instances it becomes clear that there is no direct correlation between language and ethnicity. It is not uncommon for entire societies to abandon an existing language in favour of an alternative. The incidence of this occurring does not depend merely on the relative numerical strengths of the two language groups at any stage in the process, but on a variety of comparatively complex factors which can only be touched upon in this context. The languages of secular patronage and of religious observance clearly play a part in this equation; it was after all largely the appearance of a Welsh bible that saved Welsh from extinction in the modern era. Societies in transition — in the process of fundamental reorientation — were clearly vulnerable to the introduction of a new language where that became identified with the new social fabric and the ideology and value system which upheld it. Language also plays a fundamental role as an indicator of group identity, and those wishing to confirm their membership of a specific group are likely to adopt the language by which group members communicate and identify themselves. All these facets, and more, are relevant to the interface between Britons and Anglo-Saxons.

Early Anglo-Saxon society was hierarchical, and distinctions between different ranks were of considerable legal and social importance. Anthropological differences between immigrant and indigene were entirely inadequate to divide one from another, so that distinctions between them for social and legal purposes were expressed by such indications as public notoriety, physical culture — clothing, for example — and language. When English speakers created place-names using the element *w(e)alh* ('Welshman') in a genitive plural (*wala*), they were recognizing the distinctive 'Welshness' of those living in that particular community (Faull 1975; Cameron 1979). Although it has often been stressed that this attribution did not necessarily depend on their speaking Welsh, it is likely that this was one of several factors by which they could be distinguished. A more critical factor may have been an inability to speak English.

Such names could only have been of any value as labels when Welsh speakers were few in any one area. They occur widely, suggesting that this use suggested itself quite naturally (even spontaneously) to English speakers at a specific stage in the disappearance of the British language. They were, therefore, probably created comparatively late in the process of the decline of British as a spoken language within England, at a date which will have varied with the chronology of its decline in each area. The tendency of place-names in *walh* to occur on the periphery of early territories or estates may imply that they represented the last community within a particular economic and social system to bow to a process of anglicization emanating from the centre and affecting local communities through the hierarchy of government, of tenure and of patronage.

The term *w(e)alh* was eventually to become synonymous with slavery in the Old English of the ninth to eleventh centuries. The correlation already existed but in a less extreme form in the seventh century, when even Britons credited with personal freedom by Ine's laws were denied the full wergild of their Saxon counterparts. Beneath them, the mass of the unfree population was probably indigenous. In important respects, this society was one which practised apartheid. Being British was an indication of low status and of low worth in early Anglo-Saxon society.

In such a society, the speaking of Welsh was a liability which mattered in the critical circumstances when an individual sought to defend his personal security or to better his social, economic and legal position. It seems likely that the British population remaining in territory taken over by Anglo-Saxons learned English and eventually abandoned their native language under this stimulus. One might surmise that the process was led by high-ranking Britons who successfully made the transition to the core of nascent Anglo-Saxon élites. Some of these scaled the very heights of the Anglo-Saxon social system, as evidenced by the scatter of individuals whose Celtic names – such as Cerdic and the later Cædwalla – appear as incongruous non-English elements in the (admittedly largely unhistorical) genealogies of the early Anglo-Saxon kings. Others may have been crossing the cultural divide as late as the seventh century, when Merewalh; 'illustrious Welshman' was more likely to have been a Welsh king who was a political client of the Mercian royal house, than a son of Penda who had been given an outlandish name, as Goscelin would have us believe. In the 620s the Hwicce, Wrekin-dweller and people of Elmet were all British. A century later they were 'English'. Relatively prosperous farmers within territories where leadership and patronage had fallen to English kings or warriors probably found it advantageous rapidly to follow suit so as to avoid the risk of enslavement and to gain access to the Anglo-Saxon system of patronage and protection at law; such men may have pressurized their neighbours to take the same step, since the status of the entire kindred was at risk. British slaves in English households were naturally encouraged to adopt the language of their masters.

The adoption of the English language was a prerequisite of acceptance into the warrior and élitist society that lay at the heart of the Anglo-Saxon world. Some ceorls (probably those on royal estates) were expected to serve the *fierd* and the ability to pass as English was presumably a prerequisite of social advancement or material reward (*Laws of Ine* cap. 51)

Since this category at law eventually ceased to exist, the Welshmen who were segregated by law in seventh-century Wessex were eventually integrated into the ranks of Anglo-Saxon society, though whether or not to equivalent status groups we do not know. It seems probable that the same process was occurring from the beginning in all parts of England, and on a massive scale, starting where immigration was earliest and spreading out as Anglo-Saxon élites seized further territories.

The peculiar nature of the Anglo-Saxon settlement made Englishness attractive and access to it feasible to individuals of British extraction. The early Anglo-Saxon communities were small and geographically scattered, without political cohesion on any scale. Each had its own miniature social hierarchy. Each was in competition with its neighbours. Many were land-locked. While their needs for military manpower clearly sucked in adventurers from the Continent, there was also an outward flow, with Saxon settlers from Britain perhaps establishing themselves in parts of Gaul, and more certainly maintaining contact with Germany. The manpower needs of early East Anglia, the upper Thames valley or Kent provided an opportunity for those of the indigenes who were already well placed within the social system to adapt themselves to the culture of the dominant group, so necessarily swelling the English-speaking population, just as the 'foreign Gaels' bolstered the Norse in Ireland. Such internal recruitment was probably crucial to the success of early English societies and the nature of the process means that even in areas of primary English settlement there need be no close link between language and ethnicity after the first generation or two. A similar phenomenon was not unknown on the Continent, where the Burgundian settlement in south-east France provides an obvious parallel, if one where the imposition of a Germanic language was ultimately unsuccessful.

The social circumstances of internal recruitment required acculturation on a scale which enabled erstwhile Britons to pass for Saxons. It has long been recognized that surviving Britons became bilingual and eventually abandoned their native tongue in favour of English. It is also clear that Britons adopted Anglo-Saxon with extraordinary precision:

> ... the Britons learned the language of their conquerors, and they acquired its sound-system and vocabulary very completely, their own phonetics having no discernible effect on the new language and their own vocabulary very little.

(Jackson 1953: 245)

That they sought to improve their position within the social and legal framework of early English society and pass themselves off as Anglo-Saxons provides a motive, which is otherwise lacking. The dynamics of Anglo-Saxon society provided the opportunity.

It has long been recognized that pockets of Celtic place-names survived for a considerable period inside Anglo-Saxon England, within some of which place-name formation in Celtic occurred comparatively late.

Welshmen were still a distinctive element in northern England at the end of the Saxon period, and were probably identifiable by their language. These enclaves have been described in language derived from the modern creation of reserves for indigenous ethnic groups and wild animals, but such language is entirely inappropriate. Localities where British was retained as a spoken language by the middle ranks of society were those where pressure to adopt English culture was weak. Many of these areas, like Devon and Cumbria, were only drawn into the Anglo-Saxon political system at a comparatively late date, often through land seizure by individuals and institutions whose interests and households were centred elsewhere. The estates given to St Wilfrid for the endowment of Ripon monastery included the valleys of the Ribble, the Dent and the Aire, where British communities had apparently survived virtually untouched by the usurpation of local kingship by English kings. The grant of Cartmel by King Ecgfrith to St Cuthbert included the Britons resident on the estate. These provide two relevant examples where English interest in territories was probably initially superficial, with few English speakers present. The survival of British place-names may have been rendered more likely as a result, and it is noticeable that an important group did survive near the Ribble, on the Fylde.

Many such areas may have been comparatively resistant to name changing because they contained few locations environmentally suitable for settlement. Where occupation of such environmental niches continued, place-name continuity was probably more likely than where changing demographic and economic circumstances encouraged settlement mobility. An example of such a situation might be the Wigan area of south Lancashire, under Northumbrian control from the seventh century but on second-rate land surrounded by extensive mosslands, among which sites well suited to settlement were at a premium. Yet such a circumstance might have little effect: continuous or near-continuous occupation of several sites at Wharram Percy from the Roman into the Saxon period and beyond failed to deflect at least one phase of name changing at each site.

Other enclaves were isolated by breaks in the system of patronage. Areas where British-speaking aristocracies retained control even under English kings appear generally to have maintained the British language and its place-names over a longer period. In such instances, the pressures to acculturate were centred on the household of the local leader, where they might be balanced by cultural pressures from below resulting in bilinguality only among the élite. Strathclyde and Elmet may fall within this category. The survival of place-names derived from *eccles* may be indicative of the survival of comparatively un-anglicized British aristocracies and British Christianity to the threshold of the English conversion (Cameron 1968). If so, it is worth noting that instances exist in the south-east as well as in the west, although the former may have an alternative explanation (Gelling 1977).

Areas where British-speaking aristocracies retained control under English kings were in the minority. English leaders were probably subjected to intense pressure from within their own war-bands to exercise patronage and dispense any land which became available. Conquered territory was either retained by the king or distributed among those with access to patronage, who were necessarily English speakers. The bulk of the Romano-British aristocracy was probably displaced through chieftains and early kings exercising patronage in favour of their own servants, English speakers whatever their ethnic origin. Those of the indigenous aristocracy who survived within English-dominated territory did so only by adapting to English cultural pressures, with the same ultimate result. In most instances this process brought the English language into land units and estates where it was sooner or later adopted by the middle and lower ranks of the local community.

A major complication in any discussion of the linguistic interface between Briton and German is the extent and function of Latin as a spoken language in Britain in the fifth century. This is not a question which is easily resolved. Most of the 400 or so Latin loan-words in Anglo-Saxon are common to all the west Germanic languages and so arguably entered the language prior to the *adventus*, or later as a result of the conversion. A handful, such as *ceaster*, are insular borrowings but this group is barely more numerous than borrowings from Celtic, and the existence of a score or so of Latin words adopted in Britain is certainly not proof positive that Latin was widely spoken in the south and east of Britain in the fifth century (Jackson 1953: 255; *contra* Ehret 1976–7).

However, Latin must still have been the language of government and the British Church when the *adventus* occurred. Vulgar Latin was probably Patrick's mother tongue and he certainly wrote in it. It was presumably the language of the landowners. British Latin was categorized by Jackson as archaic and many are still of this opinion, although there has been some recent dissent from it (Mann 1971; Gratwick 1982). If so, then insular Latin was not in close touch with that of Gaul or other parts of the western Empire. However, a gentleman's education included rhetoric as late as the generation of Gildas and Maglocunus, which, whatever date we assign it, was after the earliest generations of Anglo-Saxon England.

In Gaul, Latin had all but replaced Celtic even among the peasantry. It is impossible to be sure how far this process had gone in fifth-century Britain but it seems quite likely that large sections of even the rural community in the lowlands were by this stage at least bilingual. In favour of a low level of Latin are the names of two of the Saxon Shore forts, Dover and Lympne, which were plurals in both British and Anglo-Saxon and so were probably transferred by Britons bilingual in British and Anglo-Saxon, rather than Latin and Anglo-Saxon (Jackson 1953; Rivet and Smith 1979). However, these names may be a special case. Kent experienced a collapse of villa occupation in the third century and the dissemination of Latin may have been curtailed. Such coastal names could in any case have entered the Germanic languages soon after the forts were constructed, a century and a half before the *adventus*. These two instances are somewhat isolated from the remainder of the distribution of Romano-British name survivals.

British probably did not die out in any part of Britain before the Anglo-Saxon period. Latin was presumably most widely used as a spoken language in the lowland zone and particularly among the townsfolk and villa owners of the more Romanized areas, but was subject to social gradients (Hamp 1975) and unevenly distributed. The collapse of towns and villas on the eve of the English settlement can only have weakened Latin as a spoken language, although it clearly did not destroy it. However, those fluent in Latin were probably that sector of the British population least willing to live cheek by jowl with barbarian warriors, who probably had more contact with communities who spoke British first and Latin only second. Even so, existing bilingualism may have played an important role in the ease with which the British community adapted itself to Anglo-Saxon. A society which regularly used two languages may have found the assimilation of a third relatively simple.

That this newcomer eventually drove out both the earlier languages reflects the drastic nature of the social adjustment which was under way in the fifth and sixth centuries, as a society which had fallen out of the Roman system sought to stabilize internally and defend itself externally. It need not reflect the numbers of Anglo-Saxon, British and Latin speakers present at any particular time or in aggregate. The true contrast between the conquests of the Anglo-Saxons and the Normans lies in the comparative stability of the social system during the period of assimilation. Rapid and fundamental social and cultural changes in the fifth and sixth centuries contrast dramatically with the continuity of farms, fields, towns and social and tenurial status in the eleventh. So too do the declining literacy of Britain in the late fifth and sixth centuries, compared to the expanding and literate Church in the late eleventh century. Despite everything, the quantity of French which entered the insular vernacular was considerable and it was not until the fourteenth century that French was clearly in retreat as a spoken language within England. It is these contrasts which provide the key to the different reactions of the indigenes to Anglo-Saxon and Norman French, respectively.

The significant incidence of Latin loan-words in Anglo-Saxon creates further problems for those who support the theory of a mass migration from Denmark and north-west Germany. As a language, Anglo-Saxon is an integral member of the Germanic group of languages which centre on the lower Rhine, its closest parallel being with Old Frisian, rather than the Baltic language family. The notion that Frisians played a significant role in the Anglo-Saxon settlement is not popular in Holland (Bremmer 1990). Any proponent of the theory of mass migration from parts of Germany out of touch with the Roman Rhineland is left having to concoct clumsy mechanisms to explain a supposed high incidence of Latin loan-words among the communities of Schleswig-Holstein in the early fifth century.

In conclusion, language replacement within an existing community is a widespread and common phenomenon. That the British adopted Anglo-Saxon is demonstrable. That this occurred on a large scale is entirely possible. What is still at issue is the relative size of the British and immigrant communities. Placed in the context of radical social transformation in the post-Roman era, a large-scale transfer of language to a predominantly British population is plausible. Place-name scholars are now accepting the probability that entire British communities spread across whole regions of England abandoned their native tongue in favour of Anglo-Saxon. This has long been recognized as a probability in Northumbria but it has now been proposed for areas further south:

> . . . in Cheshire and Shropshire, the English language must have prevailed and been employed for a wholesale replacement of Welsh names by English ones. It seems unlikely that this can have been due to the numerical superiority of English farmers, so it has to be ascribed to the social and administrative superiority of a relatively modest number of Mercians.

> (Gelling 1989: 197)

In such circumstances English was not imposed on the indigenes but embraced by them as one element in a process of cultural integration which they believed offered advantages to themselves. It is not the superior but the inferior community which is motivated to destroy apartheid. This recognition of language transfer is an important advance on pre-existing attempts to explain the dominance of Anglo-Saxon in the place-naming process of the north-west Midlands through migration (e.g. Dodgson 1967). With that achieved, there can be no objection in principle to the same process occurring even in areas of primary English settlement. There is nothing, therefore, in the replacement of British by Anglo-Saxon which is inimical to the interpretation of the Anglo-Saxon settlement as an élitist phenomenon.

The place-names of the migration period

Between the 1920s and the 1960s, place-name scholarship operated within a fairly constant set of assumptions. The earliest English names were deemed to be those in -*ingas*, 'the people of x', followed by -*inga-ham/tun* 'the settlement of the people of x', alongside names which referred to pagan religious practices. A historical interpretation of such place-name evidence underlies much of the Germanist view of the English settlement as propounded by scholars such as Stenton, who was, himself, a leading place-name scholar.

By the 1960s, several place-name researchers were nurturing serious doubts concerning the existing chronological framework of English place-names. In a seminal paper published in 1966, the late Professor Dodgson compared the distribution of names in *-ingas* and *-inga-* in south-east England with the distribution of pagan cemetery sites, and, on that basis, suggested that these categories of place-names were separate in time, place and burial habits from the settlements of those using the pagan burial sites. His conclusions have been accepted by most place-name scholars and seem to be supported by further work in the east Midlands (Kuurman 1974–5), although it is worth remarking in passing that only his negative conclusions are convincing, while alternative interpretations of the evidence are equally possible, given a different range of assumptions.

At the same time, pagan place-names have been subjected to critical reappraisal, dubious examples rejected and a late pagan context proposed (Gelling 1961, 1973). The assumption that they belong to an Anglo-Saxon pagan context at all has since been subject to some scepticism (e.g. Bronnenkant 1984). However, the most recent analysis has reinstated certain elements (Wilson 1985), suggesting that the element *hearg* may have been specifically associated with the focal temples of tribal communities, as in the only two surviving literary references – *gumeninga hergae* and *Besingahearh* (Birch 1885–93: 201, 72; the 'temple of the Gumeningas' and 'the temple of the Besingas', respectively).

In consequence of this increasing scepticism, the search for genuinely early English place-names was resumed in the 1960s, still on the assumption that particular elements could be identified and diagnosed as contemporary with the earliest English settlement. The first element to be afforded this treatment was *-ham* (Cox 1973), which was commonly associated with monothematic personal names, thought to be early and often identified settlements on or near Roman roads. However, a detailed examination of this element in Kent, Surrey and Sussex demonstrated that it was not associated with pagan burial sites and was only peripheral to Romano-British settlement. Any discussion is necessarily bedevilled by the difficulties inherent in distinguishing between *-ham* and *-hamm*, a suffix with an entirely different meaning and without claims to chronological primacy (Dodgson 1973).

The study of Latin loan-words in English place-names has proved a more valuable exercise. There is a positive correlation between names formed from *-wicham*, a compound of Latin *vicus* and English *-ham*, and Roman roads and minor settlements (Gelling 1967, 1977, 1988a) but it remains doubtful if this implies that any such Roman-style settlement was necessarily still in use when the name was created. Like *ceaster*, the term is a generic and gives no indication that the inhabitants knew the name of whatever Roman site was referred to. *Vicus* entered the English language on the Continent, not in England. Parallels with *burh-tun* spring to mind and the *vicus* of the one could have been as much a landscape relic as the *burh* of the other, when that was a prehistoric fortification or Roman fort.

Names in *eccles, funta, port* and *camp* all reflect borrowings into English either direct from Latin or via British (Gelling 1977), but such names need not be particularly early unless they represent pre-existing names which have been accommodated into the English language. Their geography does little to suggest that they served a primary role in the formation of English place-names.

An examination of English literature written up to 731 (the date of Bede's *Ecclesiastical History*) identified 224 place-names, among which 119 names contained elements with a topographical meaning and only 75 habitational elements (Cox 1975–6). Names with certain pre-English elements made up 26 per cent of the total, a proportion far higher than from any later sample of English place-names, although clearly boosted by the use of non-colloquial Latin names by English churchmen. Topographical names using the elements *eg* (island) and *feld* (open space) were common. Habitational names utilized the elements *ham, ceaster, burh* and *tun* in descending frequency. Numerous common English place-name elements were either poorly represented or entirely absent (e.g. *-ingtun, worth, broc*), suggesting that they played little part in early place-name formation. Of the 46 river names identified, 31 (70 per cent) were certainly pre-English, reinforcing the general pattern of early name retention which is a feature of river names.

This study has created a platform from which it has been possible to revise the probability of a particular group of elements being relatively early in the chronology of English place-name formation, and it is now commonly accepted that topographical elements should be included among the earliest layers which can be identified (Gelling 1988a). However, while a cut-off date in the eighth century is necessitated by the small volume of early written Anglo-Saxon, it does mean that this place-name sample is very late, deriving entirely from the period *c.* 670 to *c.* 731, between nine and thirteen generations after the initial *adventus*. As primary evidence, therefore, the corpus leaves much to be desired, and it is not contemporary with the earliest Anglo-Saxon material remains identified through archaeology.

A welcome strand in all recent place-name analysis has been the comparison of place-name evidence with archaeological evidence. The correlation of one with another has been crucial to arguments on the meaning and role of place-names in *-wicham, -ham, -ingas* and *-inga-*. However, it does leave place-name scholarship vulnerable to a series of possible mishaps. All too frequently over the last thirty years archaeologists have wavered from one standard of dating for the fifth century to another and these alterations have an effect on place-name studies which has caused many otherwise admirable studies to become outdated.

More importantly, place-name scholars have made demands on archaeological evidence which the latter is incapable of supporting in its present state. The correlation of the distribution of particular place-name elements with Romano-British settlements is of only dubious relevance, except where settlements have been rigorously screened to exclude those which had fallen out of use before the probable date of arrival of English speakers in a particular locality. No such corpus can yet be offered with any confidence for any part of England, leaving comparisons of these two types of data without any secure chronological foundation.

Similar problems surround attempts to correlate early medieval settlements and place-names. Archaeologists can identify settlements which used a material culture which they label Anglo-Saxon. They can offer an approximate date range for such occupation, but they cannot generally demonstrate that that community spoke Anglo-Saxon or recognized a name for their own habitation site or the territory farmed from it which derived from Anglo-Saxon. The vast majority of such sites have been abandoned for more than a millennium. In most instances we can be reasonably sure that the place-name appropriate to that site when it was occupied is lost. Early English sites are customarily known by a current place-name conveniently close to the site but not specific to that settlement. Even if the actual name had survived through some accident of transfer to another site, such a process is not reconstructable and the place-name remains effectively lost.

Field survey in areas where pottery seems to have been in widespread use in the early Anglo-Saxon period has demonstrated to archaeologists that the pattern of rural settlement was comparatively dense, with several farms or hamlets within the area of a modern township. Where occupation was aceramic, archaeology is floundering in its attempts to identify any settlements at all. We can only assume that rural settlements which resembled those which have been identified elsewhere were scattered widely across the English countryside, probably occurring every kilometre or two in any direction from any one settlement. Among these sites the use of English apparently spread widely, if erratically, during a period which lasted for nearly three centuries. The distribution of the settlements so far identified need not be indicative of the relative density of Anglo-Saxon speakers in any part of England at any one time. Examining every place-name within a fixed distance of such a site will not resurrect the names current in that landscape when that site was occupied. Most are probably lost and there is not at present any certain means of separating the survivors from later Anglo-Saxon place-names. Instead of being a controlled exercise, such surveys (e.g. Copley 1986, 1988) merely offer a method of establishing an entirely random overview of English place-names without particular relevance to the fifth and sixth centuries. If such efforts have demonstrated anything, it is that we cannot certainly identify any categories of English place-names definitely of early provenance. (Gelling 1988b: 254), but even such negative conclusions may be too much.

The study of early English place-names is becoming progressively more difficult as our understanding of the problems becomes more sophisticated.

Place-names formed by English speakers eventually attained a numerical dominance over those derived from earlier languages. We know that within the sample provided by early documents this process was already well advanced by the early eighth century. We can guess that it occurred in parallel with the extensive settlement mobility evidenced by archaeology, and as the use of English overtook and drove out the use of other languages.

The starting place for an examination of the migration period must be Roman Britain. In 400, Britain was presumably covered by tens of thousands of place-names, the vast majority of which were, in origin, British or earlier, with a minority from Latin (Jackson 1953; Rivet 1970, 1980; Rivet and Smith 1979; Smith 1980). British place-names were certainly still coming into existence in the second and third centuries and probably still later.

The only place-names of which we can be sure in the migration period are those where there was significant continuity from Romano-British to English, but the numbers of these are necessarily limited by our very partial knowledge of the place-names of Roman Britain, of which only *c.* 460 have been collected. Some of these names were transferred from Roman Britain to England with little change (e.g. London) but most which survived did so in a very different form. In many, only a single element of the Romano-British name was incorporated into an English name, utilizing suffixes such as *-ceaster*, *-wic* or *-burh*, suggesting that English speakers were impatient of polysyllabic Romano-British names (Smith 1980). In others, the earlier name was subjected to extensive transliteration, resulting in a place-name which gives every appearance of being an original construction in the English language. York is the example most often quoted, the Romano-British *Eburacem* re-emerging as *Eoforwic*, 'Boar-wick', but Rochester and Salisbury are similar. Others are possible, though debated — Brougham and Burwens (Kirkby Thore) and the River Coquet are relevant examples. More examples of transliteration can be documented in the late-anglicized Cornish peninsula, where names such as Brown Willy and Rose in the Valley derive from this process (Padel 1982).

The case of Rochester is particularly important, because it became *Hrofæscæstir*, 'the fortification of a person named Hrof', and this is precisely the etymology by which Bede explained the English name. Had we not known the pre-English name of this site, then the English derivation would have been accepted and this and similar names would have been classed as English place-names rather than ones containing elements of pre-existing names. Given the well-documented mid-Saxon mania for eponymous solutions to English place-names, as at Bamburgh, Portsmouth and the Isle of Wight, folk etymologies of this kind may underlie numerous names which appear to be of English origin, but which may derive from earlier names. Personal names only known from place-names are particularly vulnerable to such an argument (Alcock 1971) and other categories have also been proposed.

Many personal names in Cornish seem to have been identical with individual common nouns. The frequent appearance of such words in place-names should be interpreted as personal names (Padel 1985). Numerous early Welsh territorial names were derived from a personal name and a suffix, including the British derived *-aco-* (Latin *-acum* as appears in *Eburacem*). Hundreds of names of this kind existed in Gaul and there were probably hundreds more in Britain.

In medieval and early modern England, the names of individual farms often incorporated a personal name and many were subject to occasional abrupt change as one owner replaced another. Such changes may have occurred widely in the fifth and sixth centuries as Anglo-Saxon personal names replaced British ones and elements such as *-acum* suffered from transliteration and translation.

In a few instances, British names have demonstrably been translated into accurate English, perhaps by bilingual Britons. The *Banno-* of *Bannovalium* and the *Horn-* of Horncastle are cases in point, and the numerous topographical place-names which feature in both languages invite the suggestion that translation may have been widespread, as was long ago suggested for many place-names in Northumberland (Mawer 1920). Very recently it has been suggested that the name Whithorn may derive from a Greek name translated into Latin and thence into Old English (P. Hill, personal communication), in which case it would seem to be the most complex example of this process so far identified.

What emerges from any discussion of fifth- and sixth-century place-names is that we can positively identify very few, while the processes of name formation among the unknown majority are a matter of possibility rather than probability. Of the processes of name survival:

> fragment, haphazard survivals, and much transformation by misunderstanding, folk-etymology and substitution, are the best we can expect.
> (Smith 1980: 34)

They are, indeed, all that we have.

In recent years, place-name specialists have wisely tended to turn their backs on these problems, and contented themselves with the more limited objective of interpreting the material which is available within the language in which it appears to have been formed, usually English, in the context of the environment in which that formation occurred. Prior to mid to late Saxon and Norman documentation, the origins of England's place-names pose problems which are at present insoluble.

Similar problems have been identified in other situations of language replacement. Writing of Lebanon, one scholar noted that:

> A large number of names must have shifted morphologically from Canaanite to Aramaic and/or from Aramaic to Arabic.... That a name cannot be Aramaic, is usually impossible to uphold. We are on even shakier ground with regard to Canaanite names.
> (Wild 1973: 328—9)

While those English place-names which are known to contain a pre-English name or language element have tended to increase in recent years (Gelling 1976a, 1988a), we are rarely in a position to state categorically that an English name does not conceal an earlier one, even where the appropriateness of a particular place-name to the landscape appears to lend weight to its originality in the English language.

Names and sites

A further complication is the variability of settlement continuity and the relationship between place-name and place. During the formative years of place-name studies, medieval villages were generally believed to have originated in the migration period, so that settlement and name could be assumed to be contemporary *ab initio*. Around these primary settlements were secondary sites with later names founded by colonists after the migration. However, recent changes in our knowledge of settlement chronology have devastating implications for place-name studies. In no instance has a medieval village been shown to have been continuously occupied in its nucleated form since the Roman or early medieval periods and 'primary' and 'secondary' sites cannot, in general, be distinguished functionally or chronologically.

Many of our corpus of place-names up to and including Domesday are habitative names, which were presumably coined initially to denote settlements. Many are still borne by villages, but it is not uncommon for a place-name to be documented at a date earlier than that at which the village is likely to have been founded. There is, in other words, a problem of the contemporaneity of place-names and the settlements which were later identified by those names. The formation of villages was a phenomenon of the late Saxon/Norman period. In many instances, they seem to have been accorded an existing place-name, which may have already become attached either to the territory or estate, or to a specific settlement within it.

Place-name mobility can occasionally be documented, as in the instance of *Letocetum* (Wall) the first element of which reappears as the Mercian diocesan centre of Lichfield. However, such examples are rare and the spatial origins of many place-names are obscure. Yet habitative place-names must often have been reallocated to settlements on sites other than those for which they were coined.

What predated the village was a pattern of smaller settlements, hamlets and farms, the early names of which are often lost, particularly where village formation was most marked. In such areas we cannot expect the majority of place-names to have survived even from the seventh to the twelfth century, simply because the farms to which they had been attached were abandoned when the population was nucleated into a smaller number of larger settlements. The loss of local names mirrors the loss of early field systems, farms and other landscape features, and only estate names were likely to survive. Yet this was only the last of a confused series of large-scale settlement shifts in the late Roman and Saxon periods. On this reasoning, we should expect few place-names of the fifth century to be present in the seventh, if only because the places to which they had been attached had been abandoned in favour of new sites.

The vulnerability of a specific place to name changes is in part a factor of its size and proprietorial status. In the early modern period, a single farm, owned or occupied by a single family, was very likely to experience a series of name changes, commonly being named from the personal name or some other attribute of the occupier, hence 'x's farm', 'the smith's tenement', and so on. This may equally have occurred in the migration period, on both individual farms and small estates, particularly where land held of a king by non-hereditary tenure periodically experienced a change in tenant, with each unrelated to the last. This would suggest that many minor places experienced one or more name changes in the fifth, sixth and seventh centuries, prior to the possibility of any one name being recorded. Personal names may have featured prominently among the elements used. As English replaced British, so English names and other name-forming elements would have attained a dominance among local place-names as an inevitable consequence of successive name changing.

The names least liable to change were those attached to sites or landscape features which were familiar to large numbers of people, or to places outside the private domain, such as large regions, major towns (occupied or unoccupied), group names and major topographical features (mountains, rivers, forests). Where the site concerned was known by name to more than one regional community, its abandonment was not necessarily detrimental to the survival of its name, as is the case at London. Where a place became specific to a particular Anglo-Saxon group or dynasty, then its name was more vulnerable. Archaeological evidence for continuous urban settlement is at its strongest at Canterbury (p. 104–5), yet the Romano-British name (*Durovernum*) was abandoned in favour of an entirely English creation, *Cantwaraburg*, 'the *burh* of the defenders of Kent', which reinforced the association of the site and the group identity of the community for whom it provided a focus. That the diagnostic element was of pre-English origin is irrelevant to the formation of the name.

Group and regional names

Bede perceived England as being divided into numerous *regiones* or *provinciae*. These terms were applied without prejudice to the kingdoms of the heptarchy or to comparatively small land units subordinate to large kingdoms or ruled by petty kings. Some of the names of these units predate the expansion of English across the British lowlands and imply the Anglo-Saxon take-over of pre-existing communities operating within a system of obligations and property rights. Such names are characteristic of Northumbria, where Bernicia, Deira, Elmet, Craven, Dent and others were all anglicized names of social groups or territories which existed prior to the rise of the English to dominance, but which were retained thereafter. Examples also occur in southern England, where Kent is the obvious example, the *civitas* of the *Cantiaci* becoming the kingdom of the *Cantwara*. *Viroconium Cornoviorum* (Wroxeter), the tribal centre of the *Cornovii*, derived from a British name for the hillfort on the Wrekin (Rivet and Smith 1979). The British people in the same region were named as the *Wocen saete*, 'Wrekin dwellers', in the Tribal Hidage. In the Viking age, the name survived to describe an entirely anglicized province of Mercia. *Lindesfarone* (Lindsey) derives from *Lindum*, the *colonia* at Lincoln, which had arguably had an extensive *territorium*, although not one which need necessarily have coincided geographically with the Anglo-Saxon kingdom. Such political and social units may even be the direct descendants of the *regiones* of St Germanus and Gildas.

In contrast, the names of many Anglo-Saxon kingdoms in the early eighth century are entirely English in formation and give every appearance of being secondary formations, post-dating the period of the English settlement. East Anglia cannot be the original name given by the earliest English speakers in the area, since, to have any meaning, there must have existed 'Anglian' settlements further west when the name was created. Bede was aware that the name 'West Saxon' had replaced *Gewisse*, although it should be noted that *Westsexene* appears in the Tribal Hidage, a document which long predates the *Historia Ecclesiastica*. Some do not predate the Christian era and were as much diocesan as royal in origin. It may be relevant that the Middle Angles are not listed in the Tribal Hidage, where, instead, there are numerous small and comparatively obscure groups with hidages in multiples of 300. The Middle Angle kingdom may have been an entirely artificial creation of Mercian kings during the seventh century.

In these circumstances, the names of the smaller units within the Tribal Hidage (Davies and Vierck 1974) are likely to predate many of the artificial kingdom names. Some of these are topographical (*Pecsæte*, 'Peak dwellers') but others are the names of groups with a degree of self-identity which may be expressed through a name in -*ingas* (the people of −), as in *Færpinga*, presumably the people who inhabited the *regio quae vocatur in Feppingum* where Bede recorded that Bishop Diuma died. Within the kingdoms around the Weald, it is possible to reconstruct early medieval subdivisions of the kingdoms, among which names in -*ingas* are significant in Sussex and Surrey, in areas where there are relatively few pagan cemeteries known, but absent from eastern Kent, where such cemeteries are comparatively common (7.1).

How old are names in -*ingas*? They were already coming into existence in the decades around 700 and the earliest documented belongs to the 620s. That they do not correlate with pagan cemetery sites (see p. 199)

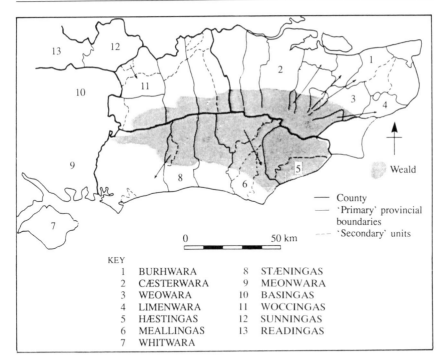

KEY

1	BURHWARA	8	STÆNINGAS
2	CÆSTERWARA	9	MEONWARA
3	WEOWARA	10	BASINGAS
4	LIMENWARA	11	WOCCINGAS
5	HÆSTINGAS	12	SUNNINGAS
6	MEALLINGAS	13	READINGAS
7	WHITWARA		

7.1 The principal divisions of south-east England in the early Middle Ages (after Blair 1989).

may be due to their function rather than the date of their creation and there is still some support among place-name specialists for the possibility that names in *-ingas* are very early (Copley 1988). In many instances, the element is found combined with a monothematic personal name, arguably of early date, which provides an eponym for the community and a folk genealogy for later generations which was probably entirely spurious. It is possible that this type of place-name was commonly given to a British community when that community and the land unit which it farmed had passed under the control of a member of the English warrior aristocracy. In such a case, a comparatively early date is credible irrespective of the presence or absence of pagan cemeteries. A place-name such as *Hæstingas* (Hastings) may have been the English name given to a pre-existing community and its territory at an early stage of anglicization. If so, it may have replaced a pre-existing British name for the territory or its people.

The link is provided by the biography of St Wilfrid (*Vita Wilfridi*, XVII), in which a British area name was anglicized as *Dunutinga*, the 'people of Dent'. British priests had fled from several petty British kingdoms in the Pennines in the face of persecution by King Edwin and Bishop Paulinus: (Higham forthcoming, e) but this narrative implies that the remainder of the population had remained and that it was productive land which Wilfrid's new church was receiving in the 670s. In other words, the *Dunutingas* were British. In the interim, such areas had presumably been directly dependent on the king and renders from them went to his court. Bede recorded names in -*ingas* and -*ingaham* for royal vills which had derived their names from the name of an area or people (Campbell 1979). A few instances occur elsewhere, hence the *Æfeningas*, 'the people of the Avon (valley)'. Otherwise, the substitution or transliteration of a British first element would have produced a typical name in -*ingas*. It seems possible that such regional names were applied at an early stage of the English land seizure to pre-existing kinship groups and their land units. If most such names were later changed or lost, in the process of estate division in the late Saxon era, then they may have been rather commoner in the sixth and seventh centuries.

This discussion of language and place-names has been undertaken for a single purpose: to explore the apparent contrast between place-name evidence and evidence of other kinds, as already laid out for the Roman/medieval interface. The conclusions reached suggest that British communities adopted the Anglo-Saxon language as part of a wider process of anglicization which began in the fifth century and continued thereafter. An attempt has been made to explain the comparative uniformity of this process and the circumstances in which many pre-existing place-names were lost or changed out of recognition, while new ones were formed. The study of place-names imposes no constraints on the numbers of Britons who became anglicized, simply because the numbers of the several language groups involved were not likely to have been the determining factor in the process of language transfer. Comparisons with Roman Gaul or Gaelic Scotland are at least as apt in this respect as the contrast between the English and Norman settlements in England. The links between language and ethnicity are far less than have often been imagined. Fluency achieved by Britons in the language and material culture of the Anglo-Saxons allowed an unknown number of them to merge with the immigrants in the formation of a society which was radically different from that of late Roman Britain. In *extremis*, it can be argued that:

> the survival or extinction of a name tells us nothing about survival or extinction of population, nor about institutions, political systems, tolerance or enmity.

> (Smith 1980: 38)

Yet this may be to overstate the case. Place-names must continue to provide one area in which the interface between Briton and German can be examined, and the transfer of British speakers to the ranks of English speakers was a crucial component in the origins of England.

CHAPTER EIGHT

ROME, BRITAIN AND THE ANGLO-SAXONS: A HYPOTHESIS

We know comparatively little about the social, political, religious or economic history of sub-Roman Britain and early England. In most respects this is a prehistoric period and it is only by marshalling the different kinds of evidence from a wide variety of disciplines that we can begin to know anything at all. The quality of that knowledge is far less than for any later period of British or English history. Much of what we do know is either anecdotal and perhaps of little general relevance, or is ambiguous and open to widely differing interpretations.

In such circumstances, the best we can hope to do is to construct hypotheses that can be subjected to critical examination, then to test their worth in ways which are neither delicate nor finely tuned. Our methods are rarely capable of doing more than redefining the parameters of probability. We can construct simple models of fifth- and sixth-century societies, consider the pressures which acted upon them and trace the course of their probable development through the period at issue. Yet we should never forget that those societies were complex and subject to multiple processes of change. Hypotheses emerging from one discipline can be tested against data or methodologies available to others, to the ultimate benefit of all, yet it is often difficult to identify points of contact at which such tests can take place.

The reconstruction which follows may 'carry conviction as an account of the kind of thing which probably happened' (Campbell 1975, commenting on Morris 1973). Equally, it may not. It is no more than a hypothesis, designed to explore and even to elucidate the particular circumstances of the Roman/English interface. Like any worthwhile hypothesis, it derives from an examination of the evidence. It might be helpful to stress at the start that the solution offered is one that allows for massive ethnic continuity from late Roman Britain to Anglo-Saxon England. However, this results not from any specific preconceptions but from the weighing of evidence of different kinds so as to arrive at a balance of probability. If it encourages discussion across the several disciplines then it will have achieved as much as can be expected.

The Roman Conquest of Britain occurred during a demographic expansion of unprecedented scale, coupled with significant improvements in productivity and in the scale of production. The élite of Iron Age southern

Britain were already in the process of developing comparatively complex and hierarchical social and economic systems which focused on control of trade with the Continent, centralized storage of surplus production and the command of patronage systems which attached the military potential of a tribal community to an individual leader. The result was a series of coin-issuing tribal dynasties, proto-urban communities and proto-states.

The Claudian invasion reached Britain along a pre-existing conduit of cultural, economic and diplomatic influence or exchange, although in itself in large part an act of imperialism uninfluenced by cross-Channel relations. The Conquest rapidly reduced to provincial status those areas in the south and east where pre-Roman social hierarchies had been. Thereafter, Roman armies slowly expanded Roman control into the tribal hinterlands of the north and west but eventually abandoned attempts to conquer the entirety of Britain, outfaced by resource and manpower shortages, the primitive and non-hierarchical social systems which they found in the periphery, and the environmental shortcomings of the highland zone. Roman Britain was henceforth bounded by a zone through which ran successive land frontiers, settling finally on Hadrian's Wall across the Tyne–Solway isthmus in the early second century.

Within the lowland zone, demographic expansion, continuing techno-logical innovation, the rapid development of new industries, skills and markets and increasing economic specialization provided the economic basis for rapid Romanization, a process which was enthusiastically embraced by the indigenous élite and the new urban classes. Comparative peace, some Continental supply of the provincial army and economic expansion within the province kept the demands of the state for taxes and other resources at supportable levels. Government contracts and expanding domestic markets created economic opportunities available to those in control of the agrarian surplus or investing in manufacturing or trade. Roman Britain emerged from a tribal past, but Roman cultural pressures were hostile to tribalism and encouraged the British aristocracy and new urban classes to conform to Continental stereotypes. One critical change was the suppression or confiscation of weapons, which left hitherto free tribesmen increasingly exposed to the patronal and proprietorial interests of their chiefs, who probably themselves abandoned customary land tenure in favour of the elevated sense of private property enshrined in Roman law. Indigenous social hierarchy was linked and adapted to the model which Rome offered, centred in the lawcourts as opposed to the field of battle.

Where communities had already long been in contact with 'superior' cultures on the Continent, significant cultural and social hierarchies had already tended to develop within British society. This had occurred in those very areas which offered the most potential for economic specialization and farming for the market, in the south and east of Britain. Here, after the Conquest, the local élite was able to develop and exploit its control of the agricultural surplus and to use it to fund its own adoption of Roman culture, characterized by a traditional Roman education, government functions, an urban life-style, and Roman dress, social habits, mortuary practices, and material culture. Key elements in this portfolio of Romanization had already begun to cross to Britain before the legions arrived, but the Conquest had the effect of opening the floodgates of acculturation.

Beneath this class, the bulk of the lowland population was 'peasantized' (Slofstra 1983) but the dynamic economic conditions of the early Roman period enabled a substantial middle group to emerge — farmers, manufacturers, tradesmen, officials, merchants and shopkeepers — in relative independence of the rural hierarchy. Guarding this system, funded by it, recruited from several echelons within it, and monopolizing the possession and use of weapons, was an army more professional and tactically more proficient than any yet seen in the western world. A significant proportion of it was stationed in Britain, though not in the lowlands which were in effect civilian areas. In control of the governmental structure was an Imperial hierarchy which monopolized key areas of decision-making, such as those relating to war and peace, hitherto resolved within a local context. A crucial aspect of the Roman state was this separation of the civil population from important political, social and military decision-making, functions which were undertaken within the central hierarchy of the Empire. Authority flowed from the top of society to the bottom throughout the state, the relationship becoming better defined and increasingly unequal during the later period.

Patterns of religious practice and belief in pre-Roman Britain were similar in many respects to the Romano-Celtic religions of the western Empire. There was ample opportunity for combining the two ideological systems during the first and second centuries, when many erstwhile British cult centres thrived beside new and more Romanized temples, the Imperial cult and exotic, eastern religions. All competed for resources in a polytheistic confusion of cult figures, within which no popular cult enjoyed the advantage of Empire-wide systematization, government support or doctrinal cohesion. However, they were also shorn of the warrior characteristics that were arguably a crucial component of pre-Roman British religion, and diverted into pre-existing but less disruptive channels such as healing or fertility.

Severe and Empire-wide stresses during the third century affected what in many respects had been a successful state system. The failure to maintain economic, demographic and territorial expansion in the second century had repercussions for the Empire and its army. A series of barbarian assaults encouraged successive rebellions which were themselves symptomatic of centrifugal political changes. The processes of Imperial centralism had peaked in the second century. During the third, the principal frontiers and their hinterlands often acted independently of one another, presaging the several prefectures of the fourth century. Changes in the balance between production and state consumption necessitated radical structural changes in society in the late third and fourth centuries, as Emperors fought to retrieve the Empire and their own role within it from economic and military disaster. This may have coincided with a Continent-wide stabilization of population, or perhaps the beginnings of significant demographic decline. The decline was accentuated by a net outflow of individuals from frontier provinces into slavery among the barbarians which reversed the substantial inward flow of the early Empire. Worsening climatic conditions damaged the supply side of the economy. Capital accumulation in many provinces had been savaged by the levies of successive Imperial contenders and by barbarian raids, and the coinage entered an inflationary spiral from which only a massive reinstatement of precious-metal content could rescue it.

Whichever factors were responsible, the solutions adopted greatly accentuated the authority and coercive powers of central government. Successful in some ways in the short, even the medium, term, in the longer term they were extremely damaging to the economic system of the Empire, imposing a weight upon it which the economy and social structure of the western provinces were unable to bear. After Diocletian, the effects of government policies progressively weakened key areas of the economy, such as the carrying and building trades, and transformed the very structure of civilian society.

In Britain, the reorganization of society around the paramount needs of the state in the period *c.* 280 to *c.* 340 introduced the worst problems of a command economy into a system within which levels of productivity had never been other than modest by comparison with other areas of the Empire. Britain lay on the edge of the Imperial trading system and, unlike the great cities of Syria, for example, controlled no rich veins of commerce with the barbarians. It lay also on the edge of the temperate climatic zone and its agricultural output was vulnerable to marginal climatic change. During the third century, London, the largest trading centre, was thrown into recession from which it never recovered probably in consequence of changes in the pattern of supply to the insular armies. Local markets declined during the fourth century as craft specialization diminished under pressure from state conscription of labour and the decline of what had hitherto been important markets for skills in government or local government employment. The civilian system of market-led craft skills was replaced by conscript labour and high levels of taxation in kind. The long-term result was the decline and ultimate death of economic specialization and the demise of the productive middle groups within society: artisans, carriers and other economic specialists. After *c.* 350, the markets for surviving artisans, industries and importers became heavily dependent on middle-ranking servants of the state whose function was to garner and redistribute the wealth of others rather than create wealth for themselves. However, such groups also obtained what they could through the system of state procurement, rather than the market-place. By the end of the fourth century, the Roman towns of Britain were experiencing severe economic decline, being little more than centres at which produce was exchanged for the coin necessary for tax payment. The Romanized villa-centred system was in retreat from whole swathes of the countryside, giving way to archaeologically obscure subsistence farming inside economic systems which barely breached the boundaries of land units or estates.

During the second and third centuries, the indigenous aristocracy of Roman Britain spent a large proportion of the wealth that reached them from the countryside within the towns, where they invested in Romanized accommodation and in the infrastructure of urban life. The pressures placed upon them by increasingly demanding governments in the late third century encouraged their departure from their ever more onerous civic duties, and, as a class, they switched their investment to the countryside. Many villas were developed into sumptuous country residences during the late third and early fourth centuries, and the commitment of the landed gentry to town life in some respects declined. Since these were the focal households within provincial society, their removal to the countryside necessarily implied a dispersal of pseudo-governmental functions and patronage from the centre to the hinterland, where many great households probably became the centres of estate-centred societies with many of the attributes of a medieval lordship. Even the *decuriones* could not escape the long-term consequences of government policies, and they, too, were affected by the decline of the market economy, and the decay of services and of cash demands for the rural surplus. Work on villas tailed off after *c.* 340, in both quantity and quality and later repairs to them, as to military fortifications, are characterized by poor quality workmanship. Under Julian, Roman Britain had been able to export skilled labour to the Rhineland. Two generations later there is little evidence that comparable skills were still available in the diocese.

By the end of the century, wealth, land and power were concentrated in the hands of a comparatively small number of great landholders (often absentee), state officers, and officials responsible for the interface between state and population. These officials had become numerous. Once a single province, fourth-century Britain became a diocese, divided between four or five provinces, with all the administrative apparatus which that entailed. A mushrooming system of social and fiscal control was established and run in the interests of the state and its officialdom. The official classes were probably very largely recruited from the gentry and the urban élite. Beside and above them the most powerful landholders flourished, extending their control over ever-increasing estates and acting as patrons of ever wider client groups. The greatest of them were pan-European landed magnates, at the apex of massive and influential systems of patronage which were able to negotiate and intervene at all levels of the state.

At the base of this society, the bulk of the population suffered reduced civil rights and shrinking economic opportunities in the face of growing demands upon their surplus production from state, officials and landowners. Population may have been in decline well within the fourth century and was probably to fall further in the fifth, while productivity and economic specialization dropped far faster, leading to a rapid fall in gross production. Yet demands for taxation were onerous in scale, disruptive of economic processes, and inflexible. The likely results were large-scale indebtedness within the client—patron system, pressures on the poor to escape from debt by flight or fire-sale and a consequent drive by the state to tie farmers to their lands. These processes accelerated the tendency for the aristocracy to amass large landholdings over which they exercised proprietorial control under Roman law. The worsening situation of the peasantry placed them increasingly within the power of those same land-owners who came to represent or even replace the authority of the state within the countryside.

The system was necessitated and guaranteed by the armed forces of the state. Yet these armed forces were dwindling, the British diocese losing soldiers at a comparatively fast rate during the third and fourth centuries, just as the bureaucracy was increasing. Since outside threats to Britain became more rather than less severe during the second half of the fourth century, the result was likely to have been increasing loss of security.

In parallel with the erection of this system of social control, the Roman Emperors adopted a state religion, Christianity, which mirrored many aspects of their system of government. Both were authoritarian; both were organized on a pan-Empire basis and regularly shared territorial divisions; both increasingly demanded quiescent conformity and took measures against dissent or schism; in the West, at least, both were élitist organizations, dominated by the aristocracy and by men with experience of government centred in the same towns as the civil administration. The spread of Christianity in later Roman Britain probably owed more to its place in the Imperial system than to its inherent attractions to the bulk of the populace, most of whom remained pagan into the fifth century.

Outside the core of Roman Britain, the west and north were far less affected by the processes of Romanization in its various forms. Geographically and climatically ill-suited to market-orientated agriculture, and devoid throughout the period of marked social stratification, neither towns nor villas made much headway and local societies remained perversely tribal. Their martial capacities were either suppressed or harnessed to the Roman recruiting office and their populations had comparatively little contact with Latin, Roman material culture, ideologies or commerce. Large swathes of ex-tribal land were probably sequestered by the military for their own use or by the Emperor for mining but such land seizures had probably ceased before the end of the fourth century. The boundary between lowland and upland, or Romanized and un-Romanized Britain, moved significantly during the Roman period. During the second century it shifted westwards but by the end all Wales and much of the Midlands had shed the characteristics of Romanization such as towns and villas. It seems unlikely that Christianity made much ground in the uplands before the fifth century, and the ideology and social structure of the upland zone were arguably closer to those of the tribal past than to stereotypes derived from the Mediterranean. Yet in some form, provincial governments extracted a part of the economic surplus from these communities, just as it did from the lowland zone.

During the late fourth and fifth centuries, the Roman system in Britain entered what was in some respects a terminal decline. The chronology of that decline varies according to the nature of the evidence examined: the date at which Imperial government in Britain ceased to be capable of coercion differs dramatically from the date at which it relinquished the right to govern, if it ever did; the Roman and Gallic Church retained an interest in British events decades after the collapse of Imperial authority, and sections of the British community remained aware of their own membership of the Roman and Christian European club for a century or more thereafter. Indeed, in important respects the chronology of the end of Roman Britain depends on the dating of Gildas's adult life. The later the *De Excidio* was written, the later could elements of the Roman system be said to have survived.

Although there were clear signs of decline in manufacturing skills and commerce two generations before, the earliest clear break was the cessation of Roman coinage. Imperial issues ceased to reach Britain in quantity *c.* 402. Those of Constantine III came to an end at his death. No large new tranches of coin reached the diocese thereafter.

The final demise of the coinage heralded the usurpation of successive British Emperors, whose bids for power temporarily replaced and made more effective Imperial authority and the legitimacy and powers of coercion which that represented. The eventual military collapse of Constantine III and Honorius's failure to resecure Britain left the British diocese and provinces without legitimate governors or provincial bureaucracies, the old ones having obligingly been evicted by the Britons in expectation of a Honorian expedition. The mint ceased its now illicit operations and never reopened, and the central administration of taxation in precious metals collapsed. Those who owned bullion buried it in expectation of securer times to come. Some of these hoards were not to be recovered until many centuries had past.

At the diocesan level, the supply system for whatever military forces remained is unlikely to have outlasted this crisis of authority, even if it had survived to that point. The field army had presumably gone overseas in 407. The collapse of the supply system to the frontier forces probably best represents the moment when regular Roman forces ceased to exist. Some may have made *ad hoc* local arrangements for supplies to continue, particularly in the north, which could have kept their communities in being for a generation or two; others may have deserted to seek a life in raiding or in the patronage of the provincial élite; others may have been reabsorbed within their own tribal kin in the local countryside whence they had been recruited.

The material culture characteristic of Roman Britain came to an end during the first half of the fifth century, and probably sooner rather than later. The large-scale manufacture of pottery and other mass-produced goods ceased, bringing to an end a process of industrial decline which can already be identified in the mid-fourth century. This may not have occurred exactly at the same time as the collapse of Imperial authority but the production and dispersal of goods certainly diminished over the next generation, with major changes occurring in the relationship between producers and consumers. To the extent that it can be observed at all, the economic system which replaced the Roman one was based on the household rather than the market-place. Again, this substitution can already be observed in the rise of the villa-house in the early fourth century but, during the fifth, the decline of urban markets was rapid and terminal. It would be a mistake on present evidence to argue for any survival of urban life, as opposed to life in what had been towns, in sub-Roman Britain. Some may have housed households of high or low status in the century or more to come and it seems likely that bishops retained an interest in the provincial capitals where their sees had been centred, at least until the threat from Saxon land seizures became insupportable. Several Roman towns, such as Canterbury, retained or rapidly re-established for themselves a degree of importance in the changing structure of settlement and social organization which may be incompatible with total abandonment.

Other aspects of Romanized life proved more resilient. The Christian Church, traditional Roman education and elements of government certainly existed within communities as destant as Gwgnedd and Verulamium, at the end of the fifth century. Their survival implies the continuing existence of the fabric of lowland society and the continuing flow of goods from the producer classes to a civilian gentry in the form of both rents and taxation (if mostly in kind or labour), and to the greater aristocracy above them who had usurped the role of Roman government. Such features of British society are either explicit in Gildas's comments on the Saxon *adventus* and on the situation in his own day, or implicit in his fabrication of an earlier (fictional) history for his own community, within which the prejudices expressed and the assumptions made arguably derive not from the past or from the author's imagination but from his own current experience.

Even without the testimony of Gildas, it is clear that the diocese was under attack late in the fourth and early in the fifth centuries from neighbouring barbarians. The Scots in Ireland, the Picts in northern Britain, the Germanic coastal tribes, all had been raiding the Atlantic shores of the Empire during the fourth century, and the governmental and military crisis in Britain in 409 to 410 created conditions which they could hardly avoid exploiting. The collapse of the diocesan system of defence left the coastal seaways unwatched from the coastal towers in the north and open for Scots or Picts to raid the richer southern shores of the province. The Channel had always been the easiest landfall for Saxon raiders who habitually crossed the narrow seas after following the Continental coastline south from Germany. The Saxon Shore forts had been placed precisely so as to deter such raids.

Britain's barbarian neighbours were tribal, with far less functional specialization within their own societies than was present in the Roman provinces. They were equipped with ideologies which positively encouraged military adventurism, and a surplus of well-equipped warriors, some of whom had a tradition of service in Roman armies or of raiding in Roman provinces.

Irish slave-raiding is well documented, and scattered settlements of Gaelic speakers were made in western Britain, from the south-west peninsula to Argyll. However, Irish society was not markedly well adapted to migration and the role of its kings as war-leaders was circumscribed by the existence of other tiers within society with important functions in religion and customary law. In general, the Irish, like the Picts (of whom we are peculiarly ignorant), may have preferred to raid rather than emigrate. However, in crucial respects early medieval Irish kingship was more capable of offensive action than the Germanic kings discussed by Tacitus in the *Germania*, and it may well be that migration might have assisted Irish kings to focus authority of several kinds on themselves as they established their petty kingships within Britain. Whether he knew of them or not (and his knowledge certainly stretched to the court of south-west Wales), Gildas omitted any reference to the Irish settlements in the west; but it was, in his opinion, the rumour of the intention of Picts or Irish to settle which led to the invitation which first brought Saxon troops into eastern Britain. We should not dismiss this causal link too lightly, even though it derives from the very earliest of those sections of the *De Excidio* dealing with events after Aquileia which have any claim to historicity.

British communities within the upland zone responded positively to the challenge posed by their barbarian neighbours and re-established a military capacity within their own societies. This was achieved through a scatter of tribal kingdoms headed by warrior kings, who surrounded themselves with war-bands of free British warriors, perhaps recruited from those same social groups within local tribal societies which had previously staffed the Roman *limitatenses*. That this was a society undergoing rapid social and ideological transition is borne out by signs of considerable experimentation in mortuary rites. Yet the restructuring of society that was necessary was slight when compared with lowland society. These communities shifted comparatively rapidly to a social system which owed as much to British precedents as to Roman ones. The results had something in common with the social organization of their tribal neighbours and competitors around the Irish Sea, yet were peculiarly Roman or British, with a Roman or British rather than an Irish view of royal authority. That this process could be achieved comparatively quickly reflects on their low level of Romanization, and particularly the ephemeral nature of its urbanizing and 'peasantizing' tendencies. Even shorn of their warlike attributes, northern and western societies had remained tribal in their structure and outlook, without the social polarization between a Romanized civilian gentry and a peasant majority which characterized most lowland regions. In the new circumstances, local men successfully secured to their own needs the flow of goods and services previously destined for provincial and diocesan governments, and attracted men keen to advance themselves by military service, who congregated around the households of the early kings. Their needs were met by exploiting resources internal to the society (by means which Gildas in part recorded) and by raiding beyond it. The methods such kings used to gain and keep power could be bloody. The tribal communities around them identified themselves with the successful dynasties. Some territories which emerged demonstrably had long roots back into the Roman period and beyond. If we knew more of the tribal structure of Roman Britain, this appearance of continuity might well be strengthened.

If Coroticus was a British-based leader (as opposed to one who had found a new base in Ireland: Thompson 1985), then the war-band which so troubled St Patrick is a sign that this adjustment had been achieved in the upland zone by the middle decades of the fifth century. When Gildas was writing, at least one generation of warrior kings had come and gone and the Celtic west was secure from the threat posed by outside raiders and small-scale, warrior colonization. The *Gododdin* poems imply that a comparable social reorganization in the north had occurred by roughly the same period, producing a court-centred society keen to hear extolled in verse the exploits of members alive and dead. The defended households at the centre of several of these British lordships have been identified and excavated, and most can be shown to have been occupied in the sixth century, the evidence for some pushing back into the later fifth.

By that stage, too, British kings on the periphery had espoused Christianity. At the start of the fifth century, most 'uplanders' were probably pagans (as in the *pagani* from whom Powys took its name) and it says much for the rapid development of British state systems that its leaders uniformly adopted Christianity within the second half of the fifth century. British kings may have consciously aped Imperial authority and patronage within the Christian Church and the ideological uniformity it offered, just as they adopted what had been an Imperial oversight of land alienations in its favour. The construction of local sacerdotal hierarchies under royal patronage contributed to and emphasized the stability of government and social systems in what had until recently been the outer periphery of a Mediterranean-centred Empire, while serving to distance ex-Roman communities from their neighbours. Complaints about secular patronage within the Church were strongly voiced in the *De Excidio*, but it was probably entirely necessary to the expansion of Christianity, whose exponents may have been very largely recruited from the refugee clergy and Christian gentry displaced from the east of Britain by the Saxon rebellion.

This restructured British kingship was at its most uncontroversial in the highland zone. It was characterized by its use of part of the economic surplus to support warriors recruited from within British society. There is little evidence of labour conscription: most of the few fortified centres which have been identified there are small in size and neither their construction nor continuing maintenance need have imposed a major strain on resources of manpower. Nor is there evidence of major ideological or social divisions within the societies over which they presided, these being characterized by a cultural and linguistic homogeneity.

There were crucial differences between these societies and those which paralleled them in the heartland of the old diocese. There, local aristocrats were eventually successful in establishing their own power within society; these are the unnamed tyrants whose justice Gildas distrusted and whose morals he abhorred (*De Excidio* XXVII). They may already have been dominant during the late fourth century. More certainly they were emerging during the 420s and 430s: Constantius's use of the term 'region' in Britain may indicate a territory over which men like Elafius, 'chief man of his region', had assumed a degree of political control by the time Germanus returned to the island for his second visit. But beside or beneath these tyrants were the estate owners of the lowland zone, the owners and occupiers of the villas in their final and often poorly dated phases of occupation. These were a class of highly Romanized and Christianized gentry, civilians to the core, whose traditional role as advocates, if not administrators, lasted well into the fifth century, and whose ranks were one source at least of clerical careerists. How else can one explain the rhetorical and Classical education of Gildas, friend of the monks but scourge of the tyrants and their compliant clergy?

The position of this gentry class required the defence provided by Roman property law, as opposed to traditional tribal land law. That Roman law remained in use is illustrated by the treatment accorded the Pelagians in Britain, as recorded by Constantius, although his comments may reflect no more than the expectations of a Continental observer transposed retrospectively to Britain. It would take a brave commentator to argue for the survival of lawcourts at the diocesan level after 410, but Gildas's own education and comments on the law in use at the time of writing imply that the lawcourts of his *civitas* (and/or the provinces) had ceased functioning only in his lifetime. Henceforth, justice was administered by the local king or 'tyrant', whose knowledge of and respect for Roman law were less than Gildas considered desirable.

We know little about such rulers. By Gildas's day, kings exercised various functions which mark them as the wielders of powers appropriate to public government, both civil and military. In this respect, they were petty Roman emperors rather than Roman-style officials of the late Roman period. They disposed of protection; they waged wars; they pursued criminals; they sat as judges; they held prisoners in gaol. They gathered around themselves soldiers or warriors and supported and entertained them within their own households. Gildas proceeded from the general to the particular in his letter, condemning in outspoken terms the qualities of five western kings by name, but these exemplars were probably never the real target of his ire. They do, however, help to localize the author, being arranged in a geographically ordered sequence starting with the next-door kingdom of Dumnonia and working steadily further away.

Gildas's condemnation of the putative British role in the construction and defence of the northern walls can be read as an implicit condemnation of the construction of comparable structures nearer home. There is a very real contrast between his veiled attacks on unnamed authority close to home and his outspoken criticism of those at a distance. The obvious conclusion must be that one or more local kings were in the process of organizing the labour and resources necessary to construct a boundary on the model of the Antonine Wall when the *De Excidio* was being written, using the late Roman system of labour corvées and of taxation in kind to achieve this. Kings and estate owners were in direct competition for the surplus from the rural community. The extraordinary demands of kings intent on the construction of boundaries, modelled however distantly on the northern walls, were unlikely to have been received sympathetically by the estate-owning classes whose income was eroded by such demands.

Is there other evidence for the survival of Roman-style taxation and social organization at this stage? Construction of the complex of buildings occupied in the fifth century at Wroxeter required the use of labour in quantities far greater than the likely number of inhabitants could have provided. Whether the remainder was recruited by the offer of incentives, the exercise of patronage or by compulsion is unclear but the last remains a possibility. Gildas himself appears to confirm that a lowland British king whose territory was vulnerable to sea-borne barbarian settlers along the eastern coasts employed barbarian warriors whom he fed from taxation in kind, perhaps transported to them by forced labour on the Roman model.

As the threat from Saxon rebels grew, kings peripheral to that rebellion appear to have adopted a variety of labour-intensive strategies to provide themselves, and to an extent the communities over which they ruled, with improved security. The large-scale refurbishment of South Cadbury and the probability that some at least of the massive earthen dyke systems (the Wansdyke, in particular) belong to this period, provides archaeological evidence as good quantitatively if not qualitatively as the inscriptional evidence for labour from the southern *civitates* working on Hadrian's Wall a century or more earlier.

Such attempts by the British élite to stave off an English take-over were ultimately unsuccessful, but they survived for several generations longer than their peer group in East Anglia and other parts of the south-east, where indigenous leadership had no time to experiment with ways of containing rebellion by its barbarian troops. On several fronts, in west Yorkshire, Wiltshire, Somerset and elsewhere, British leaders experimented with those elements of the late Roman systems of military engineering, taxation, coercion and social control which were recoverable or still to hand, in their search for solutions to the threats by which they were confronted. Variety and permutation were clearly characteristics of these transitional societies as each progressed, in their search for viability in the new circumstances of life outside the Empire, at different speeds, from different starting-points, and under different stimuli.

One of the means used to contain the Anglo-Saxon land seizure was the payment of tribute to Anglo-Saxon warrior kings. There is just a hint in the *De Excidio* that Maglocunus, himself perhaps tribute-taker over Wales and Dumnonia, was paying tribute to an English king. Such payments were clearly the norm by the seventh century, when regional 'overking-ships' emerged into history, but Bede's record of two sixth-century 'over-kings' in the south prior to Æthelbert of Kent imply that they were already then of ancient origin. Given that Roman authorities regularly paid sub-sidies to barbarian leaders, the practice probably dates to the initial Saxon rebellion of *c.* 440. It may help to explain both the appearance of objects of Celtic workmanship in Anglo-Saxon graves and the comparative poverty of the British areas, which may have resulted from demands for tribute from successive Anglo-Saxon kings.

The lowland community was ill-equipped to survive the absence of specialist soldiers under Roman control. With officialdom in decay and diocesan and provincial government in abeyance, social leadership lay with aristocrats who were comparatively few in number, cosmopolitan in origin and outlook, and distanced from the grassroots of society. Many of them were Christians, and contemporary trends within Roman Christianity were hostile to their involvement in political and military concerns, encouraging withdrawal from public life. The collapse of Romanized government co-incided with a movement within the Christian Church which sought to distance itself from the secular catastrophes of the fifth century, turning instead to the kingdom of God (St Augustine) or to now widely respected eremaic traditions first publicized by St Athanasius in the mid-fourth century. Both impulses are detectable in the *De Excidio*, although there is no evidence that Gildas had read the work of either man.

Southern Britain remained in close contact with western Christianity throughout the 420s and on to the middle of the century. The missions of St Germanus were official, sponsored by the Gallic clergy, the bishop of Rome and therefore the Emperor, to take action against Pelagianism in

Britain. Active Pelagians, under considerable pressure from the government of the western empire since 417/18, may have seen in Britain a relatively safe refuge. The Pelagian, Agricola, preached widely and gained much sympathy there for his views. The conflict between orthodoxy and heresy may have occupied the attention of many of the more important diocesan aristocrats and churchmen, whether or not it had any direct relevance to unconfirmable conflicts between pro-Empire and anti-Empire factions, or between Vortigern and Ambrosius. The latter pair need not even have been of the same generation as one another! However, Pelagian writings seem to have entered the mainstream of lowland British Christianity, and the conflict was apparently forgotten by 500. A belief in the incapacity of man to affect his own destiny was a widespread Christian view, perhaps indirectly a consequence of the sharp division between civilians and the political or military decision-making processes of the Roman world. In the *De Excidio*, Gildas made it clear that he saw barbarian inroads in Old Testament terms, comparable to the Egyptian plagues, to be combated by a new morality and an improved relationship with God rather than by force of arms.

As an ideological basis for social and military reconstruction, such forms of Christianity were at best unhelpful and at worst positively counter-productive; yet Gildas's work implies that such views, and the civilian Roman-style gentry who acceded to them, retained a key role in social leadership in areas of the lowland zone as yet unaffected by Germanic land seizures up to 500, or even beyond. The Roman form of civilian society and the Christian ideology which complemented and reinforced it long outlasted the material culture which the archaeologist identifies with Roman Britain, surviving (albeit in a shrinking territory) at least until the generation of Gildas.

Throughout the critical years between the collapse of Roman rule and the expansion of Saxon lordship into central England, this powerful, Christian and Romanophile lobby was unsympathetic to the need to adapt the social system and ideologically ill-equipped to respond to the developing crisis. They continued to preside over systems of social control which were implicitly civilian, to extract from their dependants rents in produce and labour, and they competed with the kings emerging from the ranks of the landed aristocracy for influence and for resources. They used those re-sources to sustain their own class, system of education and Church.

In contrast, kings found it necessary to recruit warriors. Gildas returned on several occasions to his scathing opinion of such men, their morals and their prowess. That Vortigern had shared part at least of his opinion is borne out by the decision to employ Saxon mercenaries. Their arrival in Britain created a core of soldiers that none of the local aristocracy could themselves have even pretended to lead to war.

Only when faced by the rebellion of barbarian mercenaries was a member of the aristocracy within the lowlands forced to take more direct action. The account of Gildas implies that, in this crisis, military action was taken with native forces, perhaps of the same kind that Germanus putatively led in the Hallelujah Victory. Ambrosius Aurelianus was probably as exceptional a figure as his behaviour suggests. Gildas believed him to be a member of the Continental, late Imperial community, rather than a Briton, albeit a man resident in Britain whose family were to remain there, and it may be significant that he avoided describing him as a king. The forces with which he resisted the barbarians were presumably grouped around his own dependants. The amateurishness of their efforts implies that their opponents were neither numerous nor particularly committed to the conquest of whatever part of Britain they controlled.

What Ambrosius achieved in Britain was probably localized in its impact since the English clearly remained within the diocese, but his deeds gave parts of the lowlands a breathing space, apparently reinforced by a long-lived *foedus* or treaty with the barbarians, during which there were no new barbarian attacks. The length of this period lends little support to the vision of massed and land-hungry German immigrants offered by some modern writers. If we may speculate about the association of written and archaeological evidence, then it may be that the peace treaty was associated with the construction of the Wansdyke in Gildas's own lifetime. It is a defensive earthwork of exceptional scale which follows a watershed, and may have been designed to oversee a major boundary excluding the Saxons of the middle Thames valley from the central south of Britain. It is tempting to place Gildas within its protection and to make this earthwork the object of his veiled hostility in the introduction to his letter.

Whatever these links, the fight back by the Britons was too little and too late to save the British lowlands for an indigenous society and culture which had been heavily influenced by Romanization and which thereafter failed to adapt sufficiently rapidly to the radically changed circumstances of the fifth century. Anglo-Saxon warriors rolled up the more westerly areas of the lowland zone during the sixth and seventh centuries, without meeting effective military opposition.

British resistance was lessened by the strong polarization of society. There was no substantial middle order in the 420s from which might have emerged a new military capacity, and time – no longer available – was needed to rectify this weakness, to convert aristocratic households into military camps united by the ties of warlord and warrior. The process was begun, certainly, but made too little headway to cope with barbarian attacks; the inadequacies of indigenous soldiers were such that Saxons were invited into Britain as soldiers only a generation after the death of Constantine III.

The bulk of the population consisted of a peasant community, whose economic, social and legal status had been severely impaired as part of the price paid over a century or more for the survival of the Roman state. In matters of ideology, language, material culture and expectations, a vast gulf separated the late Roman élite and their clients, and that gulf was now rarely crossed by the old links of tribal kinship. When pressurized by raiders or settlers from outside, local societies could not rely on the levels of social and cultural cohesion which already existed or were now developing in upland societies. Without a cohesive ideology, language or culture, and exposed to incomers by the accidents of geography and a long history of cultural receptiveness, the lowlands were ill-placed to resist even small bands of determined and competent warriors. Their aristocracies were killed or fled into exile, leaving the majority of the population they had so singularly failed to protect to make what terms they could with the aggressors.

The British field army of the very late fourth century was a section of the Gallic *comitatenses*, probably containing a high proportion of barbarian soldiers. Archaeological evidence implies that the lowland aristocracies continued to recruit such 'Roman' barbarian soldiers into the south of Britain (the Thames basin and below) for several decades, bringing with them a material culture and a rite of burial familiar in the Rhineland and northern Gaul. These soldiers do not appear to have been numerous, and evidence of their presence has not been identified in the centre of England much beyond the Thames. Their presence is a further indication of continuing contact and co-operation between the élites of southern Britain and Gaul during the first half of the fifth century. Such mercenaries came already armed and trained and probably served under their own leaders whose role approximated to that of a Roman officer. In British eyes, there would have been little to distinguish them from late Roman forces.

When did Vortigern issue his infamous invitation to the Saxons? No definitive conclusion is available to us at this stage. However, if the Gallic Chronicles were recording the result of their revolt in 441, it must necessarily have been before that date, and also earlier than the third consulship of Aëtius, an appeal to whom Gildas pretended to quote but which he could not date. How long before 441 we cannot know precisely but the arrival of the mercenaries should be placed within the period *c.* 420 to 435, leaving time for their augmentation by greater numbers and for a period during which they fulfilled the functions they were invited to perform, a detail which is unlikely to have been invented by Gildas. If the rebellion occurred in the period 435 to 441 and was centred in East Anglia (see below), spreading thence into the middle Thames valley, there seems no reason why it should have interfered with the second visit of St Germanus which should probably be located, like the first, in Kent and neighbouring districts.

If we turn now to the archaeological evidence, this suggests that the earliest influx of barbarians from northern Germany reached East Anglia during the first half of the fifth century. The new immigrants who settled north of the Thames were groups making exclusive use of Germanic material culture and mortuary rites, who appear to have had little previous contact with the Roman world. In contrast, southern Britain was characteristically settled by warrior groups practising accompanied inhumation. The augmentation and spread of these various communities began the processes from which England eventually emerged, but the pattern of burial rites which was early established was broadly that which was retained throughout the bulk of the pagan period. Exceptions to this generality do occur, as in Kent, for example, but none the less the degree of continuity of ritual in many cemeteries is impressive. Some intermixing of burial rites during the sixth century probably reflects changing social and cultural perspectives as well as movement between different areas. High-status burials, for example, within areas and cemeteries dominated numerically by cremations, tended to adopt inhumation during the later pagan period. However, these exceptions are a small minority and were probably only characteristic within the most cosmopolitan sections of society. Otherwise, the evidence for adherence to a specific rite or group of rites within a single cemetery or group of cemeteries is strong. It is difficult to reconcile this long-continuing pattern with any notion of large-scale immigration into Britain (meaning tens or hundreds of thousands of immigrants) during the late fifth and sixth centuries, which would presumably have upset this balance.

The success of these mortuary practices probably stemmed from the opportunities they offered for advertisement of the status and ethnic, social and ideological position of the deceased, a statement with obvious implications for the entire lineage of those performing the ceremony. If Britons were commonly buried with Anglo-Saxon rites, this should not surprise us. Insular communities had adapted their mortuary traditions successively to Continental practices over half a millennium before the Anglo-Saxon period and there seems little reason to think most fifth- or sixth-century Britons any less adaptable, given the opportunity. Such burial would have been essential within a kinship attempting to gain full access to the more advantageous side of the social system in any area ruled by Anglo-Saxon chieftains and their warriors.

The English in Britain retained close links with several areas of the Continent, from Scandinavia to Frankia, and travellers between them were probably commonplace from the beginning, passing backwards and forwards fashionable or innovative developments in artistry and design, clothing, weapons, ideology, mortuary rites, and many other aspects of life. Warriors probably travelled and even returned, on the model of Beowulf, loaded with high-status goods. Such movement of warriors from one people to another was earlier a feature of the Germanic societies described by Tacitus in the *Germania* (XIV). The digression concerning the Varni and the Angles recorded by Procopius provides what must be a near-contemporary record of the movement of a substantial English war-band back to the Continent, although little credit should be attached to the numbers quoted. Cultural intermixing was a natural consequence of the Germanic social system and was already present in western Germany before the *adventus*. Such mobility was characteristic of a 'heroic' society, in which the fortunes of political units were volatile and aristocratic warriors were free to seek patronage, fame or fortune in other parts of a social and cultural system which tied eastern Britain to north-west Europe.

The comparative uniformity of Germanic material culture within Britain is indicative of its aristocratic nature, with links which could not be undertaken by immigrant bands of peasants maintained and reinforced at a high social level. On the other hand some predominantly insular developments, largely in the commoner and more mundane items of metalwork, can be identified as early as the late fifth century. They emerge as local communities adopted particular motifs and forms for which they then expressed a preference over several generations. These, again, indicate a comparatively early stabilization of immigrant culture in specific areas of Britain.

Previous barbarian immigrants in the armed services of the Roman world had been expected to adopt Roman culture and eventually aspire to being Romans themselves, such was the superiority of '*Romanitas*' as perceived by both Romans and barbarians. In fifth-century Britain the situation was very different. A numerically depleted and culturally impoverished Romanized élite which had been abandoned by the Empire attempted to use Germanic mercenaries for specific purposes within or beside the local community in a context which did not encourage those mercenaries to acculturate. Among them were groups without previous experience of Rome: backwoodsmen from Denmark and Schleswig-Holstein. Their rebellion and the destruction or flight of the British aristocracy from areas where Anglo-Saxons had established permanent control over estates left Germanic immigrants without a role model from which to acquire any significant Romanization, including Christianity. These 'hill-billies' of the Germanic migrations had none of the respect or use for systems of Roman government and religion found among the immigrant Frankish or Gothic kings, whose far larger, Christian polities needed Roman-style bureaucracies to extract taxes still paid over great distances in coin. Their own small numbers, low levels of social organization, localized, uncoordinated activities and reputation for ferocity did not encourage contact with or respect for the literate classes of Roman Britain. The immigrants were thus left only with a numerous but socially and economically depressed peasant population from which they might acquire Roman or Celtic attributes.

It is not surprising that they stayed aloof from the language and life-style of this class, whose role and status were socially far inferior to what they had themselves enjoyed in the German homeland. Indeed, the social status of individual immigrants probably soon came to depend on their adherence to the material and linguistic culture of the immigrant community as a whole, as that in turn became a mark of free status or even nobility.

The acquisition of land by the new German élite and their followers implies the acquisition of the rent, in whatever form it was paid, which had sustained the British aristocracy, and from them their leaders may also have inherited a British notion of public office and of the taxation in goods and labour by which that office was traditionally supported. The experience of the first immigrants before their revolt was enough to ensure that they understood the basic system by which the agricultural surplus was extracted from the agrarian community.

Germanic warriors were devotees of a traditional north European paganism. Although we know little about the religion of pagan England, it seems certain that there was no pan-English hierarchy of priests. In the *Germania* the priesthood was hierarchical only within the individual *civitas*, and the same seems consistent with Bede's description of the conversion of King Edwin of Deira, and the role of the *pontifex*, Coifi (*H.E.* II.14). Religious practice in early England was highly localized, with an uncoordinated network of independent shrines or temples serving the religious needs of local and regional communities. It is clear that Germanic polytheism provided the immigrants with an ideology far better suited than Christianity to the pragmatism and opportunism required by those wishing to profit from the disturbed and increasingly localized political conditions of the fifth century. Early English literature derives from oral tales which extolled the warrior virtues of an inherently unstable heroic society. The worship of Woden, approximated by Romans to Mercury, offered Anglo-Saxon warriors a role model whose characteristics included trickery and lies. It is no accident that the majority of early English genealogies which have survived descended from Woden, and it seems clear that it was this god with whom the majority of the early English war-bands chose to identify. There is a good case for arguing that the form of kingship which evolved in pagan England was sacral as well as military, the king acting as the link between his community and the divine, and embodying their luck and good fortune in his own. In this respect, there is an important contrast between Germanic and Irish kingship, the former having acquired significantly more attributes than the latter by the seventh century when evidence becomes available.

The pivotal role of English kingship may help to explain the apparent cultural, linguistic and social cohesion of what would appear to have been comparatively small groups of immigrants in the migration period. Indeed, an elevated role for personal leadership probably emerged from the demands placed upon military leaders by the rigours of the migration, early Anglo-Saxon rulers combining the roles anciently held within German society by kings, war-leaders and, in part, priests. War-leadership was not, in origin, decided by birth in German society. Whether it had become so by the fifth century among the Anglo-Saxon immigrants to Britain is a moot point. If not, then the abandonment of elective war-leadership in favour of dynastic descent associated with acclamation was a crucial element in the elevation of Anglo-Saxon kingship to the heights it commanded by the late sixth century.

Both the ultimately central role of Anglo-Saxon kingship and the poverty of kinship terms in the Anglo-Saxon language are consistent with the view that Anglo-Saxon England owed its origins more to concepts of commendation than of folk membership: in many respects the origins of Anglo-Saxon society lie within the war-band. Characteristics specifically associated with free or high status tended to permeate downwards during the Anglo-Saxon period, gradually changing in shape and becoming relevant to the generality of the free population, often under pressure from government. An important example is the hundred, in the *Germania* (VI) described in some detail as an élite group within the warrior body but later to become devalued and universally applicable to freemen as a term of association and government within Anglo-Saxon England.

Despite the advantages offered by its geography, its relatively higher population levels and its greater productivity, state formation was slower in Anglo-Saxon England than in the Celtic west. It was not until the sixth century that other than the most temporary or localized kingdoms became widespread in England, with social hierarchies apparently reflecting such processes appearing initially in Kent, where Continental influences were concentrated. England began in a process of deconstruction which was more extreme than that experienced in Wales, or across most of the Continent, because of the destabilization resulting from the activities of small groups of warriors, in independence of one another, within each of which there were initially lower levels of social stratification than among the Franks or Goths. The leaders of these bands become kings and their success in establishing dynasties may imply that among the models which influenced them was Celtic Kingship.

Comparatively small groups of warriors took advantage of their near monopoly of arms and the skills of war to seize estates and groups of land units. Where they had been employed by the aristocracies of core communities, it was probably those core territories and the revenues due to them which they acquired by rebellion, in which case the territories they controlled are likely to have mirrored in most respects the geography of landownership, patronage and power of the last period of British control. Since we cannot reconstruct that, we cannot be sure of the extent of territorial continuity from one group of owners to another. However, concerning the political geography of several of the earlier areas of Anglo-Saxon lordship, from Deira in the north to East Anglia and Kent in the south, there has been much speculation suggesting wholesale or partial continuity from the British territories to the embryonic Saxon kingdoms.

The incoming Germanic families were principally in search of worked land. The British labour force cultivating the estates which they seized in the east was initially augmented by slave raiding, enabling them to maintain these territories at a high level of production and encouraging the survival of existing enclosure systems and the existing landscape. When Gildas twice mentioned in his letter the Britons' fears of enslavement by the barbarians he was probably referring to the alarms current in his own community at the time of writing.

While there are many signs of continuity in land units, in enclosed landscapes, and therefore within the rural population and the geography of exploitation, the processes by which the resultant peasant majority and immigrant minority came together to form a single people with its own material culture, language and ideology are not easily investigated. The resultant society was initially hampered by the possession of two (or more) languages and two cultures, between which the élite apparently interposed a legal barrier. This was traversed during the early English period by large numbers of the local people seeking to improve their status within the social structure, and undertaking for this purpose rigorous acculturation. This process was facilitated from the seventh century onwards by church hostility to slavery, which released an ongoing flow of Celtic farmers into the lower strata of Anglo-Saxon society. In adopting the material culture and language of the élite they did no more than had the Gallic peasantry of the Roman period.

Combined with a period of rapid settlement mobility, for reasons which relate to economic, demographic and social changes as well as environmental shifts, the widespread adoption of a new language was broadly contemporary with a massive abandonment of the existing place-name stock, in favour of names formed or re-formed in Anglo-Saxon. There are indications that translation, transliteration and phonetic drift all played their part in this process.

Outside Kent, with its early and formative links with Merovingian Gaul, early sixth-century England remained an interlocking system of small warrior lordships, in which local group loyalties may have been more to cult centres than to specific dynasties, and beneath which an indigenous but increasingly anglicized farming community funded the warrior classes. Small peoples are a feature of the south-east Midlands in the Tribal Hidage and such groups may have been typical of the century preceding. However, English society was already seeking ways of emerging from chaos by the mid-sixth century, when the earliest 'overkings' emerge from prehistory, each acting as protectors of other kings. 'Overkingship' clearly grew out of kingship and was a natural development from it. The earliest known to Bede were variously kings of the South Saxons, West Saxons and Kent, but a northern 'overkingship' was established by Æthelfrith in the years around 600 and the Mercians had probably long exercised a similar role in the northern Midlands by this date (Higham forthcoming, e). 'Overkingship' may be for earlier than surviving evidence for it.

The rise of kings is mirrored in the archaeological record. Those able to establish a heritable monopoly of political leadership adopted increasingly elaborate mortuary rites. Barrow burial was of considerable antiquity both in Britain and Germany and its use received a new lease of life as royal dynasties chose to deposit their dead in elaborate monuments surrounded by objects of the highest rarity and craftsmanship. Sutton Hoo is the ultimate expression of this process and its boat-burial probably contained the remains of the first and last pagan 'overking' to levy tribute on all that had been Roman Britain.

At the same time, 'Englishness' was spreading downwards through local social hierarchies, bringing an ever-increasing proportion of the community to participate in facets, and ultimately the whole, of the material and linguistic culture of the dominant group. As a result, pre-existing local identities were retrospectively reworked to establish kinship between the several sections of the community, becoming full-blown myths which tied the entire society to immigration as an explanation of their origins in Britain. Roman conquest had long since divested Britain of its own early history and the origin-myths with which the Germanic ones had to contend were Vergilian in inspiration, not insular.

Like the initial creation of territories under Anglo-Saxon control, state formation was preceded by conquest, the latter stages of which were, in part, recorded by Bede and various British writers. The result was an amalgamation of what had hitherto been separate and localized 'peoples', the fragmentary results of fifth-century deconstruction, each occupying its own territory and bonded by its own kinship ties, its own cult centre and its own war-leadership and patronage. Such units varied enormously in size, and could be incorporated into a larger unit at any stage in their own growth. Several were demonstrably Celtic in some sense in origin and it seems likely that most of the remainder were similar. Widespread renaming of these communities during the sixth and seventh centuries reinforced the notion that they were totally Germanic in origin.

By the end of the sixth century, the most successful state leaders had reached an impasse in their conflict with localism within their own polities. Able to suppress rival war-leadership, they were still confronted by a localized religious structure which found its expression both through the sacral nature of local kings and through local shrines. This dispersed structure was resistant to rapid centralization, and within the large political units over which they presided was a cause of fragility, exercising considerable influence inherently hostile to their own centralism. A handful of the most powerful such kings from Æthelberht to Oswi adopted Christianity, and exploited the unique opportunities this offered for the reorientation of larger political systems towards themselves and the missionaries under their patronage, who claimed to be intermediaries between mankind and a monopolistic divine power. The rise of Christianity in England owed a great deal to the secular needs of a small coterie of great kings but, with its triumph, Anglo-Saxon England had emerged from its own Dark Age.

The Anglo-Saxon settlement became unstoppable almost as soon as it had begun, because it was not only a migratory process but also a sociological and cultural phenomenon. The Anglo-Saxons were successful because their leadership style differed in crucial respects from that of existing Celtic society in the British lowlands. Significantly, they combined the two roles which had been carefully separated in late Roman society, those of aristocrat and warrior. Resistance to them was fatally weakened by the ideological and social factors which held back lowland society from the degree of social transformation necessary to produce and maintain an indigenous warrior class the equal of the Saxons. Too much of the agrarian surplus still went towards maintaining a civilian aristocracy whose rhetorical skills were irrelevant to the type of battles which generally occurred outside the lawcourts.

The successful seizure of the agrarian surplus by incoming barbarians required that they settle as a landholding aristocracy. By so doing, they simplified the social structure, substituting their own military competence for the civilian aristocracy. The defensive needs of British society had hitherto been supplied by the soldiers of the 'tyrants', whose maintenance necessarily competed with that of the aristocracy in the consumption of the agrarian surplus. One such king, Vortigern, lacked confidence in troops of this kind to the point that he invited troops from Germany to take service under him. The successful rebellion of these Saxons drove out the landholding classes and sucked in more of their own kind. In consequence, the Anglo-Saxon land seizure reduced pressure on the agrarian system to the ultimate benefit of the majority of the population, concentrated power far more effectively in the hands of local chieftains, and refocused society on the household and on a military élite dependent on the patronage of its chieftains, in direct control of the land, its workforce and its surplus.

There is some evidence that the basic fabric of late Roman renders and taxation passed from the control of the fifth-century British élite into the early English period intact. There can be little doubt that the means by which British authorities had employed and supplied Germanic mercenaries, and built one at least of the massive earthwork systems which we find so difficult to date, had descended from the late Roman system of taxation and labour corvées. In much the same way, late Roman diocesan authorities had refurbished Hadrian's Wall and, less certainly, built new walls around London. Such labour services were normally if more mundanely used for carrying taxation in kind, repairing bridges, maintaining public buildings and making up the roads.

Germanic aristocracies had traditionally been familiar with systems of unequal gift exchange as a means of support in the homeland (*Germania* XV). The obligatory element which is a standard characteristic of payments by the agrarian community to those holding the rights thereto in Britain mirrors the normal payments of the German agricultural slave to his master. The marriage of a German need for support to a pre-existing

Romano-British system of rent and taxation was a natural consequence of the Anglo-Saxon land seizure in England, while the obligatory element in even our earliest record of hidation may imply that the system operated on the interface between incoming free warriors and the unfree indigenous population.

That Anglo-Saxon kings were able to build massive earthworks reflects this late Roman system of obligatory labour and is most easily explained within a continuum rather than as an entirely new departure. Compulsory labour services on public roads, bridges and military establishments were a feature of later Anglo-Saxon society as they had been of late Roman society, and may have been either retained throughout the period of transition, or, less probably, resurrected by newly powerful English kings in the era of state creation. The system of hidation may have its origins in the late Roman *iugum*, its basis altered either in the British or early English period from a unit of land to one associated with the individual household. The assumption that the hide changed between the seventh and the tenth centuries, eventually becoming a unit of tax obligation, may be an unnecessarily complex interpretation of the evidence, since the hide arguably already carries this meaning in our earliest records. Some parts of the regalian rights of Anglo-Saxon kings even prior to the conversion may derive from the Roman governmental system.

The *adventus* and subsequent restructuring of society provided the opportunity for the late Roman peasant community to 'retribalize' under new leadership and shed the more extreme aspects of peasant status, as that had evolved under the late Roman state. A few Britons, probably of high rank, seem to have been active in the forefront of the Anglo-Saxon take-over, and they and their descendants were thereafter incorporated into Anglo-Saxon society, as Anglo-Saxon. The more successful among the producer community eventually emerged into the lower ranks of English society, to take advantage of the opportunities which membership of an expanding social system could confer. Many ceorls of the seventh and eighth centuries not just in the west but throughout England, were probably of British stock. By the seventh century, entire Celtic communities under indigenous leadership, were being absorbed into English society *en bloc*, and this process was probably also occurring earlier at a more localized level, within the primary areas of Anglo-Saxon settlement.

The arrival in lowland Britain of a material culture which was both well developed and eminently well suited to the evolving post-Roman social context provided a short-cut to the reconstruction of craft skills and industry. The range of Anglo-Saxon products seems to have been adopted by local communities as they obtained access to it. Indeed, they had only the most limited alternatives. Despite this, communities in many parts of Britain were aceramic or not far removed from that state, throughout the fifth and sixth centuries, and the use of pottery only returned to parts of western England as late as the tenth century.

The lack of British influence on Anglo-Saxon material culture need occasion no surprise. With manufacturing in any case near extinction when the *adventus* occurred, most categories of Roman artefacts were not particularly well suited to the changing social context of the fifth century. Areas where a degree of continuity can be identified lie in the production of jewellery and certain types of high-status metalwork, such as hanging bowls, the design of which developed in British rather than Roman society; these were adopted as part of the paraphernalia of a competitive, pagan social hierarchy. In other particulars, the incoming range of goods was adopted by communities ranged in social hierarchies within which Britons of low rank were keen to make upward progress. In so doing, they found it necessary to look and sound like Anglo-Saxons.

The more important buildings characteristic of the early Anglo-Saxon period are more likely to have derived from insular than from Germanic origins. If the earliest arrivals were mercenaries, then they were probably housed in existing buildings. After they had secured independent control of British territory, these may have continued to be housed in halls built by the local inhabitants as part of their obligations towards the élite, just as the poor-quality repairs to villa buildings around 400 may have been the work of the argicultural community, carried out under the patron—client relationship.

Prior to the *adventus*, Germanic communities had already evolved crucial social divisions, with the primary division being between those who worked and those who fought. Many of those who worked were from unfree agrarian households. Germanic immigrants could, therefore, call upon their own experiences in the homeland to assist them in dealing with inferior social groups and 'producer' communities. Within lowland Britain they encountered peasant communities accustomed to a system of social and economic control which was more extreme and formal than any likely to have been found in the German world. Despite an initial impact which may, locally, have seemed apocalyptic, British cultivators arguably clung to their lands in significant numbers and came under new Anglo-Saxon proprietors. Excluding those who were unfortunate enough to be killed or sacrificed in the early stages — and the élite were probably always more attractive candidates for sacrifice — rehabilitation within a German-led society was unlikely to worsen the condition of the British peasantry. Germanic notions of slavery were probably less onerous than those of the Roman colonate, and many peasants may have been enabled to improve their social and economic status in the early generations of Anglo-Saxon England. German warriors offered them one essential commodity: security.

The peasantry exchanged one alien system for another and had little choice regarding either. Their presence is barely recognized in the ar-chaeological record of settlement, yet evidence that the landscape remained very largely open is too extensive to ignore. In East Anglia and Kent, field systems and entire landscapes which had been laid out in the late pre-

Roman Iron Age were retained in use throughout the period, even in places such as Eastry (Kent) where Anglo-Saxon burials imply the presence of high-status households equipped with all the cultural apparatus of the immigrants. The retention of such landscapes is extremely difficult to explain had the British peasantry been swept away, and we must, therefore, conclude that local communities in those areas first settled by the Anglo-Saxons were not massively displaced in the process.

Ine's law codes discriminated against identifiable British members of West Saxon society. In order to obtain the full protection of the wergild appropriate to their economic status, it was necessary for British kinship groups in their entirety to adopt Anglo-Saxon customs: mortuary rites, dress, material culture and language. That they did this is not in doubt. The numbers involved remain in dispute, but it is possible to suggest that this process was fundamental in peopling Anglo-Saxon England.

How many Germanic immigrants were there? No exact number can be calculated from the evidence which is available, but they must have been numerous enough to establish core communities of high-status landholders in several areas of the south and east, and self-consciously to retain a language and culture which became totally identified with the successful communities which they headed. From these bases bands of English warriors made successive inroads into the remainder of lowland Britain, and their conquests were as successful on the cultural level as on the military. That immigrants were ever in a majority in any Anglo-Saxon kingdom, whether proto-East Anglia or Kent, is extremely unlikely, but the immigrant population was rapidly reinforced by British members of local lordships, eager to obtain a share in the advantages which were offered by acculturation within societies which were expanding at the expense of their neighbours, to the benefit of all who could enter the system of patronage. By the late sixth century, the Anglo-Saxon world was peopled by a cross-bred community with far more British than Germanic genes, the bulk of whom spoke Anglo-Saxon, worshipped Germanic gods and inhabited a material world dominated by Germanic culture.

Why did the leaders of fifth-century Britain allow this to happen? The answer must lie ultimately in their '*Romanitas*'. The British lowland élite was a characteristic provincial Roman aristocracy which shared the general social, cultural and ideological outlook common to their own class across the breadth of the western Empire. Their disinclination to accept personal responsibility for the defence of the community was a necessary corollary of this position, yet their control over the remainder of society was so firmly entrenched that, with the army of Britain a spent force after Constantine III, there was inadequate room for the emergence of an alternative, indigenous leadership. If their dependants and peasantries ultimately acclimatized to English landlords, who can blame them? Orosius recorded directly comparable attitudes in Spain:

... now among them [the barbarians] there may be found some Romans who, living with the barbarians, prefer freedom with poverty to tribute-paying with anxiety among their own people.

The Christian perspective of Gildas and his sympathizers did little to stimulate resistance to the barbarians. Orosius again:

... how does it harm a Christian who is longing for eternal life to be withdrawn from this world at any time or by any means? On the other hand, what gain is it to a pagan who, living among Christians, is hardened against faith, if he drags out his days a little longer, since he whose conversion is hopeless is destined at last to die?

(*Seven Books Against the Pagans* VII.41)

Where military leadership had to compete for resources with a civilian aristocracy and clergy who were prepared to concede this world to the barbarians in expectation of triumph in the hereafter, resistance to the Anglo-Saxons was unlikely to be effective. The collapse of British society in the lowland zone was a direct consequence of the withdrawal of Imperial authority and protection from a society which had evolved after a fashion common to the western provinces. The élite who employed barbarian mercenaries were not themselves intellectually, ideologically or education-ally equipped to confront their erstwhile employees when they rebelled. When they did so their degree of success was limited. Too little was done and too late: the Anglo-Saxon élite obtained control of wide swathes of eastern and southern Britain and no renewed effort was ever made to evict them. In the west, a series of strategies such as the refurbishment of a hillfort or the construction of a dyke, were adopted by local rulers but all such efforts were encumbered by the attitudes and prejudices of the landholding aristocracy, until they were eventually swept away or enticed within the English culture system under the twin stimuli of English 'overkingship' and the English conversion.

The spread of Anglo-Saxon estate tenure owes much to their British predecessors failure to create a viable alternative. Equally, the success of English culture was due in large part to the low levels of development within early English hierarchies and the localism of the consequent political systems, which had little interest in the protection or exploitation of an indigenous aristocracy. There is no need to postulate the numerical strength of the immigrants as a key factor: they were in any case certainly the least organized and probably the least numerous of any of the Germanic migrants of the time. On the latter point, the onus of providing proof must lie with those who prefer to interpret the foundation of England as a mass migration. There is no shred of support for such a view in contemporary or near contemporary literature, nor in the study of vegetational or landscape history, while the artefact evidence is open to varying interpretations and is far from conclusive.

In counting heads, we are left with cemeteries, which can contain no more than a small proportion of the total population of the lowland zone, and the ethnic interpretation of which is in any case contentious. The impression conveyed by Gildas and the Gallic Chronicles is of a political conquest rather than a mass migration, characterized by small numbers engaged in the seizure of estates and 'regions', together with the populations that they already contained or that could be brought to them by compulsion. Operating in territories and groups too small to require the literate organizational skills of their erstwhile employers, the Saxons were able to adopt crude methods of dealing with the British élite and to take to themselves the kingdom.

Such, I would suggest, were the origins of England.

REFERENCES

Abels, R.P. 1988. *Lordship and Military Obligation in Anglo-Saxon England.* London

Adams, W.Y. 1968. Invasion, diffusion, evolution? *Antiquity* **62**: 194−254

Adkins, L. 1986. Excavation at Prehistoric and Roman Beddington, 1984−5. *London Archaeology* **5.6**: 152−6

Adkins, L. 1987. Excavations at Beddington 1984−7: the final interim. *London Archaeology* **5.13**: 349−52

Addyman, P.V., D. Leigh and **M.J. Hughes** 1972. Anglo-Saxon houses at Chalton. *Medieval Archaeology* **16**: 13ff.

Addyman, P.V., D. Leigh and **M.J. Hughes** 1973. The Anglo-Saxon village at Chalton, Hants. *Medieval Archaeology* **17**: 1ff.

Addyman, P.V. 1974. Excavations in York, 1972−3: first interim report. *Antiquaries Journal* **54**: 200−31

Ager, B.M. 1985. The smaller variants of the Anglo-Saxon Quoit Brooch. *In* S.C. Hawkes, Campbell J. and Brown D. (eds) *Anglo-Saxon Studies in Archaeology and History* 4, Oxford: 1−58

Ager, B.M. 1987. Late Roman belt-fittings from the Marlowe and Stour St. sites in Canterbury. *Archaeologia Cantiana* **104**: 25−31

Alcock, L. 1963. *Dinas Powys.* Cardiff

Alcock, L. 1971. *Arthur's Britain: History and Archaeology AD 367−634.* Harmondsworth

Alcock, L. 1972. *By South Cadbury is that Camelot: Excavations at Cadbury Castle 1966−70.* London

Alcock, L. 1982. *Cadbury-Camelot: A Fifteen Year Perspective.* London

Alcock, L. 1987. *Economy, Society and Warfare Among the Britons and Saxons.* Cardiff

Alexander, J. 1975. The development of urban communities, the evidence from Cambridge and Great Chesterford. *In* BAR BS 15, 103−9 Small towns of Roman Britain

Allen, J.R.L. and **M.G. Fulford** 1986. The Wentlooge Level: a Romano-British saltmarsh reclamation in southeast Wales. *Britannia* **17**: 91−117

Alonso-Núñez, J.M. 1988. Roman knowledge of Scandinavia in the Imperial Period. *Oxford Journal of Archaeology* **7.1**: 47−64

Ammianus Marcellinus *Historia*, ed. T.E. Page translated by J.C. Rolfe, Loeb Classical Library, 1935 London

Archer, S. 1979. Late Roman Gold and Silver Coin Hoards: a gazetteer. BAR BS 71: 29−64 *The End of Roman Britain* P.J. Casey, (ed.)

Armstrong, A.M., A. Mawer, F.M. Stenton and **B. Dickens** 1952. *The Place Names of Cumberland, III.* Cambridge

Arnold, C.J. 1979. Wealth and social structure: a matter of life and death. *In Anglo Saxon Cemetaries.* Rahtz *et al.* (eds): 81−142

Arnold, C.J. 1982. *The Anglo-Saxon Cemeteries of the Isle of Wight.* London

Arnold, C.J. 1984. *From Roman Britain to Saxon England.* London

Arnold, C.J. 1988. *An Archaeology of the Early Anglo-Saxon Kingdom.* London

Attenborough, F.L. 1922. *The Laws of the Earliest English Kings.* Cambridge

Aubrey, John 1665−93. *Monumenta Britannica.* R. Legg (ed 1980) Sherborne

Baillie, M. 1989. Do Irish Bog Oaks date the Shang Dynasty? *Current Archaeology* **117**: 310−13

Baker, C.A., P.A. Moxey and **P.M. Oxford** 1978. Woodland continuity and change in Epping Forest. *Field Studies* **4**: 645−69

Baldwin Brown, G. 1915. *The Arts in Early England.* London

Bantelmann, A. 1955. *Tofting, eine vorgeschichtliche Warft an der Eidermündung.* Neumünster

Barker, K. 1984. Institution and landscape in early Medieval Wessex: Aldhelm of Sherborne, Malmesbury and Selwoodshire. *Dorset Proceedings* **106**: 33−42 Dorset Natural History and Archaeological Society

Barker, P. 1975. Excavations on the site of the Baths Basilica at Wroxeter, 1966−74: An Interim Report. *Britannia* **6**: 106−17

Barker, P. 1979. The latest occupation of the site of the Baths Basilica at Wroxeter. *In* P.J. Casey (ed): 175−81

Barrett, J.C., A.P. Fitzpatrick and **L. Macinnes** (eds) 1989. *Barbarians and Romans in North-West Europe from the Later Republic to Late Antiquity.* BAR, IS **471**, Oxford

Bartel, B. 1980−1. Colonialism and cultural responses: problems related to Roman provincial analysis. *World Archaeology* **12**: 11−26

Bartholomew, P. 1982. Fifth century facts. *Britannia* **13**: 261−70

Bartley, D.D. 1975. Pollen analytical evidence for prehistoric forest clearance in the upland area west of Rishworth, W. Yorkshire. *New Phytologist* **74**: 375−81

Bartley, D.D., C. Chambers and **B. Hart-Jones** 1976. The vegetational history of parts of south and east Durham. *New Phytologist* **77**: 437−68

Bassett, S. (ed) 1989. *The Origins of Anglo-Saxon Kingdoms.* Leicester

Bateson, J.D. 1973. Roman material from Ireland: a re-consideration. *Proceedings of the Royal Irish Academy* **73(c)**: 21−97

Bateson J.D. 1976. Further finds of Roman material from Ireland. *Proceedings of the Royal Irish Academy* **76(c)**: 171−80

Bateson, J.D. 1981. *Enamel-working in Iron Age, Roman and sub-Roman Britain; The Products and Techniques.* BAR BS 93, Oxford

Bede *Historia Ecclesiastica Gentis Anglorum. In* C. Plummer (ed) *Baedae Opera Historia.* Oxford, 1896

Bedwin, O. 1980. Excavations at Chanctonbury Ring, Wiston, W. Sussex, 1977. *Britannia* **11**: 173−222

Bell, M. 1977. Excavations at Bishopstone in Sussex. *Sussex Archaeological Collections* Vol. 115: 193−241

Bell, M. 1989. Environmental archaeology as an index of continuity and change in the medieval landscape. *In* M. Aston, D. Austin and C. Dyer (eds) *The Rural Settlements of Medieval England.* Oxford: 269−286

Belloc, H. 1904. *The Old Road*. London
Bennett, P. 1979. No 3 Beer Cart Lane. *Archaeologia Cantiana* **95**: 270−2
Bennett, P. 1980. 68−69A Stour Street. *Archaeologia Cantiana* **96**: 405−10
Bennett, P. 1981. 68−69A Stour Street. *Archaeologia Cantiana* **97**: 279−81
Bennett, P. 1982. Old Westgate Court Farm Site, London Road. *Archaeologia Cantiana* **98**: 220−2
Bennett, P. forthcoming *Excavations in the Castle Street and Stour Street areas*. The Archaeology of Canterbury VI
Benson, D. and **D. Miles** 1974. *The Upper Thames Valley: An Archaeological Survey of the River Gravels*. Oxford
Beresford, M. and **J.G. Hurst** 1971. *Deserted Medieval Villages*. London
Biddick, K. 1984. Field edge, forest edge: early medieval social change and resource allocations. *In* K. Biddick (ed) *Archaeological Approaches to Medieval Europe*. Kalamazoo: 105−18
Biddle, M. 1976. Towns. *In* D. M. Wilson (ed): 99−150
Bidwell, P. 1979. *The Legionary Bath-house and Basilica and Forum at Exeter*. Exeter Archaeological Reports, Exeter
Biggar, J.T.M. 1977−8. A field survey of Houndean-Ashcombe and other Downland fields west of Lewes, 1972−75. *Sussex Archaeological Collections* **116**: 143−53
Binchy, D. 1970. *Celtic and Anglo-Saxon Kingship*. Oxford
Birch, W.G. 1885−93 *Cartularium Saxonicum*. London
Black, E.W. 1986. Romano-British burial customs and religious beliefs in South-East England. *Archaeological Journal* **143**: 201−39
Black, E.W. 1987. *The Roman Villas of South-East England*. BAR BS 171
Blagg, T. 1986. Roman religious sites in the British landscape. *Landscape History* **8**: 15−26
Blair, J. 1989. Frithwold's Kingdom and the origins of Surrey. *In* S. Bassett (ed.) *The Origins of Anglo Saxon Kingdoms*. Leicester.
Blockley, K. 1980. The Marlow car park excavations. *Archaeologia Cantiana* **96**: 402−5
Blockley, K. and **M. Day** 1979. Marlow Car Park Excavations. *Archaeologia Cantiana* **95**: 267−70
Blockley, P. and **M. Day** forthcoming *Marlow Car Park Excavations and Associated Sites, 1948−1982*. Canterbury
Bloemers, J.H.F. 1983. Acculturation in the Rhine/Meuse Basin in the Roman Period: A preliminary survey. *In* R. Brandt and J. Slofstra (eds): *Roman and Native in the Low Countries: Spheres of Interaction*: 159
Böhme, H.W. 1974. *Germanische Grabfunde des 4. bis 5. Jahrhunderts zwischen untorer Elbe und Loire*. Münchner Beiträge zur vor- und Frühgeschichte 19 Münster
Böhme, H.W. 1986. Das Ende der Römerherrschaft in Britannien und die angelsachsische Besiedlung Englands im 5. Jahrhundert. *Jahrbuch des Romisch-Germanischen Zentralmuseums* **33**: 469−574
Bonney, D. 1976. Early boundaries and estates in southern England. *In* Sawyer (ed) *Medieval Settlement*: 72−82
Boon, G.C. 1986. Theodosian coins from North and South Wales. *Bulletin of the Board of Celtic Studies* **33**: 429−35
Bowen, H.C. and **P.J. Fowler** (eds) 1978. *Early Land Allotment* BAR, BS 48, Oxford

Bradley, R. 1987. Time regained: The creation of continuity. *Journal of the British Archaeological Association* **140**: 1

Brandt, R. and **J. Slofstra** (eds) 1983. *Roman and Native in the Low Countries: Spheres of Interaction* BAR, IS 184, Oxford

Brandt, R.W., S.E. van der Leeuw and **L.H. van Wijngaarden-Bakker** 1984–85. Transformations in a Dutch estuary: research in a wet landscape. *World Archaeology* **16.1**: 1

Branigan, K. 1968. The origins of cruck construction – a new clue. *Medieval Archaeology* **12**: 1–11

Branigan, K. 1977. *Gatcombe: The excavation and study of a Romano-British villa estate 1967–76*. BAR BS 44

Bremmer, R. 1990. The nature of the evidence for a Frisian participation in the *Adventus Saxonum*. *In* A Bammesberger and A Wollmann (eds) *Britain 400–600: Language and History*. Heidelberg:

Brenan, J. 1984–5. Assessing social status in the Anglo-Saxon cemetery at Sleaford. *London University Bulletin of the Institute of Archaeology* **21–22**: 125–32

Brigham, T. 1990. The late Roman waterfront in London. *Britannia* **21**: 99–184

Bronnenkant, L.J. 1984. Place-names and Anglo-Saxon paganism. *Nomina* **8**: 72

Brooks, D.A. 1983–4. Gildas' *De excidio Britanniae*: its revolutionary meaning and purpose. *Studia Celtica* **18–19**: 1–10

Brooks, D.A. 1986. A review of the evidence for continuity in British towns in the 5th and 6th centuries. *Oxford Journal of Archaeology* **5**: 77–102

Brooks, D.A. 1988. The case for continuity in fifth-century Canterbury re-examined. *Oxford Journal of Archaeology* **7.1**: 99–114

Brooks, N. 1989a. The creation and early structure of the Kingdom of Kent. *In* Bassett (ed) 1989: 55–74

Brooks, N. 1989b. The formation of the Mercian Kingdom. *In* Bassett (ed) *The Origins of Anglo-Saxon Kingdoms*: 159–70

Brown, P. 1968. Pelagius and his supporters. *Journal of Theological Studies* (new series) **19**: 93–114

Brown, P.D.C. 1971. The Church at Richborough. *Britannia* **2**: 225–31

Bruce-Mitford, R.L.S. 1975–83. *The Sutton Hoo Ship Burial* 3 vols, London

Buckland, P.C. 1980. The Roman pottery industries of South Yorkshire: a review. *Britannia* **11**: 145–64

Burgess, C. 1989. Volcanoes, catastrophe and the global crisis of the late Second Millennium B.C. *Current Archaeology* **117**: 325–9

Burgess, R.W. 1990. The Dark Ages return to fifth-century Britain: the restored Gallic Chronicle exploded. *Britannia* **21**: 185–95

Burrow, I. 1979. Roman material from hillforts. *In* Casey (ed) 1979a: 212–29

Burrow, I. 1981. Hillforts and hilltop settlement. BAR BS 91

Bushe-Fox, J.P. 1949. *Fourth Report on the Excavations of the Roman Fort at Richborough, Kent*. Oxford

Cadman, G.E. 1983. Raunds 1977–1983: An Excavation Summary. *Medieval Archaeology* **27**: 107–22

Cameron, K. 1968. Eccles in English place-names. *In* M.W. Barley and R.P.C. Hanson (eds) *Christianity in Roman Britain.* Leicester

Cameron, K. 1979. The meaning and significance of old English *Walh* in english place-names. *Journal of the English Place-Name Society* **12**: 1–53

Campbell, J. 1975. The Age of Arthur. *Studia Hibernia* **15**: 177–85

Campbell, J. 1979. Bede's words for places. *In* P.H. Sawyer (ed) *Places, Names and Graves.* Leeds: 34–54; reprinted in Campbell 1986

Campbell, J. 1982. *The Anglo-Saxons.* London

Campbell, J. 1986. *Essays in Anglo-Saxon History.* London

Carver, M. 1989. Kingship and material culture in early Anglo-Saxon East Anglia. *In* Bassett (ed) 1989: 141–58

Casey, P.J. (ed) 1979a. *The End of Roman Britain.* BAR BS 71

Casey, P.J. 1979b. Magnus Maximum in Britain. *In* Casey 1979a: 66–79

Chadwick, H.M. 1905. *Studies on Anglo-Saxon Institutions.* Cambridge

Chadwick, N.K. 1969. *Early Brittany.* Cardiff

Chambers, F.M. 1989. The evidence for early rye cultivation in north-west Europe. *In* A. Milles, D. Williams and N. Gardner (eds) *The Beginnings of Agriculture.* BAR IS S496: 165–75

Chambers, F. 1991. *A Reconstruction of the Postglacial Environmental History of Tatton Park, Cheshire, from Valley Mire Sediments.* University of Keele Dept of Geography Occasional Paper 17

Charles-Edwards, T.M. 1972. Kinship, Status and the Origins of the Hide. *Past and Present* **56**: 1–33

Charles-Edwards, T.M. 1976. Boundaries in Irish Law. *In* Sawyer (ed): 83–7

Chédeville, H. and **Guillote P.** 1984. *La Bretagne des saints et des rois Ve–Xe siècle.* Rennes

Churchill, Sir W. 1956–8. *A History of the English Speaking Peoples.* Volume I, London

Clark, G. 1966. The Invasion Hypothesis in British Archaeology. *Antiquity* **40**: 172–89

Clarke, G.N. 1979. *The Roman Cemetery at Lankhills. Winchester Studies, Vol. 3. Pre-Roman and Roman Winchester Pt. 2.* Oxford

Claudian *de Consulate Stilichonies. In Claudian,* trans. M. Platnauer, Loeb Classical Library, 1922. London

Cleere, H. 1975. The Roman iron industry of the Weald and its connexions with the Classis Britannica. *Archaeological Journal* **131**: 171–99

Cleere, H. 1989. The Classis Britannica. *In* Maxfield (ed): 18–22

Close-Brooks, J. 1984. Pictish and other burials. *In* J.G.P. Friell and W.G. Watson (eds) *Pictish Studies: Settlement, Burial and Art in Dark Age Northern Britain.* BAR BS **125**: 87–114

Cole, A. 1985. Topography, Hydrology and Place-Names in the Chalklands of Southern England: *Funta, Æwiell* and *Æwielm Nomina* **9**: 3–17

Collingwood, R.G. and **J.N.L. Myres** 1936. *Roman Britain and the English Settlements.* Oxford

Collins, R. 1983. *Early Medieval Spain, Unity in Diversity, 400–1000.* London

Collis, J. 1983. *Wigber Low Derbyshire: A Bronze Age and Anglian Burial Site in the White Peak.* Sheffield

Constantius of Lyons, 1954. The Life of St Germanus. F.R. Hoare (ed) *In*

The Western Fathers: 283−320; London and New York

Cookson, N. 1984. *Romano-British Mosaics*. BAR, BS **135**, Oxford

Cookson, N. 1986. The Christian Church in Roman Britain: a synthesis of archaeology. *World Archaeology* **18**.3: 426−33

Copley, G. 1986. *Archaeology and Place-Names in the Fifth and Sixth Century*. BAR, BS **147**, Oxford

Copley, G. 1988. *Early Place-Names of the Anglian Regions*. BAR BS **185**

Cox, B. 1973. The significance of the distribution of English Place-Names in -*ham* in the Midlands and East Anglia. *Journal of the English Place-Names Society* **5**: 15−73

Cox, B. 1975−6. Place-Names of the earliest English records. *Journal of the English Place-Names Society* **8**: 12−66

Crickmore, J. 1984. *Romano-British Urban Defences*. BAR, BS **126**, Oxford

Crowfoot, E. and **S.C. Hawkes** 1967. Early Anglo Saxon Gold Braids. *Medieval Archaeology* **11**: 42−86

Cunliffe, B.W. (ed) 1968. *Fifth Report on the Excavations of the Roman Fort at Richborough, Kent*. Oxford

Cunliffe, B.W. 1975. *Excavations at Portchester Castle I: Roman*. London

Cunliffe, B.W. 1976. *Excavations at Portchester Castle II: Saxon*. London

Cunliffe, B.W. 1978. Settlement and population in the British Iron Age: some facts, figures and fantasies. *In* BAR IS 48: 3−24 Lowland Iron Age Communities In Europe B. Cunliffe and T. Rowley (eds).

Cunliffe, B.W. 1983. *Danebury: Anatomy of an Iron Age Hillfort*. London

Cunliffe, B.W. 1988. *Greeks, Romans and Barbarians*. London

Cunliffe, B.W. and **P. Davenport** 1985. *The Temple of Sulis Minerva at Bath: I The Site*. Oxford University Committee for Archaeology Monograph No 7, Oxford

Daniels, C. 1980. Excavations at Wallsend and the 4th century barracks on Hadrian's Wall. *In* W.S. Hanson and J.F. Keppie (eds) *Roman Frontier Studies*. BAR IS 71(i): 173−93

Darling, M.J. 1987. The Caistor-By-Norwich 'Massacre' Reconsidered. *Britannia* **18**: 263−72

Davies, W. 1973. *Unciae*: land measurement in the Liber Landavensis. *Agrarian History Review* **21**: 115−17

Davies, W. 1978a. Land and power in early medieval Wales. *Past and Present* **8**: 323ff.

Davies, W. 1978b. *An Early Welsh Microcosm*. London

Davies, W. 1982. *Wales in the Early Middle Ages*. Leicester

Davies, W. 1988. *Small Worlds: The Village Commnunity in Early Medieval Brittany*. London

Davies, W. and **H. Vierck** 1974. The contexts of the *Tribal Hidage*: social aggregates and settlement patterns. *Frühmittelalterliche Studien* **8**: 223−93

Day, M. and **K. Blockley** 1979. St Margaret's Street − Marlowe Car Park. *Canterbury Archaeological Trust Annual Report 1978−9*: 6−10

Day, P. 1990. Reconstructing the environment of Shotover Forest, Oxfordshire. *Medieval Settlement Research Group Annual Report 3* for 1989: 6

Dickinson, T.M. 1982. Fowler's Type G penannular brooches reconsidered. *Medieval Archaeology* **26**: 41−68

Dickinson, T.M. 1973. Post-Roman and pagan Anglo-Saxon. *Archaeological Journal* **130**: 404−18

Dickinson, T.M. 1979. The Present State of Anglo-Saxon Cemetery Studies. *In* P. Rahtz *et al.* (eds): 11−34

Dixon P. 1982. How Saxon is a Saxon House? *In Structural Reconstruction* J. Drury (ed) BAR BS **110** 275−88

Dodgson, J. McN. 1966. The significance of the distribution of the English place names in -*ingas*, -*inga* in south east England. *Medieval Archaeology* **10**: 1−29

Dodgson, J. McN. 1967. The English Arrival in Cheshire. *Transactions of the Historic Society of Lancashire & Cheshire* **119**: 1−38

Dodgson, J. McN. 1973. Place-names from *ham*, distinguished from *hamm* names, in relation to the settlement of Kent, Surrey and Sussex. *Anglo-Saxon England* **2**: 1−50

Donaldson, A. and **J. Turner** 1977. A pollen diagram from Hallowell Moss, near Durham City. *Biogeography* **4**: 25−33

Drinkwater, J. 1989. Patronage in Roman Gaul and the problem of the Bagaudae. In: A. Wallace-Hadrill (ed) *Patronage in Ancient Society*. London: 189−203

Driscoll, S.T. and **M.R. Nieke** (eds) 1988. *Power and Politics in Early Medieval Britain and Ireland*. Edinburgh

Drury, P.J. and **W.J. Rodwell** 1978. Investigations at Asheldham, Essex: An interim report on the Church and the historic landscape. *Antiquaries Journal* **58**: 133−51

Drury, P.J. and **N.P. Wickenden** 1982. An Early Saxon Settlement within the Romano-British Small Town at Heybridge, Essex. *Medieval Archaeology* **26**: 1−40

Dumville, D.N. 1976. The Anglian Collection of royal genealogies and regual lists. *Anglo Saxon England* **5**, 23−50

Dumville, D.N. 1977a. Sub-Roman Britain: history and legend. *History* NS **62**: 173−92

Dumville, D.N. 1977b. On the North British section of the *Historia Brittonum*. *Welsh History Review* 8(3): 345−54

Dumville, D.N. 1984a. Gildas and Maelgwn: problems of dating. *In* Lapidge and Dumville (eds): 51−60

Dumville, D.N. 1984b. The Chronology of *De Excidio Britanniae*, Book I. *In* Lapidge and Dumville (eds): 61−84

Dumville, D.N. 1985. Late seventh- or eighth-century evidence for the British transmission of Pelagius. *Cambridge Medieval Celtic Studies* **10**: 39−52

Dumville, D.N. 1989. The Tribal Hidage: an introduction to its texts and their history. *In* Bassett (ed): 225−30

Dunnett, R. 1971. The Excavation of the Roman theatre at Gosbecks. *Britannia* **2**: 27−47

Eagles, B.N. 1979. *The Anglo-Saxon Settlement of Humberside*. BAR, BS 68, Oxford

Eddi(us), Stephanus *Life of Bishop Wilfrid*. B Colgrave, (ed) Cambridge 1927

Edwards, N. and **A. Lane** (eds) 1988. *Early Medieval Settlement in Wales*. Cardiff

Ehret, C. 1976−7. Linguistic evidence and its correlation with archaeology. *World Archaeology* **8.1**: 5−18

Ellis Davidson, H.R. 1968. *The Sword in Anglo-Saxon England: its archaeology and literature.* Oxford

Ellis Davidson, H.R. and **L. Webster** 1967. The Anglo-Saxon burial at Coombe (Woodnesborough), Kent. *Medieval Archaeology* **11**: 1–41

Ellison, A. 1980. Natives, Romans and Christians on West Hill, Uley: an interim report on the excavation of a ritual complex of the 1st millennium A.D. *In* BAR BS 77: Temples Churches and Religion: recent research in Roman Britain. W Rodwell (ed) part 1, 305–328

Esmonde Cleary, A.S. 1989. *The Ending of Roman Britain.* London

Evans, G. and **S. Pierpoint** 1986. Diver coffins and the bones of men. *London Archaeologist* **5.7**: 202–4

Evans, J.G., **S. Limbrey** and **H. Cleese** 1975. *The Effect of Man on the Landscape: The Highland Zone.* CBA Research Report 11, London

Everitt, A. 1986. *Continuity and Change: The Evolution of Kentish Settlement.* Leicester

Evison, V.I. 1965. *The Fifth Century Invasions South of the Thames.* London

Evison, V.I. 1968. Quoit Brooch Style Buckles. *Antiquaries Journal* **48**: 231–49

Evison, V.I. 1977. Supporting-arm brooches and Equal-arm brooches in England. *In* H.J. Hassier (ed) *Studien zur Sachsenforschung*: 127–47

Evison, V.I. 1987. *Dover: The Buckland Anglo-Saxon Cemetery.* London.

Fahy, D. 1964. When did the Britons become Bretons? A note on the foundation of Brittany. *Welsh History Review* **2**, 111–124

Faull, M. 1975. The semantic development of old English *wealh*. *Leeds Studies in English* **VIII**: 20–44

Faull, M. 1977. British survival in Anglo-Saxon Northumbria. *In* L. Laing (ed) *Studies in Celtic Survival.* BAR, BS **37**, Oxford: 1–56

Faull, M. 1980. Place-names and the kingdom of Elmet. *Nomina* **4**: 21–3

Filmer-Sankey, W. 1984. The Snape Anglo-Saxon cemetery and ship burial: current state of knowledge. *Bulletin of the Sutton Hoo Research Committee* **2**: 13–15

Finberg, H.P.R. 1957. *Roman and Saxon Withington.* (Occasional Paper, Leicester University Department of English Local History) Leicester

Finberg, H.P.R. 1972. *The Agrarian History of England and Wales.* Cambridge

Finberg, H.P.R. 1974. *The Formation of England, 550–1042.* London

Finch Smith, R. 1977. *Roadside Settlements in Lowland Roman Britain.* BAR, BS 157, Oxford

Fleuriot, L. 1980. *Les origines de la Bretagne.* Paris

Foard, G. 1978. Systematic fieldworking and the investigation of Saxon settlement in Northamptonshire. *World Archaeology* **9.3**: 357–74

Ford, S., **M. Bowden**, **G. Mees** and **V. Gaffney** 1988. The Date of the Celtic' Field Systems on the Berkshire Downs. *Britannia* **19**: 401–4

Forster, M. 1921. *Keltisches Wortgut in Englischen.* Halle

Fox, A. and **C. Fox** 1958. Wansdyke Reconsidered. *Archaeological Journal* **115**: 1–48

Freeman, E.A. 1878. *Old English History.* 2nd ed. London

Frend, W.H.C. 1982. Romano-British Christianity: Comparison and Contrast. BAR BS 102: 5–16 The early Church in western Britain and Ireland S.M. Pearce (ed)

Frere, S.S. 1966. The end of Roman Britain. *In* J.S. Wacher (ed) *The Civitas Capitals of Roman Britain.* Leicester: 87–100

Frere, S.S. 1975. The Silchester Church: The Excavation by Sir Ian Richmond in 1961. *Archaeologia* **105**: 277–302

Frere, S.S. 1978. *Britannia.* 2nd ed London

Frere, S.S. 1982. The Bignor Villa. *Britannia* **13**: 135–95

Frere, S.S. 1983. *Verulamium Excavations,* II. Society of Antiquaries Research Report 41, London

Frere, S.S. 1984. Excavations at Dorchester on Thames 1963. *Archaeological Journal* **141**: 91–174

Friendship-Taylor, R.M. and D.E. Friendship-Taylor 1989. *Iron Age and Roman Piddington.* (Upper Nene Archaeological Society) Northampton

Fulford, M.G. 1975. *New Forest Roman pottery: manufacture and distribution, with a corpus of the pottery types.* BAR BS 17

Fulford, M. 1979. Pottery production and trade at the end of Roman Britain: the case against continuity. *In* P.J. Casey (ed) The End of Roman Britain BAR, BS **71**, 120–32

Fulford, M.G. 1985. Excavations on the sites of the amphitheatre and forum-basilica at Silchester, Hampshire: an interim report. *Antiquaries Journal* **65**: 39–81

Fulford, M.G. 1989. Byzantium and Britain: a Mediterranean perspective on Post-Roman Mediterranean imports in Western Britain and Ireland. *Medieval Archaeology* **33**: 1–6

Fulford, M. and J. Bird 1975. Imported pottery from Germany in late Roman Britain. *Britannia* **6**: 171–81

Gaffney, V. and M. Tingle 1989. *The Maddle Farm Project: An Integrated Survey of Prehistoric and Roman landscapes on the Berkshire Downs.* BAR BS 200

Gallion, P. 1986 Celtic permanence or Roman change? Roman Brittany revisited *Oxford Journal of Archaeology* **5.1**: 67–76

Garwood, P. 1984–5. The Cuckmere Valley Project Fieldworking Programme, 1982–3. *Bulletin of the Institute of Archaeology* **21–2**: 49–68

Gates, T. 1981. Farming on the frontier: Romano-British fields in Northumberland. *In* P. Clack and S. Haselgrove (eds) *Rural Settlement in the Roman North.* CBA Group 3, Durham: 21–42

Gelling, M. 1961. Place-names and Anglo-Saxon paganism. *University of Birmingham Historical Journal* **8**: 7–25

Gelling, M. 1967. English place-names derived from the compound *wīchām*. *Medieval Archaeology* **11**: 87–104

Gelling, M. 1973. Further Thoughts on Pagan Place-Names. In F. Sangren (ed) *Otium et Negotium, Studies . . . presented to Olof von Feilitzen.* Stockholm: 109–28

Gelling, M. 1976a. The Evidence of Place-Names. *In* P.H. Sawyer (ed): 200–11

Gelling, M. 1976b. *The Place-Names of Berkshire.* III Cambridge

Gelling, M. 1977. Latin loan words in Old English place-names. *Anglo-Saxon England* **6**: 1–13

Gelling, M. 1978. *Signposts to the Past.* London

Gelling, M. 1984. *Place-Names in the Landscape.* London

Gelling, M. 1988a. *Signposts to the Past.* 2nd ed, Phillimore, Chichester

Gelling, M. 1988b. Towards a chronology for English Place-Names. *In*

D. Hooke (ed) *Anglo-Saxon Settlements*. Oxford: 59–76

Gelling, M. 1989. The Early History of Western Mercia. *In* Bassett (ed): 184–201

Gildas *The Ruin of Britain... together with the Lorica of Gildas*. H Williams (ed) London, 1899. Winterbottom, M. 1978.

Gillam, J.P. 1973. Sources of pottery found on northern military sites. *In* A. Detsicas (ed) *Recent Research in Romano-British Coarse Pottery*. CBA Research Report 10: 53–62

Gillam, J.P. 1979. Romano-Saxon pottery: an alternative explanation. *In* The End of Roman Britain P.J. Casey (ed) BAR BS **71**; 103–18

Gilmour, B. 1979. The Anglo-Saxon church at St Paul-in-the-Bail. *Medieval Archaeology* **23**: 214–18

Godwin, H. 1968. Studies of the post-Glacial history of British vegetation, XV: Organic deposits of Old Buchenham Mere, Norfolk. *New Phytologist* **67**: 95–107

Goffart, W. 1980. *Barbarians and Romans AD 418–584: The Techniques of Accomodation*. Princeton

Goodier, A. 1984. The formation of boundaries in Anglo-Saxon England: a statistical study. *Medieval Archaeology* **28**: 1–21

Gratwick A.S. 1982. Latinitas Britannica. Was British Latin Archaic? *In* W. Brooks (ed) *Latin and the Vernacular Languages in Early Medieval Britain* 2–79. Leicester.

Gray, H.L. 1915. *English Field Systems*. Cambridge, Mass

Green, C.S. 1982. The Cemetery of a Romano-British Community at Poundbury, Dorchester, Dorset. *In* BAR, BS 102, 61–76 The Early Church in Western Britain and Ireland S.M. Pearce (ed)

Green, C.S. 1988. *Excavations at Poundbury: Volume I: The Settlements*. Dorset Natural Historical and Archaeological Society, Monograph 7, Dorchester

Green, H.J.M. 1975. Roman Godmanchester. *In* W. Rodwell and T. Rowley (eds) BAR BS 15: 183–210 Small towns of Roman Britain

Green, H.J.M. 1982. The origins and development of cruck construction in Eastern England. *In* P.J. Drury (ed), BAR, BS 110, 87–99

Green, J.R. 1879–81. *History of the English people*. 4 vols, London

Greene, B., Rogerson, A. and S.G. White 1987. *The Anglo-Saxon Cemetery at Morning Thorpe*. 2 vols, East Anglian Archaeology 36, Dereham

Gregson, N. 1985. The multiple estate model: some critical questions. *Journal of Historical Geography* **11**, 339–51

Gresham, A. 1985. Bedd Porius. *Bulletin of the Board of Celtic Studies* **32**: 386–92

Groenman-van Waateringe W. 1983. The disastrous effect of the Roman occupation. *In* R. Brandt and J. Slofstra (eds): 147–57

Grove, J.M. 1988. *The Little Ice Age*. London

Guy, C.J. 1981. Roman circular lead tanks in Britain. *Britannia* **12**: 271–6

Haarnagel, W. 1979. *Die Grabungen Feddersen Wierde*. 2 Vols Berlin

Hall, D. 1987. The Fenland Project, No. 2: fenland landscapes and settlements between Peterborough and March. *East Anglian Archaeology* **35**: Cambridge

Hall, D. and Chippindale, C. (eds) 1988. Survey, Environment and Excavation in the English Fenland. *Antiquity* **62**: 305–76

Hamp, E.P. 1975. Social Gradience in British Spoken Latin. *Britannia* **6**: 150–62

Hanning, R.W. 1966. *The Vision of History in Early Britain, from Gildas to Geoffrey of Monmouth.* New York

Harden, D.B. (ed) 1956. *Dark Age Britain: Studies Presented to E.T. Leeds.* London

Hartridge, R. 1977–8. Excavations at the Prehistoric and Romano-British Site on Slonk Hill, Shoreham, Sussex. *Sussex Archaeological Collections* **116**: 69–141

Haselgrove, C.C. 1984. Romanisation before the Conquest: Gaulish precedents and British consequences. *In* T.F.C. Blagg and A.C. King *Military and Civilian in Roman Britain.* BAR, BS 136, Oxford: 5–64

Haselgrove, S. 1979. Romano-Saxon Attitudes, BAR BS 71, 4–13: The End of Roman Britain P.J. Casey (ed)

Haverfield, F. 1912. *The Romanization of Roman Britain.* 2nd ed, Oxford

Hawkes, S.C. 1958. The Anglo-Saxon Cemetery at Finglesham, Kent: a reconsideration. *Medieval Archaeology* **2**: 1–71

Hawkes S.C. 1974. The Monkton Brooch. *Antiquaries Journal* **54**: 242–56

Hawkes, S.C. 1979. Eastry in Anglo-Saxon Kent: its importance, and a newly found grave. *In* S.C. Hawkes D. Brown and J. Campbell (eds) BAR BS 72, 81–113: Anglo-Saxon Studies in archaeology and history.

Hawkes, S.C. 1982. Anglo-Saxon Kent, *c.* 425–725. In P. Leach (ed) *Archaeology in Kent to AD 1500* CBA Research Report 48, London

Hawkes, S.C. 1989. The South-East after the Romans: the Saxon settlement. *In* Maxfield (ed) 1989: 78–95

Hayes, P.P. 1988. Roman to Saxon in the south Lincolnshire Fens. *In* D. Hall and C. Chippindale (eds) Survey, Environment and Excavation in the English Fenland. *Antiquity* **62**: 321

Hayfield, C. 1987. *An Archaeological Survey of the Parish of Wharram Percy, E. Yorkshire. 1. The Evolution of the Roman Landscape.* BAR 172 Oxford

Heighway, C. and **P. Garrod** 1980. Excavations at Nos. 1 & 30 Westgate Street, Gloucester: The Roman Levels. *Britannia* **11**: 73–114

Higham, N.J. 1986a. *The Northern Counties to AD 1000.* Harlow

Higham, N.J. 1986b. The origins of Inglewood Forest. *Transactions of the Cumberland and Westmorland Antiquarian and Archaeological Society* **86**: 85–100

Higham, N.J. 1987a. Brigantia revisited. *Northern History* **23**: 1–19

Higham, N.J. 1987b. Landscape and land-use in northern England: A survey of agricultural potential, *c.* 500 BC–AD 1000. *Landscape History* **9**: 35–44

Higham, N.J. 1989. The Cheshire *burhs* and the Mercian frontier to 924. *Transactions of the Lancashire and Cheshire Antiquarian Society* **85**: 193–222

Higham, N.J. forthcoming a *Tatton: The History and Prehistory of One Cheshire Township.* Chester Archaeological Journal 1993

Higham, N.J. forthcoming b Gildas, the Roman walls and British dykes *Cambridge Medieval Celtic Studies* (1992)

Higham, N.J. forthcoming c Old light on the Dark-Age landscape: the description of Britain in the *De Excidio Britanniae* of Gildas. *Journal of Historical Geography* (1992)

Higham N.J. forthcoming d Tacitus, the *Germania* and the origin of 'sunken featured building'. *Annual Report of the Medieval Settlement Group* **5** (1991) 17–19

Higham N.J. forthcoming e The historical context of the Tribal Hidage. *In*

D.H. Hill and A.R. Rumble (eds) *The Burghal Hidage*. Manchester (1992)

Higham N.J. forthcoming f Medieval 'overkingship' in Wales: the earliest evidence *Welsh History Review* (1992)

Hill, C. 1977. The London Riverside Wall. *Current Archaeology* **57** (10:) 308–10

Hill, P. 1988. *Whithorn 2: Excavations 1984–1987, An Interim Report*. Whithorn Trust Whithorn

Hills, C. 1977. *The Anglo-Saxon Cemetery at Spong Hill, North Elmham, part I: Catalogue of Cremations Nos. 20–64 and 1000–1690*. East Anglian Archaeology 6 Dereham

Hills, C. 1979. The archaeology of Anglo-Saxon England in the pagan period: a review. *Anglo-Saxon England* Vol 8, 297–329

Hills, C. and **K. Penn** 1981. *The Anglo-Saxon Cemetery at Spong Hill, North Elmham, Part II: Catalogue of Cremations, Nos. 22, 41 and 1691–2285*. East Anglian Archaeology 11 Dereham

Hills, C., K. Penn and **R. Rickett** 1984. *The Anglo-Saxon Cemetery at Spong Hill, North Elmham, Part III: Catalogue of Inhumations*. East Anglian Archaeology 21 Dereham

Hills, C., K. Penn and **R. Rickett** 1987. *The Anglo-Saxon Cemetery at Spong Hill, North Elmham, Part IV: Catalogue of Cremations*. East Anglian Archaeology 34 Dereham

Hines, J. 1984. *The Scandinavian Character of Anglian England in the pre-Viking Period*. BAR BS 124, Oxford

Hinton, D.A. 1990. *Archaeology, Economy and Society: England from the Fifth to the Fifteenth Century*. London

Hodder, I. 1975. The spatial distribution of Romano-British small towns. W. Rodwell and T. Rowley (eds) Small towns of Roman Britain BAR, BS 15, Oxford: 67–74

Hodder, I. and **M. Millett** 1980. Romano-British villas and towns: a systematic analysis. *World Archaeology* **12.1**: 69–76

Hodges, R. 1989. *The Anglo-Saxon Achievement*. London

Hogarth, A.C. 1973. Structural Features in Anglo-Saxon Graves. *Archaeological Journal* 130: 104–19

Hooke, D. 1981. *Anglo-Saxon Landscapes of the West Midlands: The Charter Evidence*. BAR BS 95, Oxford

Hope-Taylor, B. 1977. *Yeavering: an Anglo-British Centre of Early Northumbria*. London

Hoskins, W.G. 1955. *The Making of the English Landscape*. London

Huggett, J.W. 1988. Imported grave goods and the early Anglo-Saxon economy. *Medieval Archaeology* 32: 63–96

Hughes, K. 1972. *Early Christian Ireland: Introduction to the Sources*. London

Hughes, M. 1986. *Excavations at Meonstoke 1985/6*. Winchester

Hutchinson, G. 1979. The Bar-lug pottery of Cornwall. *Cornish Archaeology* 18: 81–104

Hydatius *Continuatio Chronicorum Hieronymianorum* ad *a. CCCCLXVIII. In* T. Mommsen (ed) *Monumenta Germaniae Historica: Chronica Minora saec IV, V, VI, VII*. Berlin: II, 1–36

Jackson, K.H. 1953. *Language and History in Early Britain*. Edinburgh

Jackson, K.H. 1969. *The Gododdin: The Oldest Scottish Poem*. Edinburgh

Jackson, K.H. 1982. – *Varia*: II. Gildas and The names of the British Princes. *Cambridge Medieval Celtic Studies* 3: 30–40

James, S. 1984. Britain and the late Roman Army. BAR BS 136: 161–86

James, S., A. Marshall and M. Millett 1984. An Early Medieval Building Tradition. *Archaeological Journal* 141, 182–215

Jarrett, M.G. and S. Wrathmell 1981. *Whitton: An Iron Age and Roman Farmstead in South Glamorgan.* Cardiff

Jobey, I. 1979. Housesteads ware – a Frisian tradition on Hadrian's Wall. *Archaeologia Aeliana* 5th Series 7: 127–43

John, E. 1966. *Orbis Brittaniae.* Leicester

Johns, C.M. and T.W. Potter 1985. The Canterbury late Roman treasure. *Antiquaries Journal* 55: 313–52

Johnson, N. 1978. The Location of Pre-Medieval Fields in Caernarvonshire. *In* Bowen and Fowler (eds): 127–32

Johnson, S. 1976. *The Roman Forts of the Saxon Shore.* London

Johnson, S. 1989. The architecture of the Saxon Shore forts. *In* Maxfield (ed): 30–44

Johnston, D.E. (ed) 1977. *The Saxon Shore.* CBA Research Report 18, London

Jones, G.D.B. and D.C.A. Shotter 1988. *Roman Lancaster.* Brigantia Monographs, Manchester

Jones, G.R.J. 1972. Post-Roman Wales. *In* H.P.R. Finberg (ed) *The Agrarian History of England and Wales.* Vol. 1, part ii, Cambridge

Jones, G.R.J. 1976. Multiple estates and early settlement. Vol 1, *In* part 2 Sawyer (ed): 15–40

Jones, M. 1979. Climate, nutrition and disease: an hypothesis of Romano-British population. BAR, BS 71: 231–51

Jones, M. 1982. Crop production in Roman Britain. *In B.A.R.,* 103(i), 97–107 The Roman British countryside D. Nickes (ed)

Jones, M. 1986. *England Before Domesday.* London

Jones, M. and G. Dimbleby 1981. *The Environment of Man: the Iron Age to the Anglo-Saxon Period.* BAR BS 87, Oxford

Jones, M.E. and J. Casey 1988. The Gallic Chronicle Restored: A Chronology for the Anglo-Saxon Invasions and the End of Roman Britain. *Britannia* 19: 367–98

Jones, M.J. and B.J.J. Gilmour 1980. Lincoln, Principia and Forum: A Preliminary Report. *Britannia* 11: 61–72

Jones, M.V. 1974. Excavations at Mucking, Essex, a second interim report. *Antiquaries Journal* 54: 183–99

Kemble, J.M. 1849. *The Saxons in England.* London

Kent, J.P.C. 1956. Gold Coinage in the Late Roman Empire. *In* R.A.G. Carson and C.H.V. Sutherland (eds) *Essays in Roman Coinage presented to Harold Mattingley.* Oxford: 190–204

King, A. 1978. A comparative survey of Bone Assemblages from Roman sites in Britain. *Bulletin of the Institute of Archaeology* 15: 207–32

King, A. 1988. Meonstoke-Shavards Farm. *In* M. Hughes (ed) *Archaeology in Hampshire: Annual Report for 1987*: 13–16 (Hants. CC) Winchester

Kirby, D.P. 1965. Problems of Early West Saxon History. *English Historical Review* 80: 10–29

Kirk, J.R. 1956. Anglo-Saxon Cremation and Inhumation in the Upper Thames Valley in Pagan Times. *In* D.B. Harden (ed) 1958: 123−31

Kirk, J.R. and **E.T. Leeds** 1952−3. Three early Saxon graves from Dorchester, Oxfordshire. *Oxoniensis* **17−18**: 63−76

Koch, J.T. 1985−6. When was Welsh literature first written down? *Studia Celtica* **20−21**: 43−66

Kuurman, J. 1974−5. An examination of the *-ingas, -inga-* places-names in the East Midlands *Journal of the English Place-Names Society* **7**: 11−44

Lamb, H.H. 1981. Climate from 1000 BC−AD 1000 *In* M. Jones and G. Dimbleby (eds) 1981: 53−65

Lane, T. 1988. Pre-Roman origins for settlement on the Fens of South Lincolnshire. *In* Hall (ed) *Antiquity* **62**: 314−21

Langouet, L. and **M. Daire** 1989. *La Civitas Gallo-Romaine des Coriosolites.* Alet

Lapidge, M. 1984. Gildas's education and the Latin culture of sub-Roman Britain. *In* Lapidge and Dumville (eds) 27−50

Lapidge, M. and **D.N. Dumville** 1984. (eds) *Gildas: New Approaches.* Woodbridge

Lawson, A.J. 1983. *The Archaeology of Witton, near North Walsham, Norfolk.* East Anglian Archaeology 18 Dereham

Lawson, A.J., E.A. Martin and **D. Priddy** 1981. *The Barrows of East Anglia.* East Anglian Archaeology 12 Dereham

Leech, R. 1986. The Excavation of a Romano-Celtic Temple and a Later Cemetery on Lamyatt Beacon, Somerset. *Britannia* **17**: 259−328

Leeds, E.T. 1913. (repr. 1970) *The Archaeology of the Anglo-Saxon Settlements.* Oxford

Leeds, E.T. 1923. A Saxon village near Sutton Courtenay, Berks. *Archaeologia* **73**: 147−92

Leeds, E.T. 1927. A Saxon village near Sutton Courtenay, Berks. *Archaeologia* **76**: 59−80

Leeds, E.T. 1945. The distribution of the Angles and Saxons Archaeologically considered. *Archaeologia* **19**: 1−106

Leeds, E.T. 1947. A Saxon village near Sutton Courtenay, Berks. *Archaeologia* **92**: 78−94

Leeds, E.T. 1949. *A Corpus of Early Anglo-Saxon Great Square-Headed Brooches.* Oxford

Lennard, R. 1933−4. The character of the Anglo-Saxon conquests: a disputed point. *History* **18**: 204−14

Lethbridge, T.C. 1956. The Anglo-Saxon settlement in Eastern England. *In* Harden (ed): 112−22

Limbrey, S. and **J.G. Evans** 1978. *The Effect of Man on the Landscape: The Lowland Zone.* CBA Research Report 21, London

Longley, D. 1975. *The Anglo-Saxon Connexion.* BAR BS 22, Oxford

Losco-Bradley, S. 1977. Catholme. *Current Archaeology* **59**: 358−64

Loyn, H.R. 1962. *Anglo-Saxon England and the Norman Conquest.* London.

Loyn, H.R. 1984. The conversion of the English to Christianity. Some comments on the Celtic contribution. Davies, Griffiths, Jones and Mangan (eds). *Welsh Society and Nativehood.* 5−18 Cardiff.

Lynch, A. 1981. *Man and Environment in S.W. Ireland, 4000 BC−AD 800.* BAR BS 85, Oxford

Lynn, C.J. 1978. Early Christian period domestic structures: a change from round to rectangular plans. *Irish Archaeological Research Forum* **V**: 29—43

Macaulay, Lord 1867. *The History of England from the Accession of James the Second.* I. London.

Macinnes, L. 1989. Baubles, bangles and beads: trade and exchange in Roman Scotland. *In* Barrett *et al.* (eds) 108—16

Mackreth, D.F. 1978. Orton Hall Farm, Peterborough: a Roman and Saxon Settlement. *In* M. Todd (ed) *Studies in the Romano-British Villa.* Leicester: 209—28

Mackreth, D.F. 1988. Excavation of an Iron Age and Roman Enclosure at Werrington, Cambridgeshire. *Britannia* **19**: 59—151

Maitland, F.W. 1897. *Domesday Book and Beyond.* Oxford

Mann, B. and **J.C. Mann** 1973. Roman Army in Britain — Britons in the Roman Army. *Britannia* **4**: 191—205

Mann, J.C. 1971. Spoken Latin in Britain as Evidenced in the Inscriptions. *Britannia* **2**: 218—24

Mann, J.C. 1985. Two 'Topoi' in the Agricola. *Britannia* **16**: 21—4

Manning, W.H. 1975. Economic influence on land use in the military areas of the Highland Zone. *In* Evans *et al.* (eds): 112—16

Mason, D. 1988. Prata Legionis in Britain. *Brittania* **19**: 163—89

Matthews, C.L. and **S.C. Hawkes** 1985. Early Saxon Settlements and Burials near Dunstable, Bedfordshire. *In* S C Hawkes *et al.* (eds) *Anglo-Saxon Studies in Archaeology and History* 4, Oxford: 59—115

Matthews, J.F. 1975. *Western Aristocracies and the Imperial Court, AD 364—425.* Oxford

Mawer, Sir A. 1920. *The Place-Names of Northumberland and Durham.* Cambridge

Maxfield, V.A. (ed) 1989. *The Saxon Shore: a handbook.* Studies in History 25, Exeter

Mayes, P. and **M.J. Dean** 1976. *An Anglo-Saxon Cemetery at Baston, Lincolnshire.* Occasional Papers in Lincolnshire History & Archaeology 3, The Society for Lincolnshire History & Archaeology, Sleaford

Meaney, A. 1964. *A Gazetteer of Early Anglo-Saxon Burial Sites.* George Allen & Unwin London

Meaney, A.L. and **S.C. Hawkes** 1970. *Two Anglo-Saxon Cemeteries at Winnall.* Society for Medieval Archaeology Monograph Series No 4, London

Merryfield, D.L. and **P.D. Moore** 1974. Prehistoric human activity and blanket peat initiation on Exmoor. *Nature* **250**: 439—41

Miles, D. 1986. *Archaeology at Barton Court Farm, Abingdon, Oxon: an investigation of late Neolithic, Iron Age, Romano-British and Saxon settlements.* London

Miles, H. 1977. The Honeyditches Roman Villa, Seaton, Devon. *Britannia* **8**: 107—48

Miles, H. and **T. Miles** 1973. Excavations at Trethurgy, St. Austell: interim report. *Cornish Archaeology* **12**: 25—30

Millar, F. 1981. *The Roman Empire and its Neighbours.* 2nd Ed, London

Millar, F. 1982. Emperors, frontiers and foreign relations, 31 BC to AD 378. *Britannia* **13**: 1—23

Miller, M. 1975a. Historicity and the pedigrees of the north countrymen. *Bulletin of the Board of Celtic Studies* **26**(3): 255—80

Miller, M. 1975b. The commanders at Arthuret. *Transactions of the Cumberland*

and Westmorland Antiquarian and Archaeological Society, ns **75**: 96−118

Miller, M. 1978. The last British entry in the Gallic Chronicle. *Britannia* **9**: 315−18

Millett, M. 1979. The dating of Farnham (Alice Holt) pottery. *Britannia* **10**: 121−37

Millett, M. 1987. The question of continuity: Rivenhall revisited. *Archaeological Journal* **144**: 434−44

Millett, M. with S. James 1983. Excavations at Cowdery's Down, Basingstoke, Hants, 1978−81. *Archaeological Journal* **140**: 151−279

Mitchell, R.J. and E. Sunderland 1978. Genetic studies of the Population of the Isle of Man. *In* P.J. Davey (ed) Man and environment in the Isle of Man BAR BS **54**: 77−107

Morris, J. 1965. Dark Age dates. *In* M.G. Jarrett and B. Dobson (eds) *Britain and Rome: Essays presented to E. Birley.* Kendal: 145−85

Morris, J. 1973. *The Age of Arthur.* Chichester

Morris, J. 1980. *Nennius: British History and the Welsh Annals.* Chichester.

Morris, P. 1979. *Agricultural Buildings in Roman Britain.* BAR BS 70, Oxford

Morris, R. and J. Roxan 1982. Churches on Roman Buildings. *In* W. Rodwell (ed) Temples, Churches and Religion: recent research in Roman Britain BAR BS 77: 175−209

Muckelroy, K.W. 1976. Enclosed Ambulatories in Romano-Celtic Temples in Britain. *Britannia* **7**: 173−91

Myres, J.N.L. 1956. Romano-Saxon Pottery. *In* D.B. Harden (ed): 16−39

Myres, J.N.L. 1960. Pelagius and the end of Roman rule in Britain. *Journal of Roman Studies* **50**: 21−36

Myres, J.N.L. 1969. *Anglo-Saxon Pottery and the Settlement of England.* Oxford

Myres, J.N.L. 1986. *The English Settlements.* Oxford

Nash, D. 1981. Coinage and state development in Central Gaul. *In* B. Cunliffe (ed) *Coinage and Society in Britain and Gaul: some current problems* 10−17 London

Nash-Williams, V.E. 1950. *The Early Christian Monuments of Wales.* Cardiff

Neale, D.S. 1978. The growth and decline of villas in the Verulanium area. *In* M. Todd (ed) *Studies in the Romano-British Villa.* Leicester: 33−58

Newman, J. 1988. The East Anglia Kingdom Survey. *Bulletin of the Sutton Hoo Research Committee* **5**: 10−12

Newman, J. forthcoming East Anglian Kingdom Pilot Survey. *In* M. Parker-Pearson and T. Schadla-Hall (eds) *Looking at the Land.* Leicester

Nicolaisen, W.F.H. 1976. *Scottish Place Names.* London

Okun, M.L. 1989. An example of the process of acculturation in the Early Roman Frontier. *Oxford Journal of Archaeology* **8.1**: 41−54

Orosius, Paulus *Historiarum adversum paganos libri vii.* (8 volumes, Vindobonae, 1882). Quotations are from the translation by I.W. Raymond, New York 1932

Owen-Crocker, G.R. 1986. *Dress in Anglo-Saxon England.* Manchester

Ozanne, A. 1962−3. The Peak Dwellers. *Medieval Archaeology* **6−7**: 15−52

Padel, O.J. 1982. Cornwall as a Border Area. *Nomina* **6**: 18−22

Padel, O.J. 1985. *Cornish Place-Name Elements.* Cambridge

Pearce, S.M. 1982. Estates and Church Sites in Dorset and Gloucestershire: the emergence of a Christian Society. *In* S.M. Pearce (ed) *The Early Church in Western Britain and Ireland.* BAR BS 102, 117−38

Pearce, S.M. 1985. The Early Church in the Landscape: the Evidence from North Devon. *Archaeological Journal* **142**: 255–75

Pelteret, D. 1981. Slave raiding and slave trading in early England. *Anglo-Saxon England* Vol 9, 99–114

Pennington, W. 1970. Vegetational history in the northwest of England: a regional synthesis. *In* D. Walker and R.G. West (eds) *Studies in the Vegetational History of the British Isles*. Cambridge: 41–79

Percival, J. 1976. *The Roman Villa*. London

Percival, J. 1985. The Precursors of Domesday: Roman and Carolingian Land Registers. *In* P.H. Sawyer (ed) *Domesday Book: A Reassessment*. London

Pharr, C. 1952. *The Theodosian Code and Novels and the Simondian Constitutions*. Princeton NJ

Phillips, C.W. (ed) 1970. *The Fenland in Roman Times*. London

Plummer, C. (ed) 1896. *Venerabilis Baedae Opera Historica I*. Oxford

Pollard, S.H.M. 1974. A late Iron-Age settlement and Romano-British villa at Holcombe, Devon. *Proceedings of the Devon Archaeological Society* **32**: 59–162

Potter, T.W. 1981. The Roman Occupation of the Central Fenland. *Britannia* **12**: 79–133

Powlesland, D. with **C. Haughton** and **J. Hanson** 1986. Excavations at Heslerton, North Yorkshire, 1978–82. *Archaeological Journal* **143**: 53–173

Powlesland, D. 1990. West Heslerton: The Anglian Settlement. *Medieval Settlement Research Group Annual Report* **4**: 44

Preston-Jones, A. and **P. Rose** 1986. Medieval Cornwall. *Cornish Archaeology* **25**: 135–85

Pretty, K. 1989. Defining the Magonsaete. *In* S. Bassett (ed): 171–83

Pritchard, F.A. 1986. Ornamental Stonework from Roman London. *Britannia* **17**: 170–89

Procopius of Caesaria *History of the Wars*. tr. H.B. Dewing. Loeb Classical Library, 1914–40, London

Quinnell, H. 1986. Cornwall during the Iron Age and the Roman Period. *Cornish Archaeology* **25**: 111–34

Rackham, O. 1976. *Trees and Woodland in the British Landscape*. London

Rahtz, P.A. 1961. An excavation on Bokerley Dyke, 1958. *Archaeological Journal* **118**: 65–99

Rahtz, P.A. 1976a. Buildings and Rural Settlement. *In* D.M. Wilson (ed): 49–98 with an appendix, 405–52

Rahtz, P.A. 1976b. Irish settlements in Somerset. *Proceedings of the Royal Irish Academy* **76(c)**: 223–30

Rahtz, P.A. 1978. Grave orientation. *Archaeological Journal* **135**: 1–14

Rahtz, P.A. 1982. Celtic society in Somerset AD 400–700. *Bulletin of the Board of Celtic Studies* **30**: 176–200

Rahtz, P.A., T. Dickinson and **L. Watts** (eds) 1979. *Anglo-Saxon Cemeteries*. BAR, BS 82, Oxford

Ralegh Radford, C.A. 1957. The Saxon house: a review and some parallels. *Medieval Archaeology* **1**: 27–38

Ralegh Radford, C.A. 1971. Christian origins in Britain. *Medieval Archaeology* **15**: 1–12

Randers-Pehrson, J.D. 1983. *Barbarians and Romans: The Birth Struggle of Europe AD 400–700.* London

Rawes, B. 1981. The Romano-British site at Brockworth, Glos. *Britannia* **12**: 45–77

Reece, R. 1973. Roman coinage in the Western Empire. *Britannia* **4**: 227–52

Reece, R. 1977. *Burial in the Roman World.* CBA Research Report 22, London

Reece, R. 1980. Town and country: the end of Roman Britain. *World Archaeology* **12,1**: 77–92

Reece, R. 1983. Continuity on the Cotswolds: some problems of ownership, settlement and hedge survey between Roman Britain and the Middle Ages. *Landscape History* **5**: 11–20

Rees, B.R. 1988. *Pelagius: A Reluctant Heretic.* Woodbridge

Rees, S.E. 1979. *Agricultural Implements in Prehistoric and Roman Britain.* BAR BS 69, vols 1 & 2, Oxford

Reilly, P. 1988. *Computer Analysis of an Archaeological Landscape: Medieval Land Divisions in the Isle of Man.* BAR BS 190, Oxford

Renfrew, C. 1979. Systems collapse as social transformation: catastrophe and anastrophe in early state societies. *In* C. Renfrew and K.L. Cooke (eds) *Transformation – Mathematical Approaches to Culture Change.* London: 481–506

Renfrew, C. 1987. *Archaeology and Language.* London

Richards, J.D. 1987. *The Significance of Form and Decoration of Anglo-Saxon Cremation Urns.* BAR BS 166, Oxford

Richards, M. 1960. The Irish settlements in south-west Wales. *Proceedings of the Royal Society of Antiquaries Ireland* **90**: 133–62

Riley, D. 1980. *Early Landscape from the Air.* Sheffield

Rivet, A.L.F. (ed) 1964. *The Roman Villa in Britain.* London reprinted 1970

Rivet, A.L.F. 1970. The British section of the Antonine itinerary. *Britannia* **1**: 34–82

Rivet, A.L.F. 1980. Celtic names and Roman places. *Britannia* **11**: 1–19

Rivet, A.L.F. and **C. Smith** 1979. *The Place-Names of Roman Britain.* London

Roberts, W.I. 1982. *Romano-Saxon Pottery.* BAR BS 106, Oxford

Robertson, A. 1970. Roman Finds From Non-Roman Sites in Scotland. *Britannia* **1**: 198–213

Robinson, D.E. and **J.H. Dickson** 1988. Vegetational history and land-use: a radiocarbon-dated pollen diagram from Malinse Moor, Arran, Scotland. *New Phytologist* **109**: 223–51

Robinson, D.M. (ed) 1988. *Biglis, Caldicot and Llandough: 3 late Iron Age and R.B. sites in SE Wales.* BAR, BS 188, Oxford

Robinson, M. 1978. The Problem of Hedges enclosing Roman and Earlier Fields. *In* H.C. Bowen and P.J. Fowler (eds): 155–8

Robinson, M. 1981. The Iron Age to Early Saxon Environment of the Upper Thames Terraces. *In* M. Jones and G. Dimbleby (eds) BAR BS 87: 251–86

The Environment of Man: the Iron Age to the Anglo-Saxon period.

Rodwell, W. 1978. Relict Landscapes in Essex. In H.C. Bowen and P.J. Fowler (eds): 89–98

Rodwell, W.J. (ed) 1980. *Temples, Churches and Religion in Roman Britain.* Oxford

Rodwell, W.J. 1982. From Mausoleum to Minster: the early development of Wells Cathedral. *In* S.M. Pearce (ed) BAR BS 102: 49—59

Rodwell, W.J. and **K.A. Rodwell** 1986. *Rivenhall: investigations of a villa, church and village.* CBA Research Report 55, Chelmsford Archaeological Trust, Report 4 London

Royal Commission on Historical Monuments (England) 1979. *County of Northampton Archaeology Sites* 2. London

Royal Commission on Historical Monuments (England) 1981. *County of Northampton Archaeology Sites* 3 London

Royal Commission on Historical Monuments (England) 1983. West Park Roman Villa, Rockbourne, Hampshire. *Archaeological Journal* **140**: 129—50

Royal Commission on Historical Monuments (England) 1985. *An Inventory of Archaeological Sites and Churches in Northampton*

Royal Commission on Historical Monuments (England) 1989. *The Emerging Past: Air Photography and the Buried Landscape.*

Roymans, N. 1983. The North Belgic Tribes in the First Century B.C. A Historico-Anthropological Perspective. BAR, IS 184, Oxford: Roman and Native in the Low Countries R. Brandt and J. Slof Slofstra (eds.) 43—69

Rutherford Davis, K. 1982. *Britons and Saxons: The Chiltern Region 400—700.* Chichester

Ryan, N.S. 1988. *Fourth Century Coin Finds From Roman Britain: A Computer Analysis.* BAR BS 183

Ryder, M.L. 1984. Medieval Sheep and Wool Types. *Agricultural History Review* **32**: 14—28

Salamon, A. and **I. Lengyel** 1980—1. Kinship interrelations in a 5th century 'Pannonian' cemetery: an archaeological and palaeobiological sketch of the population fragment buried in the Mozs cemetery, Hungary. *World Archaeology* **12.1**: 93

Saller, R.P. 1982. *Personal Patronage under the Early Empire.* Cambridge

Salway P. 1981. *Roman Britain.* Oxford

Samson, R. 1989. Rural slavery, inscriptions, archaeology and Marx. *Historia* **38(1)**: 99—110

Savory, H.N. 1956. 'Some sub-Romano-British brooches from South Wales. *In* D.B. Harden (ed): 40—58

Sawyer, P.H. (ed) 1976. *Medieval Settlement.* Chichester

Sawyer, P.H. 1978. *From Roman Britain to Norman England.* London

Scherr, J. 1986. Names of Springs and Wells in Somerset. *Nomina* **10**: 79—91

Seebohm, F. 1890. *The English Village Community.* London

Severin, T. 1978. *The Brendan Voyage.* London

Shotter, D.C.A. 1973. *Numeri Barcariorum*: a note on *RIB* 601. *Britannia* **4**: 206—9

Shotter, D.C.A. 1989. Roman Coin-finds in Cumbria. *Transactions of the Cumberland & Westmorland Antiquarian & Archaeological Society,* **89**: 41—50

Sidonius *Poems and Letters.* W.B. Anderson (tr.) Loeb Classical Library, London, 1965

Simpson, C.J. 1976. Belt-buckles and strap-ends of the late Roman Empire: a preliminary survey of several new groups. *Britannia* **7**: 192—223

Simpson, G. 1964. *Britons and the Roman Army.* London

Sims-Williams, P. 1983a. The settlement of England in Bede and the *Chronicle. Anglo-Saxon England* **12**: 1—41

Sims-Williams, P. 1983b. Gildas and the Anglo-Saxons. *Cambridge Medieval Celtic Studies* **6**: 1−30

Sivan, H. 1987. On *Foederati, Hospitalitas* and the Settlement of the Goths in AD 418. *American Journal of Philology* **108**: 759−72

Slofstra, J. 1983. An Anthropological Approach to the Study of Romanization Processes. *In* R. Brandt and J. Slofstra (eds.) BAR, IS 184: 71−104. Roman and Native in the Low Countries

Smith, C. 1980. The Survival of Romano-British Toponymy. *Nomina* **4**: 27−40

Smith, C. 1987. Excavations at the Ty Mawr Hut-circles, Holyhead, Anglesey, Part IV − Chronology and discussion. *Archaeologia Cambrensis* **136**: 20−38

Smith, J.T. 1978. Villas as a key to social structure. *In* M Todd (ed) *Studies in the Romano-British Villa*. Leicester: 149−86

Smith, J.T. 1985. Barnsley Park Villa: Its Interpretation and Implications. *Oxford Journal of Archaeology* **4**: 31−51

Sozomen, H. *The Ecclesiastical History... From AD 323 to AD 425*. Nicene and Post-Nicene Fathers, second series, II Oxford and New York, 1957

Stafford, P. 1985. *The East Midlands in the Early Middle Ages*. Leicester

Stancliffe, C.E. 1980. Kings and conversion: some comparisons between the Roman mission to England and Patrick's to Ireland. *Frühmittelaltarliche Studien* **14** Band: 59−94

Stenton, Sir F. 1943. *Anglo-Saxon England*. Oxford

Stephens, G.R. 1985. Caerleon and the Martyrdom of SS Aaron and Julius. *Bulletin of the Board of Celtic Studies* **32**: 326−35

Stevens, C.E. 1933. *Sidonius Apollinaris and His Age*. Oxford

Stevens, C.E. 1941. Gildas Sapiens. *English Historical Review* **56**: 353−73

Stevens, C.E. 1947. A possible conflict of laws in Roman Britain. *Journal of Roman Studies* **37**: 132−4

Stevens, C.E. 1966. The social and economic aspects of rural settlement. *In* C. Thomas (ed) *Rural Settlement in Roman Britain*. CBA Research Report 7, London: 108−28

Stubbs, W. 1870. *Select Charters*. 9th ed 1913−69, revised H.W.C. Davies, Oxford

Stubbs, W. 1891. *The constitutional history of England in its origin and development*. 3 vols, Oxford

Stuckert, C.M. 1980. Roman to Saxon: Population, Biology and Archaeology. Paper presented to 45th Annual General Meeting of Society for American Archaeology, Philadelphia, Pennsylvania, 3 May 1980, quoted by Arnold, 1984

Stupperich, R. 1980. A reconsideration of some 4th century British mosaics. *Britannia* **11**: 289−301

Sulpicius Severus *Life of St. Martin*. Rev A. Roberts (ed), Oxford, 1894

Sumpter, A.B. and **S. Coll** 1977. *The Archaeology of York* 3 York

Swanton, M.J. 1973. *The Spearheads of the Anglo-Saxon Settlements*. London

Tacitus, Cornelius *De Vita Agricolae*. R.M. Ogilvie and I. Richmond (eds) Oxford, 1967

Tacitus, P. Cornelius *Germania*. M. Hutton (tr), Loeb Classical Library, 1914

Tainter, J.A. 1988. *The Collapse of Complex Societies*. Cambridge

Tallis, J.H. and V.R. Switzur 1973. Studies on southern Pennine peats. VI: A radiocarbon-dated pollen diagram from Featherbed Moss, Derbyshire. *Journal of Ecology* **61**: 743−51

Tate, W.E. 1978. *A Domesday of English Enclosure Acts and Awards*. Reading

Taylor, C.C. 1975. *Fields in the English Landscape*. London

Taylor, C.C. 1982. The Nature of Romano-British Settlement Studies − What are the boundaries? *In* D. Miles (ed.) The Romano-British Countryside BAR, 103(i), 1−15

Taylor, C.C. 1983. *Village and Farmstead*. London

Taylor, H.M. 1979. The Anglo-Saxon Cathedral at Canterbury. *Archaeological Journal* **126**: 101−30

Thomas, C. 1958. *Gwithian. Ten Year's Work*. Gwithian

Thomas, C. 1973−4. Irish colonists in South-west Britain. *World Archaeology* **5**: 5−13

Thomas, C. 1976. Imported Late Roman Mediterranean Pottery in Ireland and Western Britain: Chronologies and Implications. *Proceedings of the Royal Irish Academy* **76(c)**: 245−55

Thomas, C. 1981a. *Christianity in Roman Britain to AD 500*. London

Thomas, C. 1981b. *A Provisional List of Imported Pottery in Post-Roman Western Britain and Ireland*. Truro

Thomas, C. 1988. Tintagel Castle. *Antiquity* **62**: 421−34

Thompson, E.A. 1965. *The Early Germans*. Oxford

Thompson, E.A. 1977. Britain AD 406−410. *Britannia* **8**: 303−18

Thompson, E.A. 1979. Gildas and the History of Britain. *Britannia* **10**: 203−26

Thompson, E.A. 1980. Procopius on Brittia and Britannia. *Classical Quarterly* **30**: 498−507

Thompson, E.A. 1982a. Zosimus 6·10·2 and the letters of Honorius. *Classical Quarterly* **32**: 445−62

Thompson, E.A. 1982b. *Roman and Barbarians*. Wisconsin

Thompson, E.A. 1984. *St. Germanus of Auxerre and the End of Roman Britain*. Woodbridge

Thompson, E.A. 1985. *Who was St Patrick?* Woodbridge

Tittensor, R.M. 1977−8. A history of the Mens: A Sussex woodland. *Sussex Archaeological Collections* **116**: 347−74

Todd, M. 1970. The Small Towns of Roman Britain. *Britannia* **1**: 114−30

Todd, M. 1975. *The Northern Barbarians*. London; Rev Ed 1987, Oxford

Todd, M. 1977. *Famosa Pestis* and Britain in the fifth century. *Britannia* **8**: 319−25

Todd, M. 1987. *The South West to AD 1000* Harlow

Toller, H.S. 1980. An Interim Report on the Excavations of the Orsett 'Cock' Enclosure, Essex, 1976−79. *Britannia* **11**: 35−42

Trevelyan, G.M. 1926. *History of England*. London, New York, Toronto

Turner, E.G. 1956. A writing tablet from Somerset. *Journal of Roman Studies* **46**: 115−18

Turner, J. 1981a. The Iron Age. *In* I. Simmons and M. Tooley (eds) *The Environment in British Prehistory*. London: 250−81

Turner, J. 1981b. The vegetation. *In* M. Jones and G. Dimbleby (eds): 67−73

Turner, J. 1983. Some pollen evidence for the environment of North Britain, 1000 BC to AD 1000. *In* J.C. Chapman and H.C. Mytum (eds) *Settlement in North Britain 1000 BC–AD 1000* BAR BS 118, Oxford: 3–28

Turner, R. 1982. Ivy Champs, Witham: an interim report. *Essex County Council Occasional Paper 2*

Unwin, P.T.H. 1983. Townships and early fields in North Nottinghamshire. *Journal of Historical Geography* **9**: 341–6

Van Dam, R. 1985. *Leadership and Community in Late Antique Gaul.* California

Vince, A. 1990. *Saxon London: An Archaeological Investigation.* London

Vinogradoff, P. 1892. *Villainage in England.* Oxford

Wacher, J.S. 1974a. *The Towns of Roman Britain.* London

Wacher, J.S. 1974b. Villae in urbibus. *Britannia* **5**: 282–4

Wainwright, G.J. 1971. The Excavation of a fortified Settlement at Walesland Rath, Pembrokeshire. *Britannia* **2**: 48–108

Wallace-Hadrill, A. (ed) 1989. *Patronage in Ancient Society.* London

Warner, P. 1988. Pre-Conquest Territorial and Administrative Organization in East Suffolk. *In* D. Hooke (ed) *Anglo-Saxon Settlements,* Oxford: 9–34

Webster, G. and **L. Smith** 1987. Reply to J.T. Smith's suggested reinterpretation of Barnsley Park Villa. *Oxford Journal of Archaeology* **6**: 69–89

Welch, M.G. 1971. Romans and Saxons in Sussex. *Britannia* **2**: 232–7

Welch, M.G. 1976. *Highdown and its Saxon Cemetery.* Worthing Museum and Art Gallery Publication No 11, Worthing

Welch, M.G. 1983. *Early Anglo-Saxon Sussex.* BAR BS 112, Oxford

Wells, P.S. 1980–1. Contact and change: an example on the fringes of the Classical world. *World Archaeology* **12.1**: 1–10

West, S.E. 1969. The Anglo-Saxon Village of West Stow. *Medieval Archaeology* **12**: 1–20 Ipswich

West, S.E. 1976. The Roman Site at Icklingham. *East Anglian Archaeology* **3**: 63–126 Ipswich

West, S.E. 1985. *West Stow: The Anglo-Saxon Village.* East Anglian Archaeology 24 Ipswich

West, S.E. 1988. *The Anglo-Saxon Cemetery at Westgarth Gardens, Bury St. Edmunds, Suffolk* East Anglian Archaeology 38

White, R.H. 1988. *Roman and Celtic Objects from Anglo-Saxon Graves.* BAR BS 191, Oxford

Whitelock, D. 1952. *The Beginnings of English Society.* Harmondsworth

Whittaker, C.R. 1989. *Les Frontières de l'Empire Romain.* Université de Besançon, Annales Littéraires 390

Wickenden, N.P. 1988. Excavations at Great Dunmow, Essex. *East Anglian Archaeology* 41 Chelmsford

Wightman, E.M. 1978. Peasants and Potentates. *American Journal of Ancient History* **3**: 97–128

Wightman, E.M. 1985. *Gallia Belgica.* London

Wild, J.P. 1976–7. Loanwords and Roman expansion in northwest Europe. *World Archaeology* **8.1**: 57–64

Wild, J.P. 1982. Wool Production in Roman Britain. BAR BS 103(i), 109–22 The Romano-British Countryside D. Miles (ed.)

Wild, S. 1973. *Libanesische Ortsnamen.* Beiruter Texte und Studien, Band 8, Beirut

Wilkinson, T.J. 1988. *Archaeology and Environment in South Essex: Rescue Archaeology along the Grays By-pass, 1979–80.* East Anglian Archaeology 42 Chelmsford

Willems, W.J.H. 1983. Romans and Batavians: regional developments at the Imperial Frontier. BAR IS 184 105–28 Roman and Native in the Low countries R. Brandt and J. Slofstra (eds.)

Williams, S. 1985. *Diocletian and the Roman Recovery.* London

Williamson, T. 1984. The Roman Countryside: Settlement and Agriculture in N.W. Essex. *Britannia* **15**: 225–30

Williamson, T. 1986. Parish Boundaries and early fields: continuity and discontinuity. *Journal of Historical Geography* **12**: 241–8

Williamson, T. 1987. Early co-axial field systems on the East Anglian boulder clays. *Proceedings of the Prehistoric Society* **53**: 419–32

Williamson, T. 1988. Settlement Chronology and Regional Landscapes: The Evidence from the Claylands of E. Anglia and Essex. *In* D. Hooke (ed) *Anglo-Saxon Settlement.* Oxford: 153–75

Williamson, T. and L. Bellamy 1987. *Property and Landscape.* London

Wilson, D.R. 1975. Romano-Celtic Temple Architecture. *Journal of the British Archaeological Association* (3rd series) **38**: 3–27

Wilson, D.M. (ed) 1976. *The Archaeology of Anglo-Saxon England.* London

Wilson, D. 1985. A Note on OE *hearg* and *weoh* as Place-Name Elements Representing Different Types of Pagan Saxon Worship Sites. *In* S.C. Hawkes *et al.* (eds) *Anglo-Saxon Studies in Archaeology and History* 4, Oxford: 179–83

Winterbottom, M. (ed and trans) 1978. *Gildas: the ruin of Britain and other documents.* Chichester

Woolf, R. 1976. The ideal of men dying with their Lord in the *Germania* and in *The Battle of Maldon.* Anglo-Saxon England **5**: 63–81

Wood, I. 1987. The Fall of the Western Empire and the End of Roman Britain. *Britannia* **18**: 251–62

Woodward, A. and P. Leach 1990. *The Uley Shrines: Excavation of a Ritual Complex on West Hill, Uley, Gloucestershire, 1977–9.* London

Wormald, P. 1976. The decline of the Western Empire and the survival of the aristocracy. *Journal of Roman Studies* **66**: 217–26

Wormald, P. 1978. Bede, Beowulf and the Conversion of the Anglo-Saxon Aristocracy. *In* R.T. Farrell (ed) Bede and Anglo Saxon England. BAR **B546**: 49–58

Wright, N. 1984. Gildas's Geographical Perspective: Some Problems. *In* Lapidge and Dumville (eds): 85–106

Wright, R.P. 1964. Inscriptions: Roman Britain in 1963. *Journal of Roman Studies* **54**: 177–85

Yorke, B. 1990. *Kings and Kingdoms of Early Anglo-Saxon England.* London

Young, C.J. 1977. *The Roman Pottery Industry of the Oxford Region.* BAR BS 43

Zosimus *New History* tr. with commentary by R.T. Ridley, Australian Association for Byzantine Studies, Sydney, 1982

INDEX